INSIDE THE MULTIRACIAL POPULIST COALITION REMAKING THE GOP

PARTY OF THE PEOPLE

PATRICK RUFFINI

SIMON & SCHUSTER
NEW YORK LONDON TORONTO SYDNEY NEW DELHI

Simon & Schuster
1230 Avenue of the Americas
New York, NY 10020

First Simon & Schuster hardcover edition November 2023

SIMON & SCHUSTER and colophon are registered trademarks of Simon & Schuster, Inc.

For information about special discounts for bulk purchases, please contact Simon & Schuster Special Sales at 1-866-506-1949 or business@simonandschuster.com.

The Simon & Schuster Speakers Bureau can bring authors to your live event. For more information or to book an event, contact the Simon & Schuster Speakers Bureau at 1-866-248-3049 or visit our website at www.simonspeakers.com.

Interior design by Carly Loman

Manufactured in Canada

Jacket printed in the United States of America

10 9 8 7 6 5 4 3 2 1

Library of Congress Cataloging-in-Publication Data

Names: Ruffini, Patrick, author.
Title: Party of the people : inside the multiracial populist coalition remaking the GOP / By Patrick Ruffini.
Description: First Simon & Schuster hardcover edition. | New York, NY : Simon and Schuster, [2023] | Includes index.
Identifiers: LCCN 2023012680 (print) | LCCN 2023012681 (ebook) | ISBN 9781982198626 (hardcover) | ISBN 9781982198633 (paperback) | ISBN 9781982198640 (ebook)
Subjects: LCSH: Republican Party (U.S. : 1854-)--History--21st century. | Multiculturalism--United States--History--21st century. | Political parties--United States--History--21st century. | Populism--United States--History--21st century. | Diversity in the workplace--United States--History--21st century.
Classification: LCC JK2356 .R85 2023 (print) | LCC JK2356 (ebook) | DDC 320.56/62090730905--dc23/eng/20230517
LC record available at https://lccn.loc.gov/2023012680
LC ebook record available at https://lccn.loc.gov/2023012681

ISBN 978-1-9821-9862-6
ISBN 978-1-9821-9864-0 (ebook)

To Maggie

CONTENTS

PARTY OF THE PEOPLE

FOREWORD

Culturally, you would not peg me as an enthusiast for populist realignment. I grew up in Greenwich, Connecticut, the hometown of George H. W. Bush and a place synonymous with the East Coast Republican establishment. Most of my early career in politics was spent working for his son, the forty-third president, who today has come to represent everything the Republican party—my party—is not. In the spring of 2015, though, the turn the party would take wasn't yet clear. Republicans were out of power for eight years, and it seemed like their turn to win the next election in 2016. This expectation drew a historically large field of sixteen candidates. Then Donald Trump joined the race. At first I was amused. Then, watching Trump surge ahead in the polls, I was horrified. Trump's boorishness and profanity seemed likely to hand the election to Hillary Clinton on a silver platter. Following Trump's initial primary victories, some Republican friends and I went all in on a last-ditch Super PAC to stop Trump, pushing strategic voting either for Ted Cruz or John Kasich. Neither was my cup of tea, but at this point, it had to be anyone-but-Trump. We had successes here and there, for instance, helping in Trump's defeat in the Wisconsin primary. But if I'm being honest, even then I recognized it was too little, too late. After Trump's victory in the primaries, a feeling of dejection set in. The party had just blown the election before it had even started. We shuttered the PAC and sent the remaining funds to a set of non-Trumpy Republicans we hoped would be left to hold the line against a now-inevitable Clinton presidency. My objections to Trump were about more than one election. He threatened to do lasting damage to the ability to advance important conservative causes, needlessly antagonizing Hispanic voters, the fastest growing group within the electorate and a group Republicans desperately needed to win in the America of the future.

I turned out to be wrong about the 2016 election. A lot of us were, and so I committed to spend the next few years listening and learning. This book is the result of that effort.

I work as a pollster. Understanding where the voters stand is my job. And like others in the field, I had egg on my face after 2016. It's not that I completely discounted the probability of a Trump victory. I put the chances at 20 percent the weekend before the election. My polling had shown that even if he didn't win, the swing voter still gravitated toward his cultural views on issues like immigration—in retrospect, a harbinger of hidden support. Yet, throughout most of the election cycle, a Trump victory seemed unthinkable to me. My mistake was in substituting my own personal passions and biases—as the quintessential suburban, college-educated voter—for a neutral, clear-eyed assessment of who the actual demographic majority in America was and where they stood.

Trumpism has certainly had its costs: coarsening the public debate, damaging the Republican brand in the suburbs, and driving decent and respectable Republicans from public service. These exiles are often called the "normal" Republicans—itself a sign that we are still in denial. Yes, Trump's behavior in office was highly abnormal. But by any definition, the almost 90 percent of Republicans who supported the president of their own party were the ones acting normally, not the few holdouts like me wildly overrepresented inside the Beltway. Trump not only won the 2016 election when I predicted he wouldn't. He had done so in a way that not even our heroes—Ronald Reagan and both Bushes—could manage, running up historic margins among working-class voters and undermining the Democrats' historic claim to be the party of the workingman and -woman. We were not as surprised by the outcome of the 2020 election—Joe Biden won an election he was widely expected to—but the margin was much closer than anticipated. And the reason we came within a hair of a second Trump term was an unexpected surge of nonwhite voters—particularly Hispanic voters—his way. Suddenly, the new

Republican populist coalition was a multiracial one. This was not at all what I had expected in 2016 when I fretted about Trump throwing away the Hispanic vote for a generation.

The levelheaded, majority-building realist in me had very mixed feelings about all this. I won't recite all that I find distasteful about Donald Trump: the reasons have been endlessly recounted for eight years everywhere else, not least in the private conversations of Republican elected officials. But Trump was also accomplishing a goal I had dedicated a big part of my career to—one that the "normal" Republicans had failed to achieve—rallying working-class people and minorities in a political coalition that punched above its weight in the fight for 270 electoral votes.

Reflecting on the 2016 experience, I began to realize that my background and life experiences themselves were the problem. They had blinded me to an accurate understanding of the American electorate, especially the Republican electorate, and most especially the *new* Republican electorate. I only saw the swing voters that might be repulsed by Trump, not those drawn to him. And it was all because of a fatal, reality-blinding flaw I shared with almost everyone in politics and the media: I graduated from college.

Education was the key dividing line in 2016. Especially among white voters, the non-college majority trended toward Trump, and the college-educated minority trended toward Clinton or third-party candidates. And if we were being honest, myself and those in my peer group were unable to see objectively what was happening *because the trend was happening to us.* Virtually no one in our group possessed the demographic characteristics that would let them see the appeal of Trump's blunt-talking style. A college diploma, the most basic prerequisite for working at high levels in politics and the news media, was the very thing that blinded the elite to Trump's appeal and hobbled those who wished to stop him.

This blind spot was not only an affliction of the liberal Beltway media. A certain squishiness on cultural issues undergirded the entire Republican establishment. For us, fire-breathing cultural rhetoric was a necessary but unpleasant price to pay for the ultimate objective: electing candidates who would supercharge the economy through faster growth, less regulation, and lower taxes. This version of the official Republican Party—

highly educated, higher income, metropolitan, above all concerned with questions of strategy and electability—is now widely recognized as being on its last legs. But what is less well understood is that this was never the party's true identity to begin with. The establishment was only able to exert the control that it did thanks to a like-minded set of candidates and the weakness of the populist alternatives up to that point. In a country where a majority had not graduated from college, in a party where more and more of the voters did not graduate, rule by a consultant class that did not look like its voters was someday bound to collapse.

In the wake of this collapse, it would be easy to issue a jaded call for elites to understand "the real America," with reporting trips to diners in West Virginia and such. But the challenge is in many ways more profound. It is not merely one of considering the views of voters outside the Beltway, but of nullifying a set of beliefs indigenous to college-educated professionals who live and breathe politics—in both parties. And what are these beliefs? They boil down to being further to the left on social and cultural issues than the members of our respective parties are. This is not a problem specific to political professionals, but is a condition common to most college graduates. For Democratic elites, it's the recent fashion for identity politics, including the use of terms like "Latinx" that Hispanics themselves almost never use. And for Republican elites, it's a distaste for conservative cultural stances that leads them to run instead on a limited government economic philosophy that the average voter doesn't understand. When it comes to winning elections, the distinctive worldview of the college graduate often gets in the way.

It was the surprising outcome of the 2020 election that finally pushed me to write this book. Trump's 2016 victory had been framed by liberals in terms of white racial "resentment," thanks to his victories among working-class whites. This was never the full story: many of these same Trump-shifting voters had also shifted toward Barack Obama, making him the first Black president. Now, in 2020, the phenomenon known as education polarization—pushing non-graduates right—was expanded to include Hispanic, Asian American, and even Black voters, the most loyal Democratic group. If this trend continues, it would mean the birth of a new party system, replacing the old twentieth-century class divide between the parties—Democrats for the poor and the workers, Republicans for the rich and the professional classes. If this happened, it would signal that race-specific factors that bound nonwhites to the Democratic Party no longer matter as much, a sign of fading racial divides in society at large. With traditional Democratic constituencies voting Republican at higher rates, Democrats would no longer be able to claim the moral high ground as the tribune of workers and marginalized minority groups. The rejection of the left-wing politics of social change by formerly impoverished or discriminated-against groups would also be a sign of their improving lot—a testament to the success of the American Experiment.

Accounts of populist realignment often carry dark undertones, but the story told in these pages is a hopeful one. It is one of strivers rising through the ranks of American society through their own hard work—not looking for a government handout or no longer voting for the party of economic redistribution. The trends that in 2016 seemed to usher in a period of unparalleled racial animosity are, after 2020, pointing the way toward less racially polarized voting—and a less racially polarized society.

Heading into the 2020 election, signs that this might happen were as yet tentative. I explored this possibility in a 2019 paper for the bipartisan States of Change project, which would become the nucleus of this book. If a multiracial realignment happened, I concluded, it would not happen as a repudiation of populism or Trumpism, but as a result of nonwhite voters moving toward them, in much the same way that working-class whites had.

This book seeks to find truth in data: survey data of Americans, precinct results, voter registration records. There are other sources of truth, too, ones often seen in political books. These range from the highly anecdotal—the aforementioned West Virginia–diner style of coverage—to accounts of elite debates, the kind that play out in cleverly worded magazine essays or, less cleverly, in daily Twitter ripostes. These sources often add to our understanding of things. But they also have major shortcomings. Anecdotal reporting tells powerful stories, but is easy to manipulate to drive the narrative the reporter wants. In a closely divided country, it is easy to find anecdotes to support any point of view. All of those stories are ones worth hearing, but without rigorous quantitative analysis, they are not indicative of which side will win out in elections. Relying on the elite narrative is even worse. Elites themselves are an interested party in the story of populist realignment—and the ones on the losing side of it. So I've made it a point to focus instead on the data that can credibly say something about what *everyone* thinks: the polls that give us some insight on the public mood and the election results that serve as the final verdict. The burden of proof is on me to show that this new multiracial populism is not just a curiosity of one or two election cycles, but a logical progression of trends underway for decades, trends not easily undone. Here I hope to draw out the lessons of history, standing on the shoulders of giants whose writings fifty years or more ago foreshadowed our present politics.

Together, the data and the history tell a story. It is a story of an utterly changed electoral landscape being remade by a multiracial working-class coalition, a coalition that gives any party that can capture it the decisive advantage in national elections.

—Patrick Ruffini
Falls Church, Virginia
March 2023

1.

PARTY OF THE PEOPLE

Not long ago, the politics of America was the politics of class. This was true not only in the ways politicians spoke, but of the voters they won. In the rhetoric of Democrats in particular, there was no doubt about whose side the party was on. Trailing in the polls, Al Gore revamped a 2000 campaign initially focused on high-tech prosperity with a return to the unreconstructed politics of the workingman and -woman. "We are for the people!" Gore bellowed, sounding like an itinerant preacher. "They are for the powerful!" A technocrat at heart, Gore would prove to be an imperfect populist messenger. But the pivot seemed to work: he went from trailing by double digits to within 537 votes of winning the presidency.

Gore's rhetoric drew from a deep well: the Democratic Party's legacy as "the party of the people," one that went all the way back to its early days in the nineteenth century as the tribune of a humble agrarian class battling the coastal merchant elite. It remained a mainstay of the party through Franklin D. Roosevelt's New Deal, Harry Truman's progressive-populist comeback in 1948, Lyndon B. Johnson's Great Society, and the "I feel your pain" campaigns of Bill Clinton. For much of their history, Democrats were divided on the big social questions of the age, slavery and civil rights among them, but there was no doubt in the people's mind that they were the party of the common man. This understanding has continued into the modern era. "For us, it is the Democrats that are the party of workers, of the poor, of the weak, and the victimized," Thomas Frank wrote in his 2004 bestseller, *What's the Matter with Kansas?* "Understanding this, we think, is basic; it is part of the ABCs of adulthood."

This understanding is reflected in public opinion data. The idea that the Democrats were the party of the working class was the electorate's strongest positive association with it in every election from 1952 through at least 2004. Conversely, the strongest negative association with the Republicans were that they were the party of big business and the rich. This divide was omnipresent just two decades ago. In the 1996 election, Bill Clinton won the lowest-income voters—those making $15,000 a year or less—by 31 points. The highest-income voters went for Republican Bob Dole by 16 points, an income divide of 47 points.

Today, how much money you make no longer dictates how you vote. In the 2020 election, Joe Biden won the poorest voters—those making under $30,000 a year—by eight points, while Biden split the highest-earning voters evenly with Donald Trump—an income divide of just eight points.

A college diploma has replaced income as the new marker of social class and the key dividing line in elections. And the relationship between this new conception of class and partisanship now runs in the opposite direction: the more highly you rank, the more Democratic you vote. This shift has been so strong, so inexorable, that it has whittled down the economic divide that defined twentieth-century politics to practically nothing. Until recently, education polarization has been a white phenomenon. Most of it appeared in the 2016 election, in the starkly different ways that whites with and without degrees processed the Donald Trump candidacy, but it now thoroughly defines every election, regardless of who's on the ballot.

If politics now feels less like a contest of competing policy ideas, and more like an existential cultural struggle, education polarization is why. Something approaching half of whites now graduate from college, and this near parity between graduates and non-graduates had turned out to be a uniquely potent cultural dividing line. At the end of World War II, only a tiny fraction of young people went to college. Those who did were a narrow elite, and those who didn't were the country's mainstream. Today, college graduates represent a much larger elite, and those who don't are defined, socially and politically, as the working class. This basic divide has defined American politics in the last decade. The choice to finish college

Figure 1.1: White Education Polarization, 1980 to 2020

Lean relative to presidential election result for whites, with and without college degrees

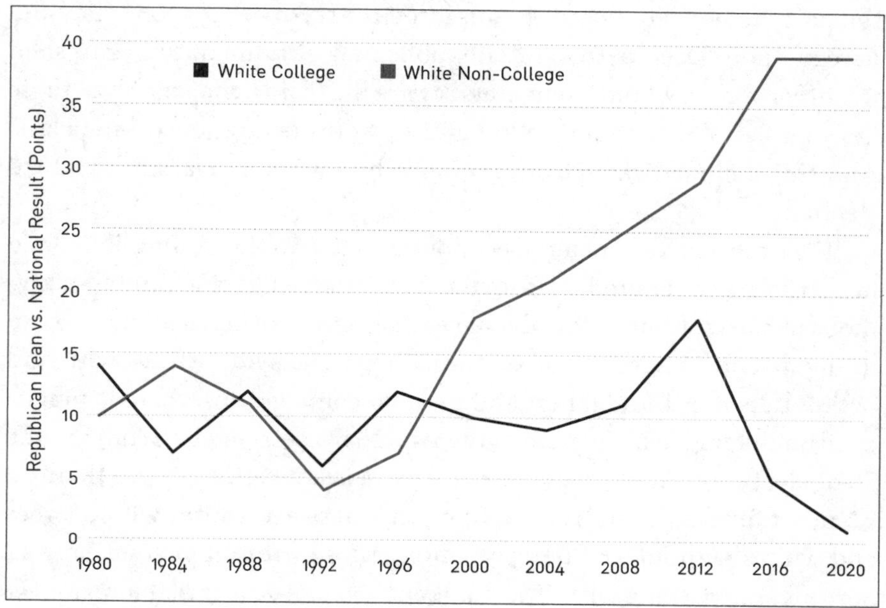

Source: VNS/NEP Exit Polls, 1980–2020

and to not finish (or even start) is now the choice that says the most about who you are and what you value in life—between self-actualization in a competitive professional field or an honest day's work mainly as a way to provide for your family; between acquiring knowledge for its own sake or staying close to the people and places you knew growing up. Among whites, this basic cultural divide translated to a modest political divide in the 2000 election—when the concept of rural red versus urban blue first came into view—and a big one in the 2016 election, when one candidate intuited a path to power that involved making implicit cultural differences between the parties very, very explicit.

Since a college diploma translates readily to higher incomes, the new education divide has upended the class divides that defined twentieth-century politics. As a result, the Republican Party now has more people in it who are in the bottom half of the income distribution than it ever has, while it bleeds votes among the wealthiest. To be clear, this is happening not because its economic message has changed. Economically, the party remains outwardly committed to free-market economics and deregulation. Despite this, the Republican coalition continues to shed wealthier voters, whom Democrats say are the main beneficiaries of these free-market policies, while adding more votes from the working class. And this included gains from the nonwhite working class in the 2020 election.

The irrelevance of material economic factors in this shift is illustrated in a striking set of numbers from the Cooperative Election Study, a sixty-thousand-person survey conducted each election that enables us to zoom in on specific subgroups of voters. When you divide whites with and without degrees into higher- and lower-income groups, there is practically no difference by income in the vote share received by Trump in the 2020 election. What drives the white vote is education, where there's a 22-point difference in Trump's vote share between whites with degrees and whites without—64 percent among those without degrees, just 42 percent among those with. The numbers also make clear that it no longer makes sense to consider white voters as a single political unit. They are only properly understood when divided by college degrees.

Because low-income whites tend to be concentrated mostly in the pro-Trump white working class, the relationship between income and vote choice is fully inverted among whites, with lower-income whites support-

Table 1.1: Income No Longer Matters to White Presidential Vote Choice

Trump-Biden margin by race and family income, with whites divided by education

	White Non-College	White College	Black	Hispanic	Asian
Lower Income ($0–$79,999)	+30%	−13%	−80%	−36%	−41%
Higher Income ($80,000+)	+31%	−15%	−82%	−25%	−43%

Source: Cooperative Election Study, 2020

ing the Republican presidential candidate at higher rates than those with higher incomes. Ohio State political scientist Tom Wood points out that this only became the case recently. In every election going back at least to 1948, through 2012, higher-income white voters always voted more Republican than lower-income ones.

Signs of the class role reversal are also present among Black and Asian American voters, where those in higher-income brackets voted a few points more Democratic than their lower-income counterparts in 2020. The crucial exception to this trend are Hispanics, the group where Donald Trump made his biggest gains in the 2020 election. On the margin, higher-income Hispanics voted 11 points more Republican in 2020 than lower-income Hispanics. In this, they resemble the white voters of the 1970s and '80s, a time when there was no appreciable education divide and higher-income members of the group were more likely to support Republicans. Back then, the GOP was defined by its support from the striving and upwardly mobile: the urban ethnic working class saw their incomes rise as they moved to the suburbs and began voting as higher-income people at the time did, for Republicans. In doing so, they were not only voting for a party that would tackle head-on the urban crime they had escaped, but one that would keep their taxes low. Their concerns were no longer those of the destitute Depression-era worker.

How did the class role reversal actually happen? Right in the title, Thomas Frank's *What's the Matter with Kansas?* talks about the phenomenon as one might talk about an unwell relative. In 2000, the country saw a hard shift to the right among rural voters, powering Bush victories in a raft of Clinton-voting border states or those on the fringes of the South, from Louisiana all the way up to West Virginia, a coal-mining state once considered the most Democratic in the country. Liberal readers craved answers about how poor, rural Americans could be tricked into voting against their economic self-interest. Frank's story centers around his home state of Kansas, where Republicans had morphed from the party of the country club into the party of Sunday service—banking the votes of lower-income, deeply religious white voters opposed to abortion and gay marriage. In Frank's telling of the story, it was the Republican bankers and donors in the wealthy Kansas City suburb of Mission Hills—where

Frank grew up—pulling the strings. "*Vote* to stop abortion; *receive* a rollback in capital gains taxes," Frank riffed. "*Vote* to make our country strong again; *receive* deindustrialization. . . . *Vote* to get government off our backs; *receive* conglomeration and monopoly everywhere from media to meatpacking. . . . *Vote* to strike a blow against elitism; *receive* a social order in which wealth is more concentrated than ever before in our lifetimes." Mission Hills donors might grumble about the rural riffraff entering the party, but that was a small price to pay for a Republican majority that would deliver on their desired economic agenda.

Frank told a compelling story of Kansas's wealthy swindling its poor—and no drama is complete without a plot twist. Almost twenty years after the publication of *What's the Matter with Kansas?*, the rich Republican string pullers of Mission Hills are hardly to be found in the party. Joe Biden won Mission Hills in the 2020 election, part of a realignment of wealthy and well-educated whites into the Democratic Party. Johnson County, home to the affluent Kansas City suburbs, is solidly blue. The old country-club Republicans are now in full revolt against Christian conservative control of the party, a split that has elected and reelected Democratic governors in this red state. For Frank and his followers, economic inequality remains the central moral struggle of the age, but the villain of the story has switched sides.

A REALIGNMENT IN TWO PARTS

Two recent developments have created a new alignment in American politics. The first was the surprise outcome of the 2016 election, where working-class whites—a group whose numbers have been in decline—nevertheless wielded enough strength to help Donald Trump engineer the largest presidential upset in decades. Rumors of the death of this voting bloc proved greatly exaggerated: they represented more than four in ten American voters, a cohesive political grouping making up a plurality of the electorate nationally and a majority in many crucial midwestern swing states. As a result, the bricks in the Blue Wall fell one by one, their names etched in memory: Michigan, Pennsylvania, Wisconsin.

Donald Trump's campaign was freakishly well targeted to win more votes in the places that mattered most on the electoral map—and lose them in the places that didn't. This re-sorting of the electorate led to a jarring result: a candidate winning the Electoral College while losing the popular vote by more than two percentage points. The Republican Party's newfound advantage in the Electoral College was no coincidence, but an outgrowth of white education polarization. College graduates have been on the rise in recent decades, but their numbers are concentrated in major metropolitan areas, the largest of which anchor solidly Democratic states like California, New York, and Illinois. Graduates' shift away from Trump made no difference to the Electoral College math, but the working-class shift toward him made all the difference.

Heading into the 2016 election, Trump's gains in the working class had been widely predicted, but their magnitude was vastly underrated. The Republican was expected to pick up Ohio and Iowa, states with at least some recent history of voting Republican. But there was little serious thought of the contagion spreading to a state like Michigan, which Barack Obama had won by 16 points in 2008. In neighboring Wisconsin, the polls showed Clinton so far ahead that she notoriously did not bother campaigning there.

The Midwest was unique, not only in its large presence of working-class white voters, but in the large numbers of voters in that group *who had voted for Barack Obama*. Republicans had hit a ceiling with the white working class in the South, where there were few left to flip. But working-class targets were ripe for the picking in old auto towns like Youngstown or Toledo, Ohio, ground zero in the contest between Obama and his opponent, Mitt Romney, in 2012.

Three major shifts characterized the 2016 election. The first was Trump's giant leap forward among working-class whites. The second was the unwinding of the Obama coalition, with steep declines in nonwhite turnout and Democratic support initially inspired by Obama's historic candidacy in 2008. And the third, though less prominent in the Midwest than in other regions, was the shift of traditionally Republican suburbs and college-educated whites into the Democratic fold.

Macomb County, Michigan, to the north of Detroit, has for decades been a reference point for those seeking to win the white working class, the home of the Reagan Democrat. It was here where Stanley Greenberg, Bill Clinton's 1992 pollster, held a famed series of focus groups to understand how Democrats could win back the working-class majority they had lost to Ronald Reagan. In the 1980s, a group of concerned moderates in the party coalesced into the Democratic Leadership Council, Arkansas governor Bill Clinton among them. The DLC warned that the party had lost sight of the broad mass of working- and middle-class Americans, fixating instead on a disparate menagerie of identity groups—women, minorities, labor, and green voters. The campaign that emerged from Macomb positioned Bill Clinton as the "Man from Hope," a candidate focused only on one group: the middle class that a large majority of Americans identified with. In his book *Middle Class Dreams*, Greenberg put the challenge in simple terms. "Democrats cannot aspire to dominate this period and lead the country unless they re-invent their links with and regain the confidence of downscale voters—working- and middle-class voters—who want nothing more complicated than a better life," he wrote. Bill Clinton thoroughly succeeded in 1992, sweeping Macomb, and doing as well nationally with working-class whites as among those with degrees. Thanks to Clinton's down-home appeal and the populist third-party candidacy of Ross Perot, the Republican Party of George H. W. Bush was drained of its Reagan-era working-class support.

Hillary Clinton was less successful than her husband in Macomb County, losing it by double digits to Trump on a 16 percent swing toward the Republicans from 2012.* She also had problems to the south, where she dropped ten points from Obama's 2012 levels in Wayne County on a double-digit drop in Black turnout in Detroit. In Wisconsin, Clinton improved Democratic margins in the Milwaukee area, most prominently in

* Margin swing, or "swing," a term to be used liberally throughout this book, is calculated by the change in margin from one election to the other. For instance, if a Democrat won a county by 10 points in the previous election, and a Republican wins it by 10 points in this election, that counts as a 20-point margin swing to the Republican. It translates to about double the change in a party's vote share. It's preferable to calculate swing based on margins, not vote shares, because it filters out changes in the level of support for third-party candidates.

the suburbs, but turnout in Milwaukee proper dropped by more than ten points, which meant fewer votes to hold back the rural red tide for Trump.

The Midwest does not lack for highly educated, high-growth areas—from cities like Minneapolis, to college towns like Ann Arbor and Madison, to fast-growing suburbs like Delaware, Ohio, or Carmel, Indiana. Like suburban and metro voters elsewhere, the voters here would find the loudmouth populist Trump a less appealing Republican option than the buttoned-up, managerial Romney, but the influence of these areas was dwarfed in the vote count by places with a working-class sensibility, whether they were heavily white or more diverse.

Table 1.2: Margin Swing and Turnout Change in the Midwest in 2016

	2012–16 Margin Swing to Trump	2012–16 Turnout Change
White Working Class		
Trumbull, OH (Warren)	+29.3%	–5.6%
St. Louis, MN (Duluth)	+17.9%	–2.7%
Stark, OH (Canton)	+17.7%	–3.4%
Macomb, MI (Detroit suburb)	+15.5%	+3.8%
Outagamie, WI (Appleton)	+10.8%	–0.8%
Diverse Working-Class Cities		
Genesee, MI (Flint)	+18.7%	–3.3%
Wayne, MI (Detroit)	+9.5%	–4.7%
Cuyahoga, OH (Cleveland)	+3.9%	–6.3%
Milwaukee, WI	–1.0%	–10.6%
Educated Professionals		
Dane, WI (Madison)	–3.6%	+1.9%
Washtenaw, MI (Ann Arbor)	–5.4%	+5.0%
Delaware, OH (Columbus suburb)	–7.1%	+5.2%
Hennepin, MN (Minneapolis)	–7.9%	0.0%
Waukesha, WI (Milwaukee suburb)	–8.0%	–2.0%

Source: Dave Leip's Atlas of U.S. Elections

The second part of the working-class realignment would arrive in 2020, when working-class Hispanic, Asian American, and Black voters joined their white working-class counterparts in their shift away from the old party of the people. As with the working-class white surprise in 2016, this shift was initially obscured by pre-election polls showing Trump losing in a landslide.

The first sign that the country was in store for another surprise came at 7:00 p.m. eastern time on election night, when vote totals from Miami-Dade County, Florida, flashed across phone and TV screens. In an instant, the political class was jolted out of a reality where Trump trailed badly all year, on track to lose the 2020 election handily. With the suddenness of an *Infinity Gauntlet* finger snap, Miami-Dade reset the conventional wisdom, thrusting the political world into a new reality, one where a second Trump term was within sight. In the largest Hispanic metropolis in America, Trump had gone from a 29-point drubbing four years earlier to just a 7-point deficit, a 22-point swing. As in 2016, Florida was off the board for Democrats, and if you gave it an hour or two, who knew where else would be? For a few hours, it felt like 2016 all over again.

As counting continued that night and in the days that followed, the decisive role of immigrant and nonwhite voters in Trump's near-victory came into clearer view. Trump had surged all along the Mexican border with Texas, including a 55-point swing in rural Starr County in the Rio Grande Valley, nearly winning a county that Clinton had captured four years earlier by 60 points. He won next-door Zapata County, the first Republican since 1920 to do so. Votes were slower to report in California, but the surprise election to the House of two Asian American Republicans in Orange County, Michelle Steel and Young Kim, indicated a surprising shift in immigrant-heavy communities that was broad-reaching and not limited to Hispanics. With Trump's coalition adding more working-class nonwhites and subtracting more college-educated whites, the pro-Republican Electoral College skew became more pronounced. Just a 0.6-percentage-point shift in the national popular vote, which Biden would still have won by some six million votes, would have been enough to reelect Trump. The new class alignment confirmed the Democrats' structural disadvantage in presidential elections, where they now needed to win the popular vote by four points to win the White House.

Trump's 2020 surge among recent immigrant groups mostly followed a consistent pattern from region to region. His Hispanic gains extended from Cubans in Miami to Mexicans close to the border, to Puerto Ricans and Dominicans in New York and Florida. He would win more votes from both Vietnamese immigrants and Chinese immigrants. The Black vote trended his way by a few points once again. Working-class losses that Democrats blamed on white racism in 2016 were not as easily explained away now.

Table 1.3: Trump's Gains in Diverse Areas in 2020

County (Metro)	2016–20 Margin Swing to Trump	% Nonwhite 2020 Electorate
Hispanic		
Starr, TX	+55.2%	96.4%
Hidalgo, TX (McAllen)	+23.4%	87.9%
Miami-Dade, FL	+22.3%	57.9%
Cameron, TX (Brownsville)	+19.3%	81.8%
Imperial, CA (El Centro)	+17.1%	83.1%
Large Asian American Populations		
Santa Clara, CA (San Jose)	+4.7%	53.6%
Honolulu, HI	+3.0%	59.7%
Diverse Urban Centers		
Bronx, NY	+11.4%	85.9%
Queens, NY	+8.4%	64.7%
Los Angeles, CA	+5.2%	58.9%
Philadelphia, PA	+3.6%	56.3%
Cook, IL (Chicago)	+3.5%	44.2%

Sources: Dave Leip's Atlas of U.S. Elections and Echelon Insights' demographic estimates of the 2020 electorate

Ideology provided a simple explanation for Trump's nonwhite gains. A long-standing paradox of public opinion is that African Americans, Hispanics, and Asian Americans vote Democratic more than their middling levels of self-reported liberalism might suggest. Racial identity plays a key role in these groups' political allegiances—and as a result Democrats win a high percentage of votes from members of these groups who lean right ideologically—similar to the high levels of support the party used to enjoy among white conservatives in places like West Virginia. If these voters were to start voting more along ideological lines, Democrats would be vulnerable to a swift, West Virginia–style collapse.

In the 2016 election, white conservatives supported Trump with more than 90 percent of the vote, but Hispanic, Asian American, and especially Black conservatives supported Republicans at nowhere near as high a rate. Hispanic and Asian conservatives supported Trump with bare majorities in the 2016 election. And among Black voters, self-described conservatives supported Hillary Clinton by 75 to 20 percent. These nonwhite conservatives are the classic cross-pressured voters, prime targets for realignment. And in 2020, Trump made a breakthrough with them: Black conservatives moved 43 points toward Trump, Hispanic conservatives moved 37 points in Trump's direction, and Asian American conservatives moved 36 points.

It needs to be repeated that Trump *lost* the 2020 election. Neither his gains in key groups nor his false narratives about a stolen election change this fact. But Trump's performance was testament to the resiliency of a Republican coalition built around the working-class voter, which in 2020 had grown to include more nonwhite voters. The rise of multiracial working-class conservatism, once on track to merit but a small footnote in the story of a landslide Trump defeat, instead became a crucial reason why the election was so close. For Republicans, this proved to be both a blessing and a curse. On the one hand, it sketched out a future road map to winning over diverse nonwhite voters on the same terms that it had won over white working-class voters. On the other hand, the closeness of the result gave Trump little reason to leave the stage, his presence clouding Republican prospects in the 2022 midterms—and the 2024 presidential race.

At a minimum, Republicans' working-class gains in 2016 and 2020 unraveled progressive hopes for an "emerging Democratic majority," a "rising American electorate," or a "coalition of the ascendant." For years, Democrats lived by the axiom that demography was destiny. They held all the growing groups in the electorate—nonwhites, the college-educated, the millennial generation—and the math grew stronger every year. Year after year, the country grew less white, less religious, and more socially liberal, with rising support for gay marriage and a growing acknowledgment of racial inequality. In 1980, 80 percent of the U.S. population was white; in 2020, that number had fallen to 58 percent. By 2045, America is projected to become a majority-minority country, with the white share of the population falling below the 50 percent mark. Unless Republicans made significant inroads with nonwhite voters, their ability to win future elections would at the very least be severely limited.

The 2012 election had seemed to vindicate this liberal narrative, with confident predictions first made in Ruy Teixeira and John Judis's 2002 book, *The Emerging Democratic Majority*, all seeming to come true at once. "Barack Obama won because he recognized a new America," went a post-election memo from the Democratic polling consortium Democracy Corps. "The President managed only 39 percent of the white vote, the lowest white percentage recorded for a winning national candidate, and suffered a 12-point swing against him among independent voters, but won both the popular vote and an Electoral College landslide by energizing voters we describe as the Rising American Electorate." Obama had attracted record turnout among Black voters enthusiastic about reelecting the first African American president, increased Democratic margins among Hispanics and Asian Americans, and was locking down millennial voters. With the electorate that was promised coming through so spectacularly, progressives reacted giddily to the possibility of no longer needing to moderate their message for a white working class fundamentally out of step with the New America.

Beltway Republicans basically agreed with the progressive Democratic analysis. A formal party autopsy was conducted following the 2012 election and the language in it was a striking public admission of fault, calling for the party to pass comprehensive immigration reform to appeal to

Hispanic voters and to soften on social issues to appeal to younger voters. "When it comes to social issues," the autopsy went, "the Party must in fact and deed be inclusive and welcoming. If we are not, we will limit our ability to attract young people and others, including many women, who agree with us on some but not all issues." One prominent business leader joined the pile-on against the party's performance that year, zeroing in on Mitt Romney's hard-line position on immigration. "He had a crazy policy of self deportation which was maniacal," said Donald Trump. "It sounded as bad as it was, and he lost all of the Latino vote. He lost the Asian vote. He lost everybody who is inspired to come into this country."

There would turn out to be another path other than the one envisioned by the GOP autopsy writers. It involved sharpening, not softening—a hard turn toward populism, verging on nativism, that not only ran up margins in the white working class beyond the party's wildest hopes but also—surprisingly—did not cost them the nonwhite voters they agonized over after 2012. If demography was destiny, perhaps it was not the destiny Democrats thought. The country's demographics may have been changing, but voting patterns within those demographics were changing faster, undermining any straight-line demographic projection of eternal Democratic rule. To illustrate how this has played out in practice, a gradually rising share of Hispanics in the electorate is of only limited help to Democrats when their Hispanic vote margins have dropped by more than half, from 44 points in 2012 to around 20 points in the 2022 midterms. Even before the 2020 election, both authors of *The Emerging Democratic Majority* conceded that their majority would no longer emerge. Judis and Teixeira reminded their fellow liberals of a crucial precondition for the theory to work: robust working-class support across racial lines, including maintaining levels of white working-class support the party had at the turn of the millennium. Now those voters were leaving the party in droves. As if this weren't bad enough, many voters in the "rising" groups—African Americans, Hispanics, and Asian Americans—started to peel off, too. The working-class shift among culturally conservative white voters has started to erode the core pillars of the Democratic coalition.

Despite a disappointing midterm election cycle in 2022, Republicans further extended their gains with working-class voters of all races. These

Figure 1.2: Nonwhite Conservatives Shifted to Trump in 2020

Trump 2016 and Trump 2020 margins among self-identified conservatives, by race

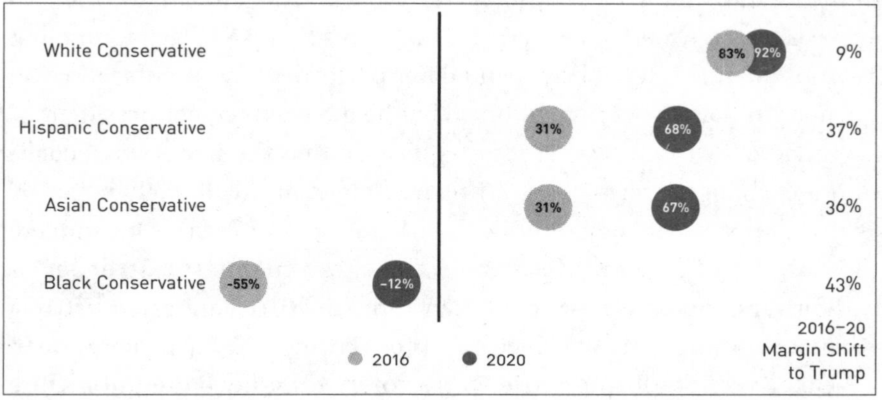

Source: Cooperative Election Study, 2016 and 2020

shifts would not ultimately prove decisive due to the influence of Donald Trump, whose involvement in the campaign turned off swing voters in competitive races. While this book lauds many of Trump's political successes—busting up the Blue Wall and realigning Hispanic voters—Trump's 2020 and 2022 performances cast serious doubt on whether or not he is the best vessel to carry forward the multiracial populist realignment he first provoked. Perhaps seeking to recapture the magic of his 2016 campaign, Trump has pivoted back to working-class populism early in his 2024 bid, attacking fellow Republicans for cutting Social Security and Medicare and making a highly touted visit to working-class East Palestine, Ohio, after a train derailment spilled toxic chemicals into the community. Whether or not these moves will help Trump win a Republican primary in 2024 remains to be seen. But a solid body of evidence from recent elections shows that the working-class realignment doesn't depend on Donald Trump appearing on the ballot. Other Republicans are having no problem winning with Trump's coalition, highlighted by the victories of Ron DeSantis in Florida and Glenn Youngkin in Virginia, and in Lee Zeldin's strong showing in the New York governor's race. These victories involved recovering many of the white suburban voters Trump lost while keeping the working-class voters Trump brought into the party—and even adding new ones. By contrast, Republicans who tethered themselves to the Trump and MAGA banners did worse in the 2022 midterms. An analysis by the American Enterprise Institute's Philip Wallach found that Trump-endorsed Republican candidates performed five points worse on the margin than those not endorsed by the defeated former president.

In victory or defeat, there is no question that the Republican coalition has changed permanently. It is no longer, and will likely never be again, the party of the country club. Different candidates or, indeed, the same candidate in different elections, can manifest a stronger or weaker version of this new coalition. Trump in 2016 manifested a strong version, winning with 304 electoral votes. Trump in 2020 brought forth a weaker version, losing more white voters than he gained nonwhite voters. And Trump was an even weaker draw in the 2022 midterms, imposing an across-the-board five-point penalty on Republicans marching under his banner.

The challenge for Republicans in 2024 is to show that they can reap the structural benefits of Trump's realignment of the American electorate without Trump's chaotic persona at the top of the ticket. Post-Trump elections show this is possible. Glenn Youngkin's victory in the 2021 race for the Virginia governorship, for example, represented a wide-ranging advance from Trump's 2020 vote in counties across the state—including a stronger performance than Trump in the state's rural, working-class southwest. Youngkin deftly threaded the needle in 2021, running on a genial business-savvy reminiscent of Mitt Romney, while meeting the populist moment with a campaign against a left-wing, "woke" agenda in the schools and a pledge to suspend the sales tax on groceries.

In Florida, Governor Ron DeSantis brought forth the strongest version of the multiracial populist coalition we have seen in any state election, becoming the first Republican to win the state's Hispanic electorate since 2006. DeSantis's victory cemented the traditionally Republican Cuban American vote with his victory in Miami-Dade County and he made particularly strong gains with the state's traditionally Democratic Puerto Rican voters in Orange and Osceola Counties. His 19-point victory, along with that of Marco Rubio for the Senate, was a rare bright spot in what was otherwise a disappointing election cycle for Republicans, making DeSantis an early front-runner for the 2024 GOP nomination.

Farther north, in New York, Lee Zeldin was not able to fully overcome the state's significant Democratic lean, but he came within six points of victory. He made his strongest gains in New York City, doubling the Republican share of the gubernatorial vote from four years earlier. Zeldin made particularly strong gains in multiracial South Brooklyn, where Asians mix freely with Hispanics, and in Asian neighborhoods in Queens, where he performed almost twenty points better than Trump did in 2020. Republicans also scored surprise upset victories in the New York statehouse, flipping three Brooklyn-based assembly districts. The biggest surprise was the victory of Lester Chang, who campaigned door-to-door in his military uniform in a heavily Asian American southwest Brooklyn district that encompasses parts of Sunset Park and Bensonhurst. The recent rise in crime, including a shocking subway shooting, weighed heavily in the shift. Crime—and Democrats' elimination of cash bail—was seized upon as an issue by Republicans running across the state. A hard-nosed law-and-order message, not a "softening" of the Republican brand for diverse communities, is what allowed Zeldin and down-ballot winners like Chang to dramatically expand the Republican base in a city where more than a third of the population was born outside the United States.

In the 2022 elections for the House, largely white suburban districts allergic to Trumpism proved to be a fire wall for Democrats, limiting their losses in what should have been a terrible year. But the national vote trends showed silver linings for Republicans. They not only scored their best performance among Hispanic voters in a midterm election, shifting the community almost ten points right from their 2020 margins, but also had their best performance among Black voters, scoring between 13 and 14 percent of the national vote, well above their previous midterm results. Rising support in diverse communities is also reflected in record numbers of nonwhite candidates selected by Republican primary electorates. There were record numbers of Hispanic and African American Republicans elected, and South Carolina's Nikki Haley and Tim Scott are poised to further test this trend in the 2024 presidential primaries. The Republican coalition is now more diverse than at any point in the party's history—and this is all happening while the party expands its majorities among white working-class voters. There are all sorts of reasons to be skeptical that a Republican popular majority for the House will translate to the next presidential campaign. But the 2022 results, uneven as they were for the party, show that the GOP's multiracial populist coalition remains intact. And it's a coalition that is there for the taking in 2024, whether or not the Republican nominee is Donald Trump.

BREAKING DOWN THE ELECTORATE

There is a natural working-class majority in American politics and those who hope to lead the country ignore it at their peril. This is something most serious observers of politics understand on an intellectual level, yet the elite obsessions of the Twitter digerati continue to dominate day-to-day political discourse in a way that suggests that this lesson has not been fully absorbed. The numbers are clear. Nearly seven in ten American adults never graduated college. The number is 64 percent among registered voters and 60 percent among people who voted in the 2020 election. These voters tend to have cultural views to the right of the average college graduate, and quite often well to the right of those college graduates who work in professional politics in both parties.

These facts are not likely to change significantly. College graduation rates are leveling off amid an affordability crisis in higher education, and nonwhites, who have lower college completion rates, are a bigger part of the demographic mix among young people of college age. For the foreseeable future, if not in perpetuity, voters without a college diploma will be in the majority.

This gives the party with momentum among working-class voters an advantage. Right now, that's the Republicans. And the midterm elections, though disappointing for Republicans, don't debunk this idea. The party's advantage, at least for the moment, is compounded by an advantage in the Electoral College and in the Senate, where large metropolitan states with lots of college graduates are on equal footing with smaller states with working-class populations.

When the divide in the American electorate is viewed in political terms—between voters trending toward the Republican Party, as opposed to those trending against them—the split is even larger in favor of Republicans. More than seven in ten voters in 2020 were in groups that had trended Republican in the last two presidential elections.

Three basic groupings define the American electorate: whites without a college degree, whites with a college degree, and nonwhites. Before we get into precise figures, you can think of this divide as existing in a rough 4–3–3 ratio, with white non-college voters the largest group.

The basic logic of the Emerging Democratic Majority was that two smaller groups would combine to overpower a larger one: Democrats were starting to do better among white college graduates, while at the same time naturally increasing their vote margins among nonwhites as these voters grew larger in the electorate, with rapid growth among Hispanics and Asian Americans. Only half of this prediction, about college-educated professionals, actually came to pass.

The New Demographic Divide*

← Trending Left	Trending Right →	
Whites College	**Whites Non-College**	**Nonwhites**
45,853,635 votes in 2020	67,430,704 votes in 2020	43,306,164 votes in 2020
28.9% of the vote	42.5% of the vote	28.5% of the vote
12 points more Democratic since 2012	8 points more Republican since 2012	12 points more Republican since 2012

* Estimates of the size of different groups in the 2020 election reflect Echelon Insights' demographic estimates, merging data from the U.S. Census Bureau's American Community Survey and Current Population Survey, as well as voter file data. Estimates of the size of voting shift come from the author's calculations using the following sources: the National Election Pool exit polls and Catalist for the 2012 to 2016 swing, and Catalist and the Pew Research Center's validated voter survey for the 2016 to 2020 swing. Exit poll data for 2020 are not included due to data quality concerns stemming from the pandemic.

If we look at things not just in terms of support levels, but shifts, the coalition math gets turned around. Nonwhites and working-class whites combine for a more than two-to-one advantage over whites with a college degree, the only group trending Democratic. In recent years, all the energy and growth in the Republican Party has come from this multiracial populist coalition.

The rightward shift of nonwhite voters in 2020 and the white working class in 2016 might seem like two discrete, unrelated events, but the two groups share a common working-class DNA and their political shifts stem from the same root. In 2016 and 2020, the electorate was polarized on cultural questions like immigration, race, and crime, over and above questions of economic or global leadership that have dominated most recent presidential elections. Intuitively, right-wing populist rhetoric on immigration or race should have coalesced more nonwhites into the party with the more liberal views of these issues. That did not happen. Instead, the only group that swung to the left in an age of racially infused populism were white people with college diplomas. Everyone else moved, in varying degrees, right: toward the side of cultural populism.

All of this happened despite Trump's 2016 rhetoric on immigration, when he said Mexicans were "rapists," "bringing drugs, bringing crime" into the country, or his off-key handling of the 2020 George Floyd protests. These shifts defy the conventional wisdom that nonwhite voters are motivated by progressive identity politics. Immigration ranks far down on the list of Hispanic voter priorities, below issues like jobs, the cost of living, and health care. Black concern about crime often comes from a place of support for a strong and consistent enforcement of the law. But a more convincing explanation for the shifts in Trump's direction lie in a fundamental divide between how ordinary American voters think about issues generally—and how that differs from political enthusiasts with high levels of formal education.

All the groups in the multiracial populist coalition are ideologically moderate. Theirs is not a boring, bland, split-the-difference moderation, but a pragmatic if ultimately eclectic one, mixing and matching positions from the left and the right. That might involve support for the construction of a border wall and for abortion rights. For whites with a college degree, politics is ideological. A majority take highly consistent ideological positions in line with their choice of party. In addition to having a more heterodox set of views generally, working-class voters also tend to be further right on cultural issues than on economic issues. This is also true within the Democratic base, where many Black voters hold socially conservative positions on abortion and LGBTQ issues consistent with their higher levels of religiosity. The sweeping left-wing stances that progressives argue are needed in order to motivate a wave of nonwhite turnout are more likely to motivate a shrug of the shoulders—if not drive these voters away.

By contrast, whites with college degrees—not nonwhites—are driving a progressive shift in the party. And when you look at the polling data, white college graduates truly are off on an island of their own. Imagine for a second a voter progressive enough to align with the Democratic or liberal position more than 90 percent of the time. Demographically, such a voter looks very different from the Democratic Party as a whole, which we can know by looking at how respondents answered a series of questions on the 2020 Cooperative Election Study. Six in ten of the most liberal voters are whites with college degrees, double their share of the electorate and the party. Just 3 percent are Black, compared to 12 percent in the electorate overall. Ryan Enos, a Harvard political scientist, captured this dynamic in comments to the *New York Times*'s Thomas Edsall. "College-educated whites, especially those with higher incomes, are not clear coalitional partners for anyone—they don't favor economic policies, such as increasing housing supply or even higher taxes on the rich, that are beneficial to the working class, of any race," observed Enos. "And many college-educated whites are motivated by social issues that are also not largely supported by the working class, of any race."

Following the party's falling short of their marks in 2020, many Democrats have begun to recognize the influence of these voters as a problem within the party. Prominent among them is David Shor, an analyst fired from the Democratic data firm Civis Analytics for tweeting out a study on racial protests deemed insufficiently woke. "The big-picture problem is that the Democratic Party is increasingly reflecting the cultural values and political preferences of educated white people," Shor told the *New*

York Times after the 2020 election. "Culturally, working-class nonwhite people have more in common with working-class white people."

Shor and others have made the case for Democrats taking a different path, emphasizing the kitchen table issues that used to define the party: taxing the rich, increasing access to health insurance, and preserving Social Security and Medicare. Looking toward 2024, Joe Biden seems more mindful of this problem, loading up his speeches with talk of infrastructure and old-age entitlements. "Those of you . . . over 40, did you ever think we'd be in a situation where blue-collar workers would vote Republican?" Biden asked in an early 2023 speech to the Democratic National Committee, adding, "A lot of them came to believe we stopped paying attention to [the] working class the way we used to." Biden's pivot has elicited comparisons to Bill Clinton in 1996 or Barack Obama in 2012, two Democratic incumbents who made inroads with working-class voters in their reelection bids. The trouble is that Biden was not exactly known as a woke warrior in 2020, going by the nickname "Scranton Joe," a generational throwback to the Democratic Party of blue-collar workers. All of this was known, and yet Biden lost ground among working-class voters against a weakened Trump.

The divide I've highlighted—college-educated whites on one side, a multiracial populist coalition on the other—is not defined by large differences in voting patterns. Both sets of voters voted for Biden and Trump at roughly the same rates. But underneath the hood, there are massive differences. College-educated whites are trending left and increasingly set in their ideological ways. The multiracial populist coalition is shifting right, but their moderation makes them politically up for grabs. These voters are more likely than not to decide the 2024 election.

THE MULTIRACIAL MAINSTREAM MAJORITY

Within the new multiracial populist coalition, most of the opportunity for Republicans lies in inspiring a further shift right among Black, Hispanic, Asian American, and mixed-race voters. Future shifts in this direction are not only possible but likely. First, as ideology becomes increasingly central to voting choices among nonwhite voters, as it already has for white voters, Republicans stand to gain among nonwhite moderates and conservatives who currently lean Democratic. The second reason is that something very similar has happened before.

Imagine a group of people initially excluded from the mainstream of American life upon arrival in this country. Businesses posted signs waving them off from applying for jobs. While they endured discrimination, two or three generations along they begin to rise from deep poverty into a decent middle-class existence. Their incomes are rising quickly and soon expected to reach the national average. The most recent census data shows them moving out of the old ethnic enclaves in the cities and out to the suburbs.

This immigrant community is family oriented and deeply religious. Nativist elements have occasionally questioned their loyalty to the United States, but they join the military at rates matching the general population. Their traditional values stand in contrast to the country's educated elite, whose politics are outwardly concerned with reducing the inequities they face, but who in practice understand little of their day-to-day life.

Politically, they often organized as a bloc, banding together as outsiders to elect people who would stand up for their specific interests against the majority hostile to their advancement. This did not mean they automatically supported the Democratic Party, but in most of the cities where they lived, this was the natural choice. When one of their own was on the ballot for president, they supported him overwhelmingly, with nearly 80 percent of their votes.

Lately, support for the party of their ancestors has waned. Elections are held, and magazine feature writers are astounded to learn that they have abandoned the party that once stood, above all other things, for the working person. A vibrant debate emerges among Democrats and the culturally like-minded in the media about how to get these voters back. The task is urgent, for some predict that within the next few years the Democratic advantage among these voters could be greatly reduced or even disappear.

All of these might describe the Hispanic or Asian American immigrant voter of 2022, but the group I am actually describing is the white Catholic voter of the 1960s and '70s. Their political unity reached a high with 78 percent of the vote for John F. Kennedy in 1960, but then trended steadily Republican in the decades that followed. By 2000, you could no longer call them a Democratic group. In 2020, they were voting Republican by double digits.

The story of white Catholics' political shift is tied inexorably to a social shift: toward greater economic opportunities and convergence with the mainstream, then defined as white Anglo-Saxon Protestant. Today, the idea of WASP dominance of elite institutions is an anachronism. Religious barriers that used to divide Americans no longer do. As a result, white Catholics entered the mainstream, both socially and politically, living and voting the same as their counterparts.

Something similar is happening with the outsiders of today, specifically the post-1965 wave of immigrants from Latin America and Asia. In the five years from 2014 to 2019, the incomes of Hispanics and Asian Americans grew by 23 percent and 21 percent, respectively. All racial groups are living in more integrated communities than they did a generation ago. Close to one in five marriages and one in six babies born in the United States are the result of an interracial or interethnic relationship. A version of all of this happened with the new American groups who originally came here in the nineteenth century. Progress has been uneven across the racial spectrum, however. African Americans have a different origin story in America and do not show the same intergenerational progress in incomes as do Hispanics and Asian Americans. Nevertheless, some signs of progress are there, with declining rates of residential segregation—a central goal of the 1960s civil rights laws.

Theories of Democratic demographic dominance rested on a united front of "people of color." But this was not necessarily the political future that people of color were hungering for themselves. Instead, we are seeing a growing convergence toward a multiracial mainstream majority, with more voters of color taking their place in the middle class and the suburbs, forming families across racial lines, and voting closer to the national average.

Aspiration is the key ingredient of this wave of realignment. A "party of the people" might imply that the parties will now switch roles, with Republicans adopting Democratic rhetoric of class resentment. This would be a mistake. To be sure, the decamping of affluent elites should be an occasion for the GOP to reevaluate some of its old policy commitments, particularly on tax cuts for the wealthiest. The Republican Party should have more than the occasional thing to say about health care. Social Security and Medicare should not be first on the list for spending cuts. But, at their best, Republicans have also been the party of the upwardly mobile and the strivers, people who see the path to a better life in their own hard work, not a government handout. This message has resonated for generations of outsiders, the new Americans who want a springboard more than a safety net.

The Republican performances in Little Havana and Little Saigon give lie to the idea that Republicans made their gains by talking like social democrats. Instead, the linkage Republicans drew between the Democratic Party and socialist ideology was clearer than ever in 2020. At the same time, the Republican Party under Trump moderated on entitlement cuts and health care, largely abandoning plans for a root and branch repeal of Obamacare and supporting multiple rounds of pandemic stimulus checks. This balance has proved an especially important one to strike with Hispanics, who, as the largest and most electorally fluid group of nonwhite voters, are the linchpin of any future Republican gains.

The diploma divide has given Republicans a shot at a long-sought-after realignment of nonwhite voters to truly become a multiracial party rooted in the working and middle classes. All of this sounds good—if you're a Republican. But if you're not, why should this matter? The story I am telling in these pages is not just about our two political parties, but about how we are changing as a country. We commonly hear that the country is more divided than ever. In many ways, that's true. But statistically, the country is growing less divided on racial lines. We see it in rising rates of intermarriage, declining residential segregation, rising incomes—and shifts in voting trends that flow from these social changes. Equality of economic opportunity is not yet a reality for people of all races and ethnicities and making them such should be a central goal of policy. But as of now, we are seeing signs of a repeat of what happened with nineteenth-century immigrants to America and their descendants, who steadily became part of the American mainstream. To be clear, the logical end point of this shift is not that the post-1965 immigrant groups will become Republican-leaning, but that they will steadily converge toward the middle.

This new multiracial mainstream majority may not result in Republican electoral majorities in any given election. Our politics seems destined to remain closely competitive, with a healthy aversion to one-party rule. What does seem clear is that the Republican Party will evolve into the home of a new voter coalition: multiracial, multiethnic, and working class. Because realignment is a two-way street, the Democrats will change, too. We could also see Democrats win more of the white vote, especially among the college-educated, in response to the shift among Republicans.

Unlike the mainstream of the nineteenth and twentieth centuries, the mainstream we are moving toward is not just a white one. For the first time in our history, we are seeing the rise of a multiracial mainstream majority where people of different races and ethnic backgrounds are now more likely than ever to live closer together, in suburbs rather than cities, finding love and starting families together. That's a far cry from the Balkanized big cities in which these groups started out, where political machines and ethnic bloc voting—usually for Democrats in general elections and for "our kind" of Democrat in primaries—were the norm.

The merchants of racial division on both the left and the right won't find much to like in these pages. This includes the cottage industry of race essentialists on the left whose ideology has pervaded schools and major corporations, inculcating an obsession with racial differences at a time when integration is on the rise. On the right are the various proponents of white "replacement theory," former Fox News host Tucker Carlson most prominent among them, who preach fear of demographic change as undermining the essential (read: white, or "Western") character of the country. To them, diversity itself is a nefarious left-wing plot to undermine what's great about America. What they ignore is that immigrants who once crossed the southern border are becoming a more reliable bulwark for conservative values than the leftward-shifting college-educated establishment with its "inclusive language" and stacks of Ibram X. Kendi and Robin DiAngelo books. Those immigrants came here because they believe in the greatness of America, a greatness that many whose families have been here for centuries have lost sight of. This shared belief in the greatness and goodness of the country is what's forging a multiracial populist conservative politics, one poised to reshape American politics for decades to come.

2.

THE COSMOPOLITAN TRAP

In this house we believe
Black lives matter
Women's rights are human rights
No human is illegal
Science is real
Love is love
Kindness is everything

Driving around the northern Virginia suburbs of Washington, D.C., in the weeks before the 2020 election, one could hardly miss this multicolored manifesto on a yard sign. The Biden signs they appeared alongside told you who the person inside the house was voting for. The "In this house we believe" sign told you why. And the reasons had little to do with the animating purpose behind the Democratic Party of yesteryear: standing up for the common man and woman against the predation of big business and the rich. Instead, the issues it raised were ones of identity, promoting equality for marginalized groups. Nowhere on this list was a clarion call for the *economically* disadvantaged: for raising the minimum wage, for collective bargaining rights, for reducing income inequality, or for single-payer health insurance. And in a place like Falls Church, Virginia, a place with a median household income of $155,071 and the highest rate of postsecondary educational attainment in the nation, perhaps this made sense. It's not that the liberally minded voters here aren't left-leaning on economics also. But it's not the thing that animates them, that they post about, that they signal to their neighbors with a yard sign over. Bernie Sanders, who did all he could in two successive primary campaigns to refocus the Democratic Party back on the class struggle, did not do particularly well in these wine-track precincts. Donald Trump activated his base on social and identity questions like immigration. Now the resistance to him would respond in kind.

The political transformation of the prosperous, highly educated American suburb is happening practically everywhere, not just near me. Some of these places, like the northern Virginia suburbs, were already very liberal, going from something like a 60–40 Democratic advantage to a 70–30 edge. Others are politically more mixed, and even varying hues of red. The key fact that unites practically all of them is their pro-Democratic *shift*. If there is a cost to the gains Republicans made in places like Youngstown, Ohio, or Flint, Michigan, in recent elections, it is being borne in places like the D.C. suburbs, Buckhead and Sandy Springs outside Atlanta, and the Johnson County suburbs outside Kansas City, Kansas.

Upscale suburbs like these were once considered to be the unassailable fortresses of the late twentieth-century Republican strength, nowhere more so than in the South and West. These include neighborhoods like West University in Houston, the first in Texas to turn Republican with the election of a young congressman named George H. W. Bush. Or Preston Hollow, the Dallas neighborhood where his son, George W. Bush, lives. Or the Cobb County suburbs of Atlanta, once represented in Congress by Newt Gingrich. Or, expanding our aperture to the Midwest, to Thomas Frank's Mission Hills, the embodiment of rock-ribbed Republicanism in the liberal imagination just two decades ago.

In popular culture, no place better embodies the kind of affluence that lent itself to easy support for Republicans from Reagan to Romney than the northern Chicago suburb of Winnetka. John Hughes, the 1980s movie director and Winnetka native, shot classics like *Home Alone* and *Ferris Bueller's Day Off* here. The local high school, New Trier, is routinely rated one of the best in the country, sporting an illustrious roster of alumni including Donald Rumsfeld, Charlton Heston, the Emanuel brothers (Rahm, Ari, and Ezekiel), and Hughes himself. There are political mapmakers on Twitter dedicated to tracking the electoral swings

Table 2.1: The Blue Shift in America's Educated Suburbs

Swing to Republican Presidential Candidate, 2012–20

County (Metro)	2012–20 Margin Swing, Romney to Trump	% 2020 Voters with Bachelor's Degree or Higher
Forsyth, GA (Atlanta)	−29.6%	58.8%
Hamilton, IN (Indianapolis)	−27.5%	70.6%
Gwinnett, GA (Atlanta)	−27.5%	48.9%
Collin, TX (Dallas)	−27.2%	61.5%
Cobb, GA (Atlanta)	−26.8%	53.0%
Johnson, KS (Kansas City)	−25.6%	61.1%
Falls Church, VA (Washington, DC)	−24.7%	85.6%
U.S. average	**−0.3%**	**37.6%**

Source: Dave Leip's Atlas of U.S. Elections and Echelon Insights' demographic estimates of the 2020 electorate

in the precinct where the stately McCallister family house from *Home Alone* is located. The results are striking. From 2012 to 2020, Winnetka went from voting for Mitt Romney by 12 points to supporting Joe Biden by 36 points, a margin swing of 48 points. In an even shorter period, from 2018 to 2022, this wealthy lakeside hamlet shifted from supporting the moderate Republican governor (and town resident) Bruce Rauner by 21 points to favoring his Democratic successor by 28 points. This came about despite the fact that Chicago-centric Cook County, where Winnetka is located, barely budged in these two elections.

Whether the denizens of these upscale suburbs started out as liberals or moderate Republicans, the resistance to Trump transcended old party battles over tax policy or the role of government. In the eyes of these voters, Trump was much worse than your typical Republican stooge for wealthy CEOs: he was a racist, a misogynist, a threat to American democracy itself. Joe Biden spoke of the choice as a "battle for the soul of the nation." Four years earlier, Hillary Clinton tried to forge a transpartisan pro-decency coalition with mantras like "Love trumps hate" and "Love and kindness." Places like Winnetka and West University cheered, but the audience for such airy slogans in 2016 proved to be relatively limited, constrained as it were to upscale voters clustered in states that were unlikely to flip in the Electoral College.

Joe Biden in 2020 showed one could run up the score in educated suburbs and metros just enough to flip key swing states like Arizona and Georgia, centered around the large metros of Phoenix and Atlanta. Despite his victory, Biden's electoral performance was even less electorally efficient than Clinton's was, requiring a large popular vote majority to barely squeak by in the Electoral College. In Congress, the Democratic suburban advantage rests on firmer ground. There, swing districts, not states, are the unit of measurement, and many of these swing districts are in suburbs that have been trending left, including the Dallas and Houston seats that had been home to the Bush family, the suburban Atlanta district from where Newt Gingrich launched the Republican Revolution, and four Orange County, California, districts that had once served as a political launchpad for Barry Goldwater and Ronald Reagan.

Political analyst David Wasserman, the nation's leading expert on the politics of House districts, has developed perhaps the stickiest heuristic for describing the new geographic divide: Whole Foods versus Cracker Barrel. By Wasserman's tabulations, Biden won 85 percent of counties with a Whole Foods Market, the upscale grocery chain, and 32 percent with a Cracker Barrel, the roadside eatery popular in rural America—a Whole Foods–Cracker Barrel divide of 53 points, the highest ever. Wasserman traces this divide through the last three decades and finds it has increased in every presidential election since 1992, when the gap was 20 points. It is possible to widen this divide even further. Biden won 95 percent of counties with *just* a Whole Foods and no Cracker Barrel, and won only 18 percent of counties with a Cracker Barrel and no Whole Foods, a gap of 77 points.

Conservatives routinely poke fun at the kinds of people who shop at Whole Foods, imagining them as a tiny, out-of-touch liberal elite filling their carts with organic fruits, expensive wines, and soft cheeses. I have news for them: this elite isn't tiny. Broad-based prosperity in the United States over the last several decades makes the Whole Foods and Whole

Foods–adjacent voter a considerable force not to be ignored. Its growing size allows for one political party to be increasingly organized around the liberal cultural views of the college-educated voter, an impossibility when just a tiny fraction of voters had degrees. This new cosmopolitan voter isn't just the CEO or banker of Thomas Frank's Mission Hills. Broadly speaking, it encompasses the entire professional class: the doctors, lawyers, and software engineers ensconced in every major metro area in the United States. Professionally, we know them as knowledge workers, those who make their living not with their hands or servicing people's daily needs, but in rearranging ideas and bits into units of ever-greater value in a free-market economy. They are not the 1 percent. They are the top 20 percent, but they are living the life of someone in the top 1 percent one or two generations ago.

This voter has changed the politics of the American suburb, and moved the Democratic Party left. Within the Democratic Party, college-educated voters—and especially white voters with degrees—have social values well to the left of the average Democrat. College-educated voters have been increasing as a share of the voting public over the last several decades, rising even faster within the Democratic Party. And the public has gotten more liberal on many cultural questions in tandem with the rise of the college-educated voter, the increase in support for gay marriage being one prominent example.

Liberal ideology, once the view of a minority faction of Democrats, has now become dominant within it. The numbers here tell a clear story. In 2000, liberals made up just 27 percent of Democrats, barely more than the 24 percent who identified as conservative. By 2019, liberals had grown to 47 percent of the party, with conservatives whittled down to just 14 percent. Partly as a result of this shift among Democrats, liberals have become more of a force in the electorate, rising from 19 to 26 percent of all voters during this time. The years between 2014 and 2016 accelerated the trend. This was the time of the "great awokening," kicked off by the first Black Lives Matter protests in Ferguson, Missouri, and culminating in the election of Donald Trump. During this time, liberalism among Democrats accelerated its upward trajectory as Democrats set aside the old-school blue-collar economics that once united the party and prepared to do war with Trumpism under the banner of democracy and social liberalism.

Aside from being utterly convinced they were in the right, liberals had many victories to celebrate in this period. The *Obergefell v. Hodges* decision in 2015 legalized gay marriage throughout the land. A few weeks later, the Confederate flag was lowered on the South Carolina capitol grounds, ending decades of controversy. History seemed to be on their side. And inevitably, that would mean a new political majority, not just for Democrats, but for the entire equality agenda espoused on the "In this house we believe" sign. As a result, Democrats were more comfortable placing issues of racial and gender identity at the forefront of their campaign in 2016, replacing the blue-collar economic focus that helped Obama sweep the midwestern battlegrounds in 2012.

In doing so, they had wandered into a trap. Progressives were strong enough at last to control the Democratic Party, but still in a losing position in the general electorate, where they trailed conservative-identifiers by 10 points—36 to 26 percent. The Democrats might still have had a shot at winning over a majority of the country. But the distinctive politics of the Whole Foods voter did not. And that politics was growing increasingly influential among Democrats, with plenty of talk in the 2020 primary debates about decriminalizing border crossings and seizing guns. The growing assertiveness of the liberal, college-educated Democrat also created a disconnect with moderate, working-class Black and Hispanics, whom Democrats actually relied on to win elections. Further deepening the liberal predicament, the Democrats' suburban gains mostly came in places that would do nothing to help them in the Electoral College, aiding in the election of Trump with a minority of the vote.

RISE OF THE METROPOLITAN ELITE

The rivalry between the elite and common folk is as old as the country itself, but the nature of it changed dramatically in the mid-twentieth century. In his 2012 book, *Coming Apart,* Charles Murray pinpoints 1960 as the year things began to change. The deep social fissures that up to that point mainly divided whites from Blacks began to work their way through white America, leading to today's political divide between whites with and without college degrees. In 1960, social maladies like drug use or illegitimacy affected upper- and lower-class whites about equally—and the rates for both groups were low. By 2010, a yawning socioeconomic gap had opened among whites, with much higher rates for lower-class whites. Murray's shorthand for this divide, upper-class Belmont versus working-class Fishtown, was a precursor to the Whole Foods–Cracker Barrel divide that would serve as a metaphor for Trump-era politics.

The size and scale of the country's elite was a major point of distinction between the America of mid-century and that of today. Murray paints a picture of an elite that was much smaller in numbers, but more intricately interwoven into the country's mainstream middle-class majority. The rich then were just a tiny fraction of the population. Just eighty thousand were millionaires, worth $7.3 million or more in 2010 dollars. Neighborhoods filled with mansions and consisting entirely of wealthy people could be found only around New York, Chicago, and Los Angeles. Elsewhere, business executives tended to live in modest homes in middle-class neighborhoods. Murray grew up in Newton, Iowa, population 15,381, and Newton was headquarters to the Maytag Company. The company's president, Fred Maytag II, lived in a nice home in a more affluent part of town, but not that much nicer than the typical house in Newton. His neighbors were doctors, attorneys, and other Maytag executives—but also insurance agents, civil servants, and factory workers. In the 1960s, the professional class was a tiny sliver of American society. It didn't make sense to build neighborhoods for them. Retail businesses didn't cater to their tastes and interests. Rich people didn't drink fancy espresso drinks and very few drove luxury vehicles. They were apt to drink the same type of coffee and drive the same kind of car as the blue-collar worker next door.

We idealize the postwar boom years as a period of fast growth marked by high social mobility. Those who came from humble origins with no more than a high school degree could rise to become CEOs or cabinet secretaries. Even on Wall Street, it was possible to have a successful career without a college diploma. "If somebody with an MBA degree applies for a job, we will certainly not hold it against them, but we are really looking for people with PSD* degrees," wrote Bear Stearns chairman Alan Greenberg in a 1981 memo. The asterisk is his, not mine, and it stands for "poor, smart, and a deep desire to become rich." Past legends at the firm, he noted, made a mark with only a high school diploma and a PSD.

Colleges and universities of the era had a much different—and more limited—role than those of today. In 1950, the typical student at one of the top universities—Harvard, Princeton, and Yale—was socially and economically privileged, but not necessarily academically distinguished. These schools were playgrounds for the kind of decadent elite one found depicted in works like *The Great Gatsby.* So long as one belonged to the right social circles or went to the right prep school, admission at a top school was virtually assured, with Harvard admitting 94 percent of applicants from Phillips Exeter and Phillips Andover Academies in 1950. An objective measure of academic fitness did not appear until the precursor to the SAT was introduced in 1929, and its use did not become widespread until after World War II. Now a booming postwar economy required a highly educated, professional workforce, with demand for scientific, technical, and managerial skills to oversee ever-growing and more complex enterprises. This sounded the death knell for the elite university as an old-money playground. In just eight years, from 1952 to 1960, Murray writes, the average SAT verbal score at Harvard jumped from 583 to 678. College admissions began to be more about skill than connections. A meritocracy was born.

The number of Americans going to college grew steadily. In 1960, just 8 percent of the population over age twenty-five had a bachelor's degree or higher. Today that figure is 35 percent. While a simple college diploma may have been enough to ensure a successful career in the mid-twentieth century, only graduation from a high-ranking college or university can now reliably provide that assurance. Today, a bachelor's degree—a credential that more than six in ten American adults don't have—is considered a bare-minimum requirement for even the least promising white-collar jobs. Higher-status jobs require even higher graduate-level credentials. And in top fields like the law, only a degree from a top twenty school allows one to recoup the six-figure investment in tuition needed to earn the degree.

Much is better about the world we live in now. Social climbing is no longer as big a factor driving professional success. Women have opportunities to join the workplace and become fulfilled in their careers. Minorities are protected by law in hiring. And this all would be entirely good but for one fact: this new elite is becoming just as calcified and self-perpetuating as the old-money elite it replaced. The professional class now sorts itself into separate communities from blue-collar workers. Those with college degrees tend to only marry each other, a process known as assortative mating, passing along their advantages to their offspring. Those who don't go to college are prone to get trapped in a self-perpetuating cycle of misfortune, barred from white-collar employment and more easily exposed to the ills of drug addiction and family breakdown. This calcified state, with an aristocracy of education reigning supreme, means people don't move up the economic ladder as easily as they used to. Instead of the middle-class American culture of Newton, Iowa, we now have two cultures perpetually at war with each other, divided by lines of class, education and, increasingly, politics.

The sorting of America is manifesting itself in place and geography, rooted in the changing nature of the professional opportunities available to the American worker. Up until 1980, college graduates were evenly distributed across the major metropolitan areas of the country, write Bill Bishop and Robert G. Cushing in *The Big Sort.* After 1980, technology-focused metros like San Francisco and Boston began attracting more than their fair share of the country's college graduates. This was a change from the mid-twentieth century, where lifetime employees might move across the country if corporate headquarters moved. After 1980, companies began to chase talent rather than the reverse. In *The Rise of the Creative Class*, Richard Florida finds something even more striking about how these high-tech hubs first got going. Cultural amenities, more than an existing concentration of jobs, were what attracted smart, creative people to a city. These amenities included a thriving music and arts scene—and also vibrant gay communities. Florida stresses that this is not because the newcomers themselves were gay, but because the presence of these communities signaled something about the openness of a place that appealed to young creatives. Three factors quantified by Florida—the Gay Index, the Bohemian Factor, and the Tolerance Index—could predict high-tech growth. Cities did not just grow indiscriminately based on preexisting industry clusters, but in part because of newcomers selected for liberal values, further increasing liberal voting in these cities. And, once it came time to raise kids, the slightly older, liberal-not-leftist version of these young creatives would begin to populate the suburbs outside the city.

The abundance of opportunities available to those with a postsecondary credential has permanently changed the shape of the income distribution curve. Income inequality is commonly understood as a divide between two fixed and unchanging groups: the 1 percent at the top and the 99 percent at the bottom. Yet the reason that the fortunes of the 1 percent appear to be growing so fast is that a larger share of the population now qualifies as high-income, as defined by the standard of living that buys. The upper-middle class, with its swelling ranks of college-educated professionals, is poaching people who were formerly in the "middle" middle class. Those purely in the ranks of the middle class shrunk from 50 percent in 1967 to 36 percent in 2016. The much-bemoaned "hollowing out" of the middle class was driven by middle-middle-class kids earning college diplomas and becoming richer. The birth of a mass upper-middle class is a cause for celebration. But it came at a steep cost, leaving those without college diplomas barricaded from entry, a far cry from Alan Greenberg's PSDs.

Now more numerous and prosperous than ever, the professional class is able to cluster together in a way that they weren't able to in Charles Murray's Newton, Iowa. The large-scale social sorting we've seen in higher education and employment also defines the housing market, with larger and larger clusters of high-income neighborhoods that only someone with a multiple six-figure income can afford to move into. Murray calls these places SuperZips—zip codes in the top 5 percent of the distribution of education and income. In 2000, 63 percent of those in SuperZips had college degrees and the median family income was $141,400. When he updated the definition based on data from the 2010 census,

Murray found that the SuperZips had consolidated even further, meaning that well-off people were even more likely to live there as opposed to middle-income places, and they formed larger, more cohesive geographic clusters, making it easier to live and go to work without ever crossing a low- or middle-income neighborhood. In racial terms, the SuperZips were whiter and more Asian than the metro areas they were part of. The insularity of the new elite becomes apparent when one looks only at graduates of top-ranked universities. Using class directories, Murray found that more than 40 percent of a sample of graduates of Harvard, Princeton, and Yale lived in a SuperZip and 74 percent lived in a zip code in the top 20 percent of the socioeconomic distribution. Within more elite graduate programs, the skew was even more pronounced: over 50 percent of Harvard Business School graduates lived in a SuperZip.

You might be thinking of a SuperZip as a *rich* neighborhood with elites hobnobbing at cocktail parties and sneering at the rubes in Middle America—stereotypical places like the Upper West Side in Manhattan or Georgetown in Washington, D.C. That's misleading: in New York and Washington, D.C., SuperZips encompass large swaths of the suburbs, including towns like Springfield and Chantilly in northern Virginia that Georgetown elites hardly ever venture into. In the Washington, D.C., area, Murray's SuperZip cluster is indeed vast, with a population of 1.7 million people in 2010. The cosmopolitan elite is growing more physically distant from the rest of society, with a decreasing likelihood that they will have a meaningful encounter with someone outside the educational or occupational elite. A college diploma, not necessarily a high income, is the ticket to SuperZip living and ways of thinking. Within the SuperZips, there certainly are class divides between the truly wealthy and the college-educated rank and file, like teachers or medical professionals. In political terms, it is educational—not economic—privilege that counts. The college-educated metro-area elite is becoming a cohesive voting bloc, serving as a bulwark against populist revolts from Brexit to Trump.

This was not the case until recently. *Coming Apart* gave us a bracing portrait of a society deeply divided, but this had not yet been actualized politically until the 2016 Trump candidacy. As a whole, the 2000 and 2010 SuperZips leaned left, but not uniformly so. The pre-2016 view of professional class politics was encapsulated in David Brooks's *Bobos in Paradise.* Writing at the turn of the millennium, Brooks described a world in which left-leaning bohemian cultural values were only just starting to displace crusty bourgeois conservatism as the dominant ideology of the nation's elite. The 2000 election provided a small foretaste of the divides that would come to define modern politics. Urban-rural polarization reached new highs and our modern understanding of red-blue tribalism was born. In that election, the northern Virginia suburbs of Washington, D.C., began voting Republican just outside the Capital Beltway, and many of the 2000 SuperZips were red. Today, the blue-to-red transition happens just beyond Leesburg—thirty-five miles from the center of D.C. and an hour drive in good traffic, and twenty-five miles farther out than the old border. Nearly all of the SuperZips are now blue.

Encompassed within that newly blue territory are all the population centers of Loudoun County, which embodies the wholesale political and economic transformation of the American suburb. In 2000, one would have described the county as an "exurb," a growing community far out from the city, attracting families who wanted more space at an affordable cost and were willing to sacrifice a shorter commute to get it. Working on George W. Bush's reelection campaign, places like Loudoun were happy hunting, full of "values voters" who prioritized family life over urban amenities. In 2000, Loudoun County cast 75,653 votes for president, and George W. Bush carried the county 56 to 41 percent, winning all but one precinct. By 2020, Loudoun's electorate had nearly tripled in size, to 224,862 votes. It backed Joe Biden in a landslide, 62 to 37 percent, with the Democrat coming out on top in all of the county's densely populated areas, and only the still-undeveloped countryside east of Leesburg was left as a Republican rump.

The Loudoun of today is no longer a distant bedroom community of Washington, but a jobs mecca in its own right. Thanks to a technology boom, the typical resident has plenty of jobs to choose from nearby, from government contracting firms to the data centers that power most of the internet traffic on the East Coast. Satellite imagery from 2005 to 2015 shows the rapid transformation into suburban sprawl of nearly all the farmland on the western boundary of Dulles airport. The county has the highest median household income of any large county in the country, at $142,299, according to 2019 estimates. It is increasingly diverse, with Asian residents as the largest minority group at 20 percent, and Hispanics making up a further 14 percent. It embodies perfectly a shift in the country's metropolitan regions that John Judis and Ruy Teixeira described in *The Emerging Democratic Majority*. While different parts of the country used to be cleanly partitioned—cities for manufacturing, rural areas for agriculture, and suburbs for home life, places like Loudoun embody a burgeoning "postindustrial metropolitan area" that "combines city and suburb in a seamless web of work and home."

The county's economic transformation has paved the way for more liberal politics, at both the local and national levels. When the debate over critical race theory flared up in 2021, it did so not in leftist redoubts like San Francisco or Seattle, but in Loudoun County. "Anti-racism" training for teachers came to light with materials dividing groups based on whether they "experienced privilege" (men, adults, white people, Christians) or whether they "experienced oppression" (women, children, nonwhite people, non-Christians). School board members themselves felt they were on solid ground enough politically to overcome the opposition, with a majority of them belonging to a private Facebook group called "Anti-Racist Parents of Loudoun County" that plotted a strategy to discredit parents who questioned the curriculum. Throughout the summer and fall of 2021, the debate over critical race theory coalesced into a broader debate over politically powerful teachers unions subverting parents' role in their children's education. Republican gubernatorial candidate Glenn Youngkin moved quickly to claim the mantle of the concerned parent. In a victory that saw Virginia as a whole move a net of 12 points right from the results of the 2020 election, Youngkin improved by 15 points in Loudoun County.

Recent trends in Loudoun County could signal that education polarization has reached a high-water mark. Moderate voters in places like Loudoun County might conclude that they are becoming politically too much like the big cities its residents were trying to escape, and as a result, we might see the suburbs course correct in 2024. This could well happen, and there's a better-than-even chance that some version of it will happen without Donald Trump at the top of the Republican ticket. But in the long term, education polarization with a leftward shift among the well-to-do is not a trend we should bet against. We also thought it had reached a high-water mark in 2000 and 2016, but polarization only continued apace. To better understand where it might go, we need to understand the political roots of this divide, roots that long predate Donald Trump.

DAVID SHOR'S WARNING

In May 2020, David Shor was fired by his employer for a tweet. A few months later, he found himself the most influential election analyst in the country.

Before his brush with cancel culture, Shor was a minor celebrity to those working in the field of political analytics, but was little known outside this small group. Working for Obama's reelection campaign at the age of twenty, he developed the forecasting model that predicted the candidate's margins in battleground states more accurately than the best pollsters. Shor was not only a committed Democrat but a member of the party's left flank, sporting on his Twitter bio a rose emoji popular among Democratic socialists.

The controversy around Shor began with a tweet amid the 2020 protests around race and policing. Shor had a knack for tying obscure academic research to the events of the day, and the work of Omar Wasow seemed relevant to what was then unfolding. Studying the aftermath of the 1968 riots following the assassination of Dr. Martin Luther King Jr., Wasow, a Princeton University political scientist who is Black, found a connection between counties where riots took place and a drop in the Democratic vote share that fall. "Post-MLK-assassination race riots reduced Democratic vote share in surrounding counties by 2 percent, which was enough to tip the 1968 election to Nixon," tweeted Shor. Nonviolent protests in 1968, on the other hand, increased Democratic vote share. The implication was clear: images of escalating violence risked reelecting Donald Trump, a disastrous prospect for Democrats and progressives, while peaceful protests would elicit sympathy for the cause the marchers represented and might help remove Trump.

Many on the left did not appreciate the advice, quickly barraging Shor with accusations of insensitivity. The next week, Shor was out of a job. Whatever hiatus Shor may have had planned didn't last for long, and he reemerged in a July interview with Eric Levitz, a writer for *New York* magazine. The interview itself is an amazing document, a sweeping tour of the landscape of politics and public opinion. His stark warnings to Democrats spawned a wave of follow-up interviews, podcast appearances, and even approving words from Barack Obama. Shor had gone from pariah to prophet.

Rising Democratic support in the professional classes was a poisoned chalice, Shor would argue. "Over the past 60 years, college graduates have gone from being 4 percent of the electorate to being more like 35. Now, it's actually possible—for the first time ever in human history—for political parties to openly embrace cosmopolitan values and win elections," he said. "And so Democratic elites started campaigning on the things they'd always wanted to, but which had previously been too toxic. And so did center-left parties internationally." What follows next from Shor's argument is that consolidating this base of 35 percent makes it harder to get to 50 percent. This is due to features unique to America's constitutional design: a president elected via a state-by-state Electoral College tally and a Senate where small rural states were on equal footing with population powerhouses like California and Texas.

As politics polarized on educational lines, the Democrats' problems only grew. They were now winning many cities and the surrounding suburbs by wider margins, but losing entire states key to winning 270 electoral votes. The 2020 election results bore out that Democrats could win the popular vote by as much as four points and still lose the White House. Also that year, thirty-one states, combining for sixty-two Senate seats, voted more Republican than the country—the number of seats Republicans would be expected to win in a tied national vote. This basic pattern is not new. In 2016, Trump won thirty states, while still losing the popular vote by two points. In winning the popular vote by two points in 2004, George W. Bush won thirty-two states with sixty-four senators.

For now, the Senate remains narrowly Democratic. Hopes of a Republican Senate supermajority have been frustrated over the years by two developments: first, Democrats evading the wrath of conservative red-state electorates by selecting popular local moderates as candidates, and second, Republican overreach, most recently picking novice Donald Trump–style candidates that cost the party as many as four Senate seats in the 2022 midterms. The 2024 election, though, remains a key test: their ranks thinned over the last decade, the remaining red-state Democrats—Joe Manchin, Jon Tester, and Sherrod Brown—will all face voters in a presidential year, the kind of election where split ticket voting is lowest.

The fact that Democrats have managed to hang on for so long is vindication of Shor's proposed remedy: run popular candidates and do popular things. Shor's insight isn't exactly new: it's what pretty much every political consultant I know tells their clients. But the parties' internal dynamics often lead them to act irrationally. The fervor surrounding Shor's firing in 2020 was a prime example of it, happening at a time when progressive organizations convinced themselves that it was a good idea to issue statements in favor of defunding the police. Republicans tethering themselves to Donald Trump in the hopes of gaining his endorsement, while sound advice for winning the primary, was general election poison.

Shor's back-to-the-future approach went by the label of "popularism." Progressive wonks keen to offer up friendly advice to Democrats in the wake of the 2020 near-disaster liberally copy-pasted from Shor's *New York* interview. On their Twitter feeds and Substack newsletters, popularism was all the rage. The success of Barack Obama's 2012 campaign was a central tenet of Shor's gospel. That year, the country's first Black president had shown how to win white working-class midwesterners, who later flocked to Donald Trump, voters that progressives now casually discard as racists. As he often did, Shor was able to boil down political success to simple numbers: voters who agreed with Democrats on universal health care but opposed them on immigration issues swung from supporting Obama with 60 percent of the vote to only supporting Hillary Clinton with 41 percent. Shor's straightforward solution: make politics about health care, and avoid making it about immigration, as Obama did in 2012.

Republicans have their own issues, but for Democrats specifically, a danger remains that they will be pulled left by cosmopolitan elites populating the upper ranks of their party. A 2021 study by the progressive polling firm Data for Progress found that opinion elites in both parties were consistently to the left of their party's members on nearly all issues the pollsters studied. The ranks of party activists, donors, staff, and even candidates themselves are drawn from these "opinion elites." While this reflects a certain symmetry between the parties—elites across the ideological spectrum are college-educated and have more cosmopolitan values—this has asymmetrical effects: pushing Democrats further left and Republicans toward the ideological middle. One of the largest gaps in the views of elites as compared to rank-and-file Democrats was on the issue of increasing deportations of illegal immigrants, which had the support of four in ten rank-and-file Democrats but just one in ten elites. Because polarized cultural debates are more likely than boring economic ones to generate social media eyeballs and clicks, not to mention donations, it is hard for parties to avoid talking about these issues entirely. And these cultural issues drive the geographic polarization that hurt Democrats.

This is not to say that the Democrats don't have an advantage on some social questions. One such issue is abortion rights, with the *Dobbs v. Jackson* decision overturning *Roe v. Wade* providing a boost to the party in the 2022 midterms. But more often, Democrats find themselves on the losing side on issues where opinion is driven by the cosmopolitan-traditionalist divide, public safety and border security among them. Surveys show that the Democratic base is internally more divided by cultural issues, even on abortion, than they are on economic questions. And cultural questions are more and more central to how people vote these days.

Shor and I do similar work on opposite sides of the partisan divide, and we had a chance to catch up for an interview for this book about a year after the summer 2020 brouhaha. Shifting topics at one point, Shor teased that I was probably not the type who liked to read European sociologists. Thanks to reading a previous Shor missive, I actually knew exactly where he was going with this. He then launched into a riff on the academic literature on postmaterialism.

A term coined by political scientist Ronald Inglehart in the 1970s, postmaterialism explained why wealthier voters increasingly chose parties of the left. In the industrial era, the struggle between capital and labor dominated politics, one that manifested in the brief prominence of socialist Eugene Debs in early twentieth-century U.S. politics and the rise of communist parties in Western Europe. But within a few decades of the war ending, Inglehart noticed the class struggle abating. From the antiwar movement to environmentalism to gender equality, debates with no direct connection to the material well-being of the working class were increasingly at the center of politics. These values seemed to grow more and more important as societies grew more prosperous, which they were at a fast clip in the postwar period. With the material needs of the working class no longer a concern, and demands for confiscatory taxation of those at the top lessened, people across the class divide increasingly felt freer to vote their social values.

Inglehart measured postmaterialism using a series of survey questions that contrasted how much people valued material and security aims (a "high level of economic growth," "making sure this country has strong defense forces," "fighting rising prices") with postmaterialist aims ("trying to make our cities and countryside more beautiful," "protecting freedom of speech," "seeing that people have more say about how things are done at their jobs and in their communities," "progress towards a society in which ideas count more than money"). When Inglehart first measured postmaterialism in the Nordic countries in 1970, he found a stark divide between the old and the young: the older generations scarred by wars and depressions still worried about material scarcity; the postwar generation was increasingly focused elsewhere. Over time, this generational trend has worked its way through every Western society, with the values of the young gradually taking over. Thirty years later, with rising prosperity, levels of postmaterialism had shot up in every Western country. The tie between postmaterialism and prosperity is also seen in the economic divide between countries like the United States, Sweden, Austria, and Canada scoring highest on postmaterialism, and emerging economies like Ethiopia, Pakistan, and Bulgaria scoring lowest.

Politically, postmaterialism shifts rich people to the left from a starting point on the right, and poor people to the right from a starting point on the left. Where politics used to be sorted on an economic axis, it is now sorted on a cultural axis. The rising importance of values like openness and self-expression creates an opening for left-wing politics among the wealthy and well-educated that didn't exist before. These voters are increasingly building their politics around their liberal cultural values, and working-class voters are doing the same around religious and nationalist values. A cross-national study by Amory Gethin, Clara Martínez-Toledano, and Thomas Piketty finds the polarization trend growing stronger in each decade from the 1940s through the present, measuring support for parties of the left by the upper 10 percent of voters socioeconomically. The leftward trend among elites has been strongest in northern European and English-speaking countries—those most like the U.S.—with America seeing the strongest shift in the last decade under Donald Trump.

This is the politics of "morals as luxury goods," to borrow the title of a recent paper by Benjamin Enke, Mattias Polborn, and Alex A. Wu. Contrary to Thomas Frank's *What's the Matter with Kansas?,* the paper's authors find it's not the poor who are most likely to "vote against their self-interest." It's the rich. While 70 percent of "rich moral liberals" vote Democratic, only a slight majority of "poor moral conservatives" vote Republican. And they found a sharp acceleration in culturally driven voting after 2004, a period marked by the rise of the internet and cable news. In the American National Election Studies, the longest continuously running study of voter attitudes, the importance of social-issue voting has risen dramatically, specifically among voters in the top third economically. From 1988 to 2000, whether one held socially conservative or liberal views was only modestly predictive of who one would vote for, and the effect was the same regardless of income. Starting in 2004, social issues became more predictive of vote choice across the board, but they became *a lot* more predictive of how wealthier people voted. Meanwhile, economic issues mattered no more to voters than they did in the late eighties. This explains the shift to the left in wealthier places like Buckhead, Winnetka, and Loudoun County during that time. It used to be fashionable for country-club Republicans in these places to say that they were "fiscally conservative and socially moderate." Now most of the rank-and-file voters who describe themselves this way have another name: Democrats.

The sea change in the values of the upper class is magnified by how much larger and more cohesive that upper class is today. They always had outsize influence and financial power; now they have real voting power and are wielding it for Democrats. That's very different from the world we started with. "In the postwar era, college-educated professionals were maybe 4 percent of the electorate," Shor noted in his *New York* interview. "Which meant that basically no voters had remotely cosmopolitan values. But the flip side of this is that this educated 4 percent still ran the world. Both parties at this point were run by this highly educated, cosmopolitan minority that held a bunch of values that undergirded the postwar consensus, around democracy and rule of law, and all these things."

Mid-century college graduates were self-aware of their own inability to advance their cosmopolitan views in the political arena. Their first try was in the counterculture of the 1960s, which culminated in the 1972 campaign of George McGovern that ended in the worst defeat for a single party in postwar America. Yet McGovern's coalition was a vanguard for what the Democratic Party would later become. He did relatively better among professional elites than Hubert Humphrey had. Urban and rural counties polarized to a degree that would not be seen again until decades later. He did well with Black voters. This new coalition fell woefully short in raw numbers, but it was the shape of things to come.

The majority of us don't remember what politics was like sixty years ago, but most readers will remember the politics of twenty years ago, and it was very different from that of today. At the turn of the century, the politics of issues like gay marriage leaned toward the traditionalist right. In 1996, Bill Clinton ran radio ads targeted at evangelical Christians touting his signing of the Defense of Marriage Act, defining marriage as between a man and a woman. Discussions of race and policing had died down following the Rodney King case and the ensuing 1992 riots in Los Angeles. Then the fatal shooting of Michael Brown in Ferguson, Missouri, happened. Gay marriage became the law of the land. Donald Trump was elected. Equality became "equity." Catering to the changing values of their professional-class workers, corporations began taking progressive stances in the culture wars. All of this reflects the growing strength of cosmopolitanism within the electorate. Progressives in the national political arena no longer had to bottle up their beliefs. They could proclaim them loudly.

But what if progressives overshot? What if this is just a trap? The rising share of cosmopolitan voters in the electorate hasn't lessened the allure of populist politics, which recently succeeded in electing a president, where it had failed before. Bloc voting in cosmopolitan metro areas has been matched—and sometimes outmatched—by a countervailing trend in rural America for the right. At the same time, Black and Hispanic voters left behind by the rise of the Whole Foods suburb seem less enthused by this new version of the Democratic Party. These dueling realignments suggest a kind of self-regulating equilibrium where new divisions result in roughly the same competitive politics. But the rules of the game as written, which empower rural states over urban ones, place this new cosmopolitan bloc at a disadvantage.

3.

THE MAJORITY THAT FAILED

Barack Obama's 2008 election as the forty-fourth president heralded the coming-of-age of a new demographic majority. Not only had Obama notched the biggest electoral landslide since Bill Clinton's victory in 1996, but he did so with a coalition that seemed to portend a permanent changing of the guard: winning almost two-thirds of voters age eighteen to twenty-nine, inspiring record Black turnout with expanded Democratic margins, and winning nearly seven in ten Hispanic voters. The financial crisis that struck Wall Street just six weeks before the election certainly had something to do with the decisiveness of the result. But for many analysts, the issues and events of the day are never the sole explanation for why Americans vote the way they do. Obama's victory was also one prophesied six years earlier by two Washington writers who argued that the country was on the verge of lasting Democratic rule.

The Emerging Democratic Majority, by John Judis and Ruy Teixeira, attempted to do more than answer which party would win the next election, but which one would win the next generation. Its title echoed Kevin Phillips's *The Emerging Republican Majority*, which posited a durable Republican majority anchored by the shifting allegiances of whites in the South, the growth of the Sunbelt, and the exodus of working-class ethnic northerners from the Democratic Party. Phillips's theories looked prophetic just a few years later when Richard Nixon romped to a 23-point victory against the liberal George McGovern.

And so, too, for the new Democratic majority of Judis and Teixeira, even if its day in the sun would be delayed until 2008. The Judis-Teixeira majority rested on three pillars, all areas of growing Democratic strength. The first was the growth of the country's professional class, centered in what the authors called "ideopolises"—major metropolitan areas centered around the knowledge economy, not manufacturing. The second was the growing Democratic allegiance of women, building on the gender gap that first developed following the entrance of women into the workforce. And the third was the growth of racial and ethnic minorities in the electorate, especially Hispanics and Asian Americans.

This last prophecy was underlined with an exclamation point following the Obama victory. In conjunction with Obama's strength among Black voters, this evolved into the axiom that "demography is destiny," with the inexorable growth of a more diverse electorate spelling doom for Republicans. This simple idea would become conflated with the entirety of the Judis-Teixeira thesis, but actually, rising diversity was just one part of the authors' larger, more nuanced argument—and it was not even the most important one. While "demography is destiny" has fallen out of favor in the wake of Donald Trump's 2016 victory, Judis and Teixeira's first prediction—growing professional-class support for Democrats—actually came true. While these trends are now spoken of mostly in terms of a diploma divide between those with college degrees and those without, Judis and Teixeira were actually making a more nuanced case about the changing nature of the workforce, in the shift from factories to offices, and in the shift to more creative kinds of work within those offices. A creative professional might eschew the narrow profit maximization goals of upper management—goals that had previously tethered a slew of professionals to Republicans as the party of business. Wrote Judis and Teixeira:

> While corporate and financial executives, accountants, and property managers are creatures of the private market who tend to gauge their own success in profit-and-loss terms, many professionals identify their success with the quality of the service they offer or the idea they produce. Software programmers worry about the "coolness" of their code; architects about the beauty and utility of their buildings; teachers about whether

their pupils have learned; the doctor and nurse about the health of their patient.

This new professional class did not necessarily hew to a liberal stereotype—latte-sipping, Volvo-driving, NPR-listening. Rather, this group had shifted to the Democrats in the 1990s because of Bill Clinton's "progressive centrism," with its attentiveness to suburban quality-of-life concerns like education and crime. This focus was driven by Clinton's 1996 pollster, Mark Penn, a centrist who had taken over from the progressive-populist Stanley Greenberg. Penn's lodestar was "wired workers"—new-age knowledge workers moderate in their politics.

Judis and Teixeira's majority also had a fourth pillar that was forgotten about in the wake of Obama's victories: working-class whites. While progressives crowed about the decline of this traditional and Republican-leaning segment of the electorate, Judis and Teixeira warned that they remained crucial to any Democratic majority. Though white working-class voters were shrinking, not growing, in the electorate, they were close to a majority at the time of the book's publication, so Democrats would need to stay competitive with them. The 2000 election, with its white rural swing to George W. Bush, was a warning sign of what happened when they didn't. As the party then still strongly identified with the working class and organized labor, Judis and Teixeira were hopeful that 2000 was but a temporary blip, predicting that states like West Virginia would revert to Democratic form following the early 2000s recession. Instead, West Virginia would only continue to slip further and further to the right, favoring Bush by 11 points in 2004, on its way to becoming the nation's most Republican state under Donald Trump. Judis and Teixeira's Democratic majority as originally envisioned ran straight through coal country and the old manufacturing hubs. The party's collapse in these areas imperiled the whole project, a fact ignored by Obama-era progressives. As they wrote in laying out the conditions for their majority to emerge, "[I]t is fair to assume that if Democrats can consistently take professionals by about 10 percent, working women by about 20 percent, keep 75 percent of the minority vote, and get close to an even split of white working-class voters, they will have achieved a new Democratic majority." Democrats haven't been competitive with working-class whites since the book was published, the consequences of which were papered over temporarily by their Obama-specific strength among nonwhites.

In the wake of Obama's victory, progressives saw Democratic majorities as far as the eye could see, powered by the country's changing demographics. The Democratic group Women's Voices, Women Vote coined the term the "Rising American Electorate," which they defined to include unmarried women, young people, and nonwhites, which were all growing and leaned more Democratic than the country as a whole. When progressive groups touted their "rising" coalition, it was usually in service of a mobilization strategy—one that relied on turning out groups that leaned Democratic but only sporadically voted—as opposed to a persuasion strategy of convincing more traditional segments of the election who reliably voted, like white male factory workers in the Midwest. To this new wave of Obama-era Democrats, mobilization looked like the ultimate cheat code, rendering obsolete the need to persuade voters by moving to the middle. Since the mid-2000s, the Rising American Electorate has been mentioned at least fourteen thousand times, per Google, with related ideas featuring prominently in Democratic thinking. The "coalition of the ascendant" was another term, which was coined by columnist Ronald Brownstein, a collection of "millennials, minorities, and socially liberal whites (especially college-educated and single women)" who were ascendant because they were "all growing within the electorate, boosting Democrats."

The heyday of the Emerging Democratic Majority drew its lifeblood from this arithmetic. Because Democratic-leaning groups were ever expanding, and Republican-leaning groups shrinking, Democrats would own the future. Serious observers could not contest this basic math: nonwhites are in fact growing in the population, and we have recently passed the point where a majority of newborns in the U.S. are nonwhite. Yet other aspects of the Rising American Electorate rely on actuarial trickery, like corralling every millennial or member of Generation Z into it, when these groups will naturally expand as more voters turn eighteen and their political preferences may change as they age. When you look at things in terms of fixed age cohorts, the electorate is growing older, not younger, and today's thirty- to forty-four-year-olds support Democratic candidates by a narrow single-digit margin, a far cry from when they were eighteen to twenty-nine in 2008 and backing Obama by 34 points.

What Barack Obama showed is that a majority built around minorities and young people could be assembled, at least temporarily. But the idea that the traditional white working-class electorate could be discarded would prove to be a terrible miscalculation—especially given their large numbers, making up a near-majority of voters at the time of Obama's election and four in ten today. *The Emerging Democratic Majority* warned about this and Barack Obama himself understood it. But the lesson was lost in the post-2008 progressive euphoria.

THE REAL OBAMA COALITION

Obama's reelection to the presidency in 2012 further cemented the rightness of betting on the "coalition of the ascendant." Leading up to the 2012 election, Washington had operated under the conventional wisdom that Obama was, if anything, a slight underdog for reelection. Mitt Romney's internal polling had him ahead, and his team confidently predicted a victory with over three hundred electoral votes. Instead, Obama cruised to a relatively comfortable four-point victory. The political class quickly scoured the exit polls for explanations and settled on Obama's continued strength among nonwhites as the key to his victory, with historic Black turnout once again and the Republican share of the Hispanic vote cut to just 27 percent. A striking finding from the exit polls is that Obama had assembled a national majority while falling to just 40 percent of the white vote. The "Rising American Electorate"—one that relied on minorities and young votes to do the heavy lifting—was alive and well.

The stories that political parties tell themselves about how they won or lost deeply influence the path for years to come. An unexpectedly large victory or defeat serves as a triumphal reaffirmation of the existing strategy or a shock to the system forcing change. Three successive presidential defeats forced Democrats to chart a more moderate course with Bill Clinton in 1992, and the same looked like it might be true for Republicans with their post-2012 autopsy. However, this dominant interpretation of how Obama won in 2012 had a fatal flaw not fully understood at the time.

The idea that Barack Obama won while doing dismally among white voters is a "whoa, if true" observation that happened not to be true. A thorough analysis published by *New York Times* data journalist Nate Cohn six months before the 2016 election laid out why: there were more white voters—and specifically white voters without a college degree—than recorded in the exit polls. Traditionally serving as the final word on how the winners won, the exit polls painted a picture of an electorate that was less white, more educated, and younger than the U.S. Census Bureau's survey on voting—a set of numbers routinely overlooked, since they came out six months after the fact. When the exit polls were reconciled with actual results in the weeks following the election, their top-line number was weighted to line up with the final election result, but problems with sample composition threw off their estimates of how various demographics voted. Exit poll errors compounded to dramatically underestimate the number of older white voters, placing the number of white voters over the age of forty-five with no college degree at 23 percent of the electorate, when more reliable government surveys and estimates from the Democratic political data firm Catalist placed it at 30 and 29 percent, respectively. Having disappeared nearly one in four older white working-class voters—the same voters who would form the core of Trump's base—the exit polls understated Obama's key inroads with those voters. Specifically, the larger number of these voters meant that Obama had not lost them as badly as thought. Cohn estimated that Obama did at least two points better among whites than the exit polls stated in every midwestern state except for Iowa. In Pennsylvania, Obama was thought to have gotten 42 percent of the white vote and likely got 46 percent. In Michigan, exit polls said Obama got 44 percent, when he actually got 47 percent. This was underscored by an analysis of county election results: Obama had done consistently better than John Kerry had eight years earlier in heavily white counties in the North, while doing worse in those same kinds of counties in the South and the border states.

Because the exit poll had underestimated the share of white votes Obama won, it overstated the contribution of nonwhite voters to his victories. For instance, the exit poll estimated that the Black vote in Ohio jumped four points from 11 percent of the electorate in 2008 to 15 percent in 2012, which is implausible when you look at voter file data showing that turnout in heavily Black neighborhoods in Ohio was down from its 2008 highs. By publishing blowout numbers for Obama among nonwhite voters in the direct aftermath of the election, the exit poll furthered a flawed narrative that led Democratic strategists to overestimate the Rising American Electorate and underestimate the staying power of the white working class.

An examination of the campaigns that Obama actually ran in 2008 and 2012 tells a very different story of the strategy he actually used to win. Obama certainly did make gains with a diverse coalition of voters that enabled him to add states like Colorado and Virginia to the Democratic column. But another key ingredient was his reassuring economically downscale white communities that he had their backs in the middle of the biggest financial collapse in a generation. In tone, the general election campaigns of 2008 and 2012 departed from the mythology of Obama as a transformational agent of change ushering in a new generational coalition of millennials and minorities. In 2008, Obama's "hope and change" from the primaries gave way in the general election to an image of a coolheaded Obama who would stabilize the economy and look out for regular working folks. Speaking directly to the camera in his first ad of the 2008 general election, Obama drove home these themes.

> America's a country of strong families, and strong values. My life's been blessed by both. I was raised by a single mom and my grandparents. We didn't have much money, but they taught me values straight from the Kansas heartland where they grew up. Accountability and self-reliance. Love of country. Working hard without making excuses. Treating your neighbor as you'd like to be treated. It's what guided me as I worked my way up, taking jobs and loans to make it through college. It's what led me to pass up Wall Street jobs and go to Chicago instead, helping neighborhoods devastated

> when steel plants closed. That's why I passed laws moving people from welfare to work, cut taxes for working families, extended health care for wounded troops who'd been neglected. I approve this message because I'll never forget those values. And if I have the honor of taking the oath of office as president, it will be with a deep and abiding faith in the country I love.

Obama was, in his own words from his famous 2004 Democratic convention speech, a "skinny kid with a funny name." He had grown up partly in Indonesia. Internet conspiracy theories abounded that he was not born in the United States or was secretly a Muslim. Even the true facts of Obama's story—his work as a community organizer and constitutional law professor—did not suggest he would have an easy job appealing to the white working class. Hence, most of his advertising played up reassuring themes that spoke to tradition-minded Americans: Kansas values, welfare reform, patriotism. In the stretch run of the election, with his victory increasingly assured, this gave way to reinforcing core Democratic themes on health care and jobs. Obama ran 155,452 ads on health care to John McCain's 11,033. On jobs, the tally was 132,247 for Obama to 15,526 for McCain—a conspicuous difference given the economic collapse unfolding in the last six weeks of the election. Obama's most-aired ad of the 2008 campaign—and in political TV advertising history up to that point—did not feature a soaring Obama rally speech calling forth a new generational coalition. It was a boilerplate attack ad against McCain's health care plan.

Obama's 2012 campaign was even more singularly focused on the American worker. Looked at from a distance, the entire campaign seemed to be a referendum on the fate of steel- and autoworkers. The economy had recovered from the depths of the 2008 recession, but job growth was sluggish and Republicans had won the House in 2010 with a sixty-two-seat gain asking a simple question: "Where are the jobs?" As a successful businessman, Mitt Romney seemed ideally positioned to exploit Obama's economic vulnerabilities.

A Mormon who now serves as a senator from Utah, a former governor of Massachusetts, and a son of Michigan, Romney was poised to press regional advantages across the country. In the Midwest, the most crucial region, it was as the son of the former Michigan governor and American Motors CEO, George Romney. The son had made his own fortune as an expert in turning around failing businesses for Bain Capital, a private equity firm. With millions of Americans defaulting on their mortgages and putting off car purchases, automakers were looking for their own turnaround, and Romney was oft-touted as their savior. Two weeks after the 2008 election, Romney took to the *New York Times* op-ed page to offer his prescriptions for the auto industry: reining in exorbitant union contracts, cutting retiree benefits, and bringing in new management from other industries. The piece closed with a call for a "managed bankruptcy" that would allow the companies to restructure and emerge from the crisis stronger than before. Romney's suggestions would soon be forgotten; what was remembered was the headline the *Times* editors put above his byline: "Let Detroit Go Bankrupt." The attack ads practically wrote themselves.

Romney's *New York Times* op-ed conjured every bad image of the greedy, bean-counting CEO, the kind who boosted profits by firing workers and then cutting pay and benefits for those who remained. This was the portrait that Obama and his allies would paint in the 2012 campaign, starting with a barrage of advertising that spring. An Obama campaign ad showed Romney crooning "America the Beautiful" set to headlines of Bain companies outsourcing jobs to foreign countries. Ads from the main pro-Obama Super PAC featured scores of testimonials from workers laid off at the hands of Bain and Romney. Former paper plant worker Mike Earnest recounted being asked to build a thirty-foot stage that would be used days later to announce the closure of the plant. "Turns out that when we built that stage, it was like building my own coffin," said Earnest. "And it just made me sick." Another featured the story of steelworker Joe Soptic, who lost his job and his family's health insurance after a Bain layoff. The ad went further, laying the death of Soptic's wife from cancer at Romney's feet. "I do not think that Mitt Romney cares what he has done to anyone, and furthermore, I do not think Mitt Romney is concerned," said Soptic. As political theater, the ad was masterful. It was also misleading and manipulative: Soptic's wife died years after Romney had left Bain. In Democratic attacks, Romney was held up as someone straight out of *Lifestyles of the Rich and Famous*. Mocking the car elevator in Romney's San Diego home, Michigan governor Jennifer Granholm told the Democratic convention, "In Mitt Romney's world, the cars get the elevator and the workers get the shaft."

In September, Romney played into all of these attacks when he was caught on tape at a private fundraiser dismissing low-income taxpayers, saying, "There are 47 percent of the people who will vote for the president no matter what. All right, there are 47 percent who are with him, who are dependent upon government, who believe that they are victims, who believe the government has a responsibility to care for them, who believe that they are entitled to health care, to food, to housing, to you-name-it—that that's an entitlement." Romney added, "My job is not to worry about those people. I'll never convince them they should take personal responsibility and care for their lives." In the exit poll, Obama won 81 percent of voters who said their most important quality was someone who "cares about people like me."

The 2012 debate over jobs and the auto industry recovery happened mostly in Ohio. Romney's former home state of Michigan saw little campaigning, as Obama's sixteen-point margin in 2008 seemed all but insurmountable. Ohio was a different story: it historically leaned a few points to the right of the country as a whole and was a must-win for Romney. The auto industry also had a strong presence there, with Toledo a major manufacturer of Jeeps and General Motors' Lordstown manufacturing plant in the Youngstown area. In late October, the Romney campaign sensed an opportunity for a counterattack, seizing on a media report about Jeep restarting production in China. Obama's critics jumped on it as evidence of offshoring and proof that the vaunted auto industry recovery was not all it seemed. "Who will do more for the auto industry? Not Barack Obama," a Romney ad began. "Obama took GM and Chrysler into bankruptcy and sold Chrysler to Italians, who are going to build Jeeps in China. Mitt Romney will fight for every American job." Like the Soptic ad, Romney's Jeep ad was a stretch. Jeep was reopening manufacturing in China, but would also keep its Toledo plant open.

Despite Romney's last-minute Hail Mary, Obama was reelected comfortably with a hat trick straight out of the original Judis-Teixeira playbook. First, he maintained and expanded Democratic margins among white professionals, enough to turn states like Virginia (centered around the D.C. suburbs) and Colorado (centered around Denver and the heavily populated Front Range) a darker shade of blue. Second, Black support and turnout for Obama held up near 2008 levels and Obama grew his share of the Hispanic vote. And third, his relentless pummeling of Romney as the enemy of the working class paid dividends in keeping enough midwestern whites in his camp, with Obama sweeping every battleground in the region. Education polarization diminished, reversing a decades-long trend. Lucas County, Ohio, home of Toledo and the Jeep Liberty plant, shifted 11 points to the Democrats between 2004 and 2012.

Beyond his specific campaign tactics, how did Obama do it? If it is true that Donald Trump motivated white working-class voters with racial resentment, how did the first Black president win so many of their votes? The answer lies deeper than any attack ad, and gives lie to the idea that the 2016 shifts were about racism. The explanation goes back to the Midwest's leadership in the antislavery movement and industrial unionism, explains the noted political historian Michael Barone:

> There's a tradition of equal rights for Blacks, which could easily translate into the idea that it's a good thing to have Black presidents. In the outstate regions of those states, there's a tradition in the Republican Party that goes back to 1854, in the opposition to the Kansas-Nebraska Act on slavery in the territories, and it's a position of the industrial union heritage of the United Auto Workers, and the steelworkers, and other unions, who made a big point of equal rights for Blacks more than their white membership was really demanding. So, people with those long-standing partisan allegiances have more reason to be more sympathetic to Blacks than, say, the South, where there is no tradition of the industrial unions, and no tradition of the pre–Civil War Republicans.

Lost in all of the jubilation surrounding the "Rising American Electorate" was just how instrumental working-class white voters in the

Midwest were to the final outcome. It was these voters, in combination with strong support from racial and ethnic minorities, that hardened the so-called "Blue Wall," creating a supposedly insurmountable *Democratic* advantage in the Electoral College. In the interpretation of these results, this part of the story was lost, with all the hubbub around the segments of the Obama coalition that were "emerging" and "ascendant." These blind spots would lead the Democrats to the doorstep of failure four years later.

THE RECKONING

Bewilderment abounded in the aftermath of the 2016 election at how Donald Trump could possibly have won an increasingly diverse, secular, and educated America. Demographics were all moving in the right direction for progressives, and while this certainly didn't rule out a Republican winning the odd election or two, that Republican should have been someone who had made peace with these trends and could appeal to nonwhites and college-educated suburbanites—the very opposite of a candidate like Trump.

"Demography is destiny" emphasized the size of groups within the electorate, and this certainly matters. But what matters even more is the level of support a candidate receives within each group—as well as their political skill and appeal to voters across the board. In basic algebra, we are taught about slopes and intercepts, which come together to form an equation or a model that in politics dictates how well a candidate will perform. The slope represents the degree to which support for a candidate grows in tandem with the share of people in any given demographic. For example, the more whites without a college degree in a county, the higher the share of the vote for Donald Trump. But there is another part of this equation: the intercept. That represents the contribution a candidate makes, positive or negative, to the electoral performance of their party—independently of how well they do within demographics. Different candidates can bring forth stronger or weaker versions of party coalitions; someone more viscerally charismatic can persuade more voters across the spectrum, resulting in a higher intercept, an across-the-board gain regardless of demographic factors. The intercept is shorthand for a candidate's overall political appeal. Bill Clinton and Barack Obama were high-intercept Democratic candidates; Hillary Clinton was a low-intercept Democratic candidate. Donald Trump was a higher-intercept Republican standard-bearer in 2016 than he was in 2020.

The varying nature of slopes and intercepts can frustrate attempts to create a single formula that can predict a permanent Democratic or Republican majority. Holding enough variables constant proves to be impossible, making it difficult to say anything about the future performance of a party beyond the current election cycle. The level of support a candidate receives within a demographic group turns out to matter more than whether the group is growing or shrinking in the electorate. Shifts in support levels from election to election tend to overwhelm the effects of group growth, and these shifts are harder to predict.

"Demography is destiny" fails as a theory when it assumes that a group will vote the way it does in perpetuity. As we've seen with the diploma divide among whites, that's a flawed assumption. It's also a flawed assumption as it relates to nonwhite voters, for instance among Hispanic voters who have become more divided in their loyalties as they've grown as a share of the electorate. There is a well-established dynamic here at play, one we've seen before with past ethnic white immigrants in the nineteenth and early twentieth centuries, who used to exhibit very distinctive voting patterns and gradually regressed toward the political mean. Small, embattled minorities are likely to vote more cohesively as a bloc than a fast-growing group that is becoming thoroughly enmeshed in the mainstream of society, a set of forces I'll examine further on in these pages.

And so, with evidence mounting against the idea of a permanent Democratic majority, Ruy Teixeira published an essay a few months before the 2020 election trying to explain why. The shortcoming, he explained, rested upon a misinterpretation of the theory by Democrats in the rush of enthusiasm following Obama's victories:

After Obama's historic victory, our theory morphed from provocative projection to sacred gospel. Instead of focusing on the fact that this emerging majority only gave Democrats tremendous potential *if they played their cards right*, many progressives started to interpret it as a description of an inevitable future. The new Democratic majority, they believed, had already arrived. All they had to do to win election after election was to mobilize the growing segments of the electorate, and the demographic changes that favored them would take care of the rest. Sometimes explicitly, sometimes implicitly, our thesis turned into the simplistic argument that "demographics are destiny."

But our argument had been much more complicated than that. We had always envisaged the new Democratic majority as a *coalition* between growing segments of the population and the party's traditional electorate. To be sure, this coalition would include a lot of the voters progressives now chose to focus on: minorities, professionals and the young, and unmarried and highly educated women. But in addition to this "rising American electorate," it would also have to include a significant minority of the white working class, a group that—though its numbers were in decline—would continue to constitute a very large electoral block for the foreseeable future. (In 2008, 51 percent of eligible voters belonged to the white working class; in the 2020 elections, 44 percent will.)

In stark contrast to the Clinton era, or even the Obama era, the new racial politics on the left made it impossible for Democrats to genuinely appeal to the white working class by moderating their positions. Many on the left were suspicious that these voters were motivated by racism and so catering to them was immoral. Hillary Clinton hinted at this line of thinking when she uttered her "basket of deplorables" comment before the 2016 election, casting around half of Trump's voters in this racist and misogynistic bucket. "The voters you romanticize are not persuadable, and they haven't been for a very long time," wrote Peter Birkenhead in the *Daily Beast* before the 2016 election, adding,

"The Democrats don't need them, they shouldn't want them and they should once and for all stop coddling them." After the election, liberals doubled down on the idea that the racism of the white working class fueled the shift to Trump. "The country is under conservative assault because Democrats mistakenly sought support from conservative white working-class voters susceptible to racially charged appeals," wrote Steve Phillips, a senior fellow at the liberal Center for American Progress. "Replicating that strategy would be another catastrophic blunder." Author James Surowiecki framed this in zero-sum terms, as a choice between working-class white voters and the party's historic commitment to racial equality. "Ppl. worry the concern with working-class whites will lead to PoC [people of color] being marginalized for good reason: it's happened so many times before," Surowiecki wrote in a Twitter thread two weeks following the 2016 election. From Reconstruction to Bill Clinton, who "talked tough about crime and welfare and had [his] Sista Souljah moment," appealing to conservative whites invariably came at Black voters' expense.

The emotional responses to Trump's victory reflect a core liberal belief that race is the central driving force of today's politics. This is voiced in the liberal view that the modern Republican Party is built on anti-Black racism, an idea that long predated Donald Trump. And Trump himself often did little to disabuse the GOP's critics, from his extremely poor response to the 2017 events in Charlottesville to the 2020 George Floyd protests. But liberals have their own inconvenient truths to contend with. The first is how Obama won over many of the same working-class whites lost to Trump in 2016, showing it was possible for a Democrat to assemble the required number of Black and white working-class voters in the same coalition. And the second is how the electorate has become more racially *depolarized* in its voting patterns in the Trump era, with a populist candidate slinging so-called racial dog whistles doing better among Black voters than respectable establishment Republicans who didn't. These are facts that undermine the progressive narrative of race as the driving force behind the political shifts of recent years. Indeed, the trends go in the opposite direction, with more voters of color choosing the Republican Party side by side with working-class whites. Culture, not race, is the key driving force behind these recent shifts. That cultural divide is between cosmopolitans and traditionalists, and here, nonwhites and working-class whites stand together on the side of tradition.

The intraparty agita about the role of working-class whites in the Democratic Party also exposes a tension of managing any majority coalition: to get to 51 percent, the coalition needs to not entirely make sense. Majority coalitions are built more often by sheer force of charisma, but with charismatic leaders like Ronald Reagan, Bill Clinton, and Barack Obama gone, groups at odds with each other start to fall out of the coalition. And this is a core reason why *The Emerging Democratic Majority* was too optimistic, even at the time it was published. The party's ability to appeal to disparate parts of the electorate all at once—liberal college-educated whites and minorities *along with* working-class whites—is akin to the task of a juggler keeping one too many balls in the air at once. Without working-class whites, the majority fell apart. But this was essentially a foregone conclusion once the party cast its lot with college-educated whites without a charismatic leader holding things together. "The white working class and the upper middle class are two groups that will always be difficult to keep in the same coalition," notes Sean Trende in his 2012 book, *The Lost Majority*. "Their interests are widely divergent, and policies that appeal to one group are likely to push the other group away."

Without a political unicorn at the helm, parties will find it impossible to please every group in a coalition all at once. And demographic changes within a party can reorder the power dynamics enough to change the nature of the party itself. At the turn of the millennium, Judis and Teixeira accurately predicted the central role the professional class would play in the future of the Democratic Party. What they did not foresee, Teixeira told me, were the knock-on effects this would have on the way the party itself was viewed by the working class. Teixeira notes that a "cultural hegemony of the professional class, particularly the younger, highly educated professional class, has really shifted the brand of the Democratic Party" and the forces that are shaping it, including "the politics of a lot of the activists and the politics of the media and a lot of other things that we did not anticipate." The emerging majority hypothesis rested in part on Democrats staying the same kind of party they were in the Clinton era, but this would prove impossible due in part to the very demographic shifts first heralded by Judis and Teixeira. The party's new orientation toward the professional class, and away from the working class, has proven a fateful choice. It was all the more so because of all the ways it ignored that the working class was and would remain a decisive majority of the American electorate.

4.

THE WORKING-CLASS MAJORITY

Mistaken assumptions about the future dominance of upscale workers or "ascendant" demographics fall prey to the "What you see is all there is" fallacy. Or, rather, what the analyst would *like* to see is all there is. These collective illusions are common to the Beltway media, and living in a place like the Washington, D.C., metro area, they are hard to escape. Here, the region continues to prosper and the liberal bubble continues to expand farther and farther outside the city. Near me, *another* Whole Foods is going in. The range of dining options available on Fourteenth Street in the city continues to expand. Neighborhoods gentrify with "five over one" apartment complexes that serve as dormitories for the laptop class. And minorities displaced by this gentrification move farther and farther out into the suburbs, making those areas more Democratic. The story is much the same in major metro areas throughout the country.

After the 2016 election, we were awakened to the fact that this wasn't the only reality in America. There was another half moving in the opposite direction, and as we now know, this tendency was strongest in the swing states. The national media's glaring failure to see this invited a period of self-reflection. For many journalists, this meant pilgrimages to diners in rural West Virginia to understand what they had gotten so wrong about the Trump phenomenon. On the one hand, this willingness to self-correct showed uncharacteristic humility, an acknowledgment that the cultural milieu inhabited by most journalists was hindering their ability to accurately understand and report on the true direction of American politics. In another sense, the fixation on West Virginia as the epicenter of Trumpism led the media down another narrative rabbit hole no better than "demography is destiny." The focus on one demographic extreme to counter another, in this case on rural, pickup-driving, economically downscale, and highly religious coal country, led to an overly simplified portrait of the Trump voter. This stereotype ultimately made it easier for liberals to import their own judgments of Trump backers as "racially resentful," filled with cultural "grievances," pining nostalgically for a past that never really existed with the motto "Make America Great Again."

On the other side of this cultural gulf lay the "optimistic" and "ascendant" places inside major metros, the places booming with new jobs and population growth that would ultimately define the future. And what was so convenient about West Virginia as Trumpian archetype is that a Beltway-based reporter could easily cross this cultural chasm in a ninety-minute drive.

Such story lines ignore all the places literally and figuratively in between Washington, D.C., where Trump won 6 percent of the vote in 2020, and Grant County, West Virginia, 147 miles away, where he won 88 percent. Yes, we are becoming more geographically divided by politics, with more people living in "landslide counties," where one candidate wins the lion's share of the vote. People and places in the middle are less common these days, but they still exist and are worth understanding better. And once we do, we realize that the problem isn't just one of elites who are out of touch with the West Virginias of the world. It's that they have no conception of how people in the middle live. Politically, America is divided almost evenly down the middle, and election statistics make the divide easy to grasp and quantify. But this creates the illusion that the cultural divide is also fifty-fifty, and that's not quite true. Because minorities lean culturally further to the right than they vote in elections, and there are more moderate Democrats than moderate Republicans, this makes cultural politics or the "culture war" tilt slightly more to the right. More broadly than one's point of view on school curriculum fights or the right to abortion are the habits and experiences of society writ large. What are the educational and life experiences of the average American? Where did they go to school? Where do they go to work? How much do they earn and what does this mean in practice for how they live their lives? And how might these ideas lead them to a place politically that is different from where they are right now? The middle ground on this spectrum is not defined in ideological terms, but in terms of educational attainment, the master key that unlocks all of the others.

The basic thing to know here is that barely over a third of American adults have graduated from college—and a college education is an increasingly important driver of political behavior. Culturally, those who occupy the middle ground have been trending right in their voting. For either side to win, they need to know who these people in the middle are socially, not just politically.

THE MEDIAN VOTER

Meet Jenn, America's median voter. Jenn is a married fifty-two-year-old woman living in Lehigh County, Pennsylvania, outside Allentown, who attended two years of college but didn't graduate. Her mother was a homemaker and her father a machinist, but she is part of the movement of women into the workplace. Jenn works in a real estate office as a title examiner, making $48,000 a year. Some things might not be so surprising about Jenn to someone three hours to the south in Washington. She is middle-aged, middle-class, married, and lives in a suburb, all things that fit within our understanding of who the average American is. Otherwise, we have questions. Which way did Jenn vote, for instance? As an avatar of the "real America" outside of the Beltway, you might be expecting to hear that she is a die-hard Trump voter donning a red MAGA hat. In fact, as the median voter, there's a slightly better than even chance she voted for Joe Biden. Jenn is also not from the "flyover country" of the Midwest, which would be the *geographic* middle of the country. She lives in the county closest to the political and demographic midpoint of the United States as calculated by my Echelon Insights colleagues in our Middle America Project, factoring in numerous political, social, and demographic indicators.

As stated, Jenn attended but did not complete college, the middle point in terms of educational attainment. She is fifty-two because that is the median age of a voter in the 2020 election. Her occupation situates her within the 41 percent plurality of the workforce that does white-collar work, but she is in the bottom half of that 41 percent, below the upper half who are in jobs where having a college degree is either required or preferred. Her job as a title examiner is the one that most closely matches the educational profile of the workforce at large: 35 percent of title examiners have a bachelor's degree or higher, 39 percent have some college education or an associate's degree, and 26 percent have no more than a high school diploma. Her earnings of $48,000 might jump out at an inside-the-Beltway observer as modest, but they are at the national average for someone in her line of work. Between her income and that of her husband's, the family has no trouble making the mortgage on their $300,000 home. Jenn's world is not West Virginia, but it's not Bethesda, Maryland, either. It's at the midpoint between those two places.

Writing in 1970, Richard M. Scammon and Ben J. Wattenberg undertook a similar thought experiment to find the median voter. In *The Real Majority*, they defined the "Middle Voter" as a forty-seven-year-old machinist's wife from Dayton, Ohio, and a homemaker. Some things about this portrait are similar: a middle-aged married woman from a middle-class community. Other things are different: our median voter is a woman in the workplace; the one in 1970 did not work and never went to college. Her social milieu was blue-collar, while Jenn's is in an office. Race is left out of my assessment because of the inherent problems in assigning normality to one race in a multiracial society, while Scammon and Wattenberg's "Middle Voter" was white in a country where nearly ninety percent of voters were like that. In their words, she was a "middle-aged, middle-income, middle-educated Protestant, in a family whose working members work more likely with hands than abstractly with head." More dated early-1970s references aside, this description mostly rings true of Jenn today.

CULTURE

Not captured by census statistics or precinct voting results are the cultural surroundings in which one grows up, the stuff that strengthens bonds between neighbors and friends. As a former reality TV show host swept the Republican primaries in 2016 based largely off support from people outside of large metropolitan areas, elites began to ask why they didn't see it coming. Charles Murray's "Bubble Quiz" from his 2012 book, *Coming Apart*, was designed to help them understand just how out of touch they had become from their fellow Americans. This disconnect went beyond one's views of issues like immigration to the simple day-to-day realities of life. More than 140,000 people took the quiz on the National Public Radio website in early 2016,* answering questions like:

> *Have you ever lived for at least a year in an American neighborhood in which the majority of your 50 nearest neighbors did not have college degrees?*
>
> *Have you ever held a job that caused something to hurt at the end of the day?*
>
> *During the last year, have you ever purchased domestic mass-market beer to stock your own fridge?*
>
> *How many times in the last year have you eaten at one of the following restaurant chains? Applebee's . . . Waffle House . . . Denny's . . . IHOP . . . Chili's . . . Outback Steakhouse . . . Ruby Tuesday . . . T.G.I. Friday's . . . Ponderosa Steakhouse*
>
> *Have you ever watched an episode of any of these shows all the way through? Wendy Williams . . . Dr. Phil . . . Ellen*

Quiz takers scored an average of 40 points out of 100. The higher the score, the more mainstream your tastes, like stocking your fridge with

* Murray does qualify that the questions are designed to measure American *white* culture, as the socioeconomic divide among whites is the subject of his book. Had questions about nonwhite culture been included, elite whites' disconnection from the mainstream would presumably be even greater.

Miller Lite. Murray asked respondents to add additional demographic details about themselves, such as their age and the zip codes where they live now and where they grew up. He then set to work connecting zip code demographics to the quiz results to find patterns.

What he found was a striking connection between the socioeconomic status (or SES) of the place where one grew up and how "mainstream" one's tastes were, tangible evidence that our education and income divides also form a cultural divide. The differences were not small, either. People who grew up in the most well-educated and wealthiest zip codes, in the 99th SES percentile, scored a 27 on the quiz. Those in the poorest and least well-educated zip codes scored around 45 points. And the scores only drop off modestly through the 80th percentile of income, where they then start dropping dramatically, from around 40 points to below 30. Murray found that there was something unique about how disconnected people in the top 20 percent were from the mainstream. In percentile terms, the quality of being in touch with middle-American cultural norms does not decline in a straight line. The scores don't decline gradually; they drop off a cliff.

When you look at absolute levels of education or wealth, though, the falloff is more gradual and linear. In particular, each percentage point increase in the number of people in a zip code with a college degree is associated with a drop in the average Bubble Quiz score of 0.4 points. This is the same basic phenomenon pointed out by critics of income inequality: someone in the 99th percentile isn't just a little different than someone in the 80th percentile; they are a lot different—specifically, a lot richer and a lot more highly educated. These are basic power-law dynamics in action.

Education—not income—is the factor that explains the Bubble Quiz scores more than any other. Using zip-code-level quiz data Murray released publicly, I built a multivariate regression model to predict quiz scores. Both education and income levels are correlated with the quiz results, but education is much more strongly coupled with a lower quiz score. Just like the recent voting shifts, the cultural divide is really an educational divide, not an income divide. The higher average age of a place also adds explanatory value. Including income in the equation adds nothing. Variation by income level is solely a function of better-educated places being wealthier.

Murray's data from the spring of 2016 foreshadowed the political upheaval we would see that November, with education, not income, explaining large shifts in voting patterns among whites.

Figure 4.1: The Education Divide Equals a Cultural Divide

Average Bubble Quiz score by education and family income by ZIP code growing up

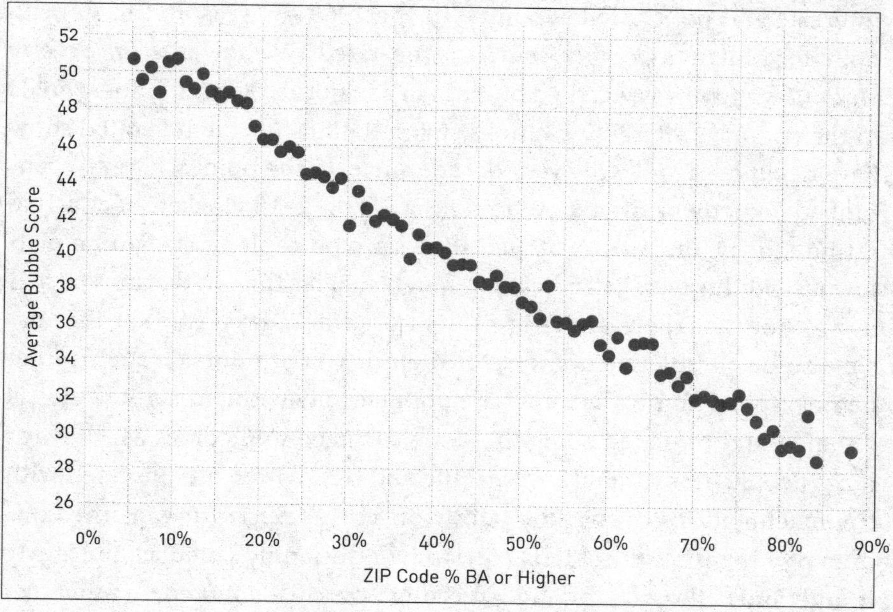

Source: Charles Murray's Bubble Quiz

In small pockets, elites are even more disconnected from mainstream culture. The 10023 zip code on the Upper West Side of Manhattan scored 12.3 points. The 20016 zip code in Northwest Washington, D.C., scored 21 points and 20817 in Bethesda, Maryland, scored 21.5. If the test were to be administered to a representative sample of Americans, Murray believes the average score would be 45 points, higher than the average of the sample of people responding on the NPR website, one of the media outlets most strongly preferred by the college-educated. The very places that scored lowest on the quiz, well below what simple demographics would predict, are the zip codes that are home to the political and media elite in New York City and Washington, D.C. While there has always been a disconnect between elites and the working class, it is now all-pervasive, with people on either side of the divide living in vastly different cultures.

Television has historically defined mainstream culture. There, we have gone from a single mainstream to one fragmented across countless streaming platforms and cable channels, each designed to cater to niche interests and political viewpoints. In the 1963–64 season, the starting point for Murray's *Coming Apart*, the top-rated TV show was *The Beverly Hillbillies* and it was watched by close to a majority of the TV households in the country, with a 39.1 ratings share. Ratings for the top-rated show have declined steadily in every decade since, to the point where the top-ranked comedy or drama on broadcast TV in 2018 clocked in at a 10.6 rating. Today, the most-watched shows are on cable or streaming platforms, and the average audience is much smaller than in decades past.

It's not that there aren't hit TV shows these days; it's that it's possible to be completely unaware of them if you are outside their target demographic. Some TV shows are popular only within discrete cultural bubbles, and these fall along the same socioeconomic lines as Murray's quiz. People in my bubble, in real life and on Twitter, are obsessed with the machinations of the Roy family on HBO's *Succession*, as the children plot to topple the elderly patriarch of the family's media empire. My friends and colleagues, by and large, don't watch *Yellowstone*, a ranch-set Western on the basic-cable Paramount network. If you are in the coastal *Succession* bubble, you likely aren't aware that *Yellowstone* is a vastly more popular show. Just 2.3 million people tuned in to the season four premiere of *Succession*, while 12.1 million watched the *Yellowstone* season five premiere. TV critics have picked up on this disconnect, with Roger Friedman of Showbiz411 writing, "The success of 'Yellowstone' is interesting because it has no 'buzz,' gets no awards, doesn't merit endless write ups and speculation and psychological theses about its characters. It's the opposite of HBO's 'Succession,' which has all of the above and minuscule ratings by comparison."

Google search interest lets us see precisely where each show is more popular. Over a period from March 2021 to March 2022, encompassing one full season of each show, *Yellowstone* holds an 8-to-1 edge in search interest, which closely matches its lead in the ratings, with more popularity in all fifty states and the District of Columbia. But some places are closer than others. In D.C. proper, *Yellowstone* has just a 51-to-49 lead. In the highest-SES suburbs, *Succession* manages to score some wins (with a 60 percent share in Falls Church, 52 percent in McLean, and 50 percent in Arlington). But, go farther afield of a high-SES metro and interest in *Succession* practically vanishes. It's 97 percent for *Yellowstone* and 3 percent for *Succession* in the Charleston-Huntington, West Virginia, media market, and 90 percent to 10 percent in the Harrisburg-York, Pennsylvania, market. *Succession* does not need monster ratings to be a commercial success, particularly with an upscale clientele paying $14.99 a month to watch it on HBO's streaming service. But it's a clear example of an elite bubble, in contrast to *Yellowstone.* Is there a political lesson here? "Politicians beware: 'Yellowstone' is a Heartland, GOP, 80s like show," writes Friedman. "It's a very Reagan era response. And that could spell trouble in elections."

Blind spots abound when it comes to the rest of what's watched on streaming platforms. In the 2021 ratings, every critically acclaimed "original" show ranked below mainstream fare that had previously run on network TV. The top-ranked show on Netflix and in all of streaming was the CBS crime procedural *Criminal Minds,* with 33.9 million U.S. viewers. The top six was rounded out by shows including *Grey's Anatomy*, *NCIS*, *Heartland*, and *Manifest.* It's not that people in elite circles are unaware that shows like *Grey's Anatomy* and *NCIS* exist. It's that few would think of them as being vastly more popular (in reruns) than critically acclaimed shows like *Squid Game*, *The Crown*, and *Ted Lasso.*

If you are reading a book like this one, the chances are that you have a college degree and are also part of this disconnect. The numbers back this up. As of 2016, the median college graduate read seven books a year compared to a median of two for those who had only graduated high school. Traveling abroad at one point in someone's lifetime is also something we assume that nearly everyone has done but is far from universal among those who haven't graduated from college. Just 7 percent of college graduates have never traveled anywhere abroad, five times less than the

37 percent of people without college diplomas. Meanwhile, 70 percent of college graduates have traveled to three countries or more, while just 27 percent of those without a college degree report having done the same. Experiences that we in the bubble assume are common are far from the norm for the majority of Americans who never graduated college.

SCHOOL

Education is now a main driver of political divides in America, and our median voter, Jenn, stands at the midpoint of this divide as someone who attended college but did not graduate. Elites may have a clear conception of the underprivileged voter who never went to college, but arguably, the Some College voter is hidden to them, as dropping out from prestigious universities—and I'm including in this category the main campuses of state universities—is a rare occurrence. At colleges and universities with less than a 25 percent admission rate, dropping out is rare; 89 percent of students at these selective schools will graduate within six years. At Ivy League schools, the graduation rate is over 95 percent; at the largest state universities it's generally over 80 percent. Contrast these figures with the numbers in the country overall, where only 60 percent of undergraduates finish their degree in six years. For hundreds of schools, this figure is below 50 percent. The record of most two-year institutions is even worse: barely 30 percent will complete their degrees.

That's for those who even start college. Around a third of college-age young people won't. Combined with a 60 percent completion rate among those who start, the share of people who will have attained a bachelor's degree by the time they are thirty is less than 40 percent. It is commonly assumed the share of college graduates is still rising, leading to a future electorate that will be more educated (and left-leaning) than ever, but government data says otherwise. In the last fifteen years, there has been no upward trend in the rate of young people earning a college diploma. Indeed, higher education has begun to slide backward. Overall college enrollment in the 2021–22 school year was down 9 percent from 2019–20. In Pennsylvania, public university enrollment was down 12 percent and community colleges saw a 23 percent drop in attendance. If colleges and universities were prepared to graduate a majority of young Americans, there's no evidence for it in new schools being built or existing institutions expanding enrollment. And when the University of California, Berkeley tried to build new student housing, it was stymied by "Not in my backyard" forces next to campus, forcing it to rescind three thousand admissions offers. While the number of college students declines, school administrations only grow, driving a surge in tuition costs that makes college even less attractive as an investment.

The end result is that the college graduation rate is only slightly higher today than it was forty years ago. Rates of college education have risen for younger age groups, but not dramatically so. According to the Census Bureau's American Community Survey, 32 percent of those just entering their retirement years in 2019 had a college diploma, compared to 39 percent of thirty- to thirty-four-year-olds, the highest level of any five-year age cohort. Across age groups, there's about a 15-point gap between the share of non-Hispanic whites and nonwhites with a degree; among thirty- to thirty-four-year-olds, 45 percent of whites have a degree, compared to 30 percent of nonwhites. As the country approaches demographic parity between whites and nonwhites, lower nonwhite graduation rates will tend to push down the overall share of those with degrees.

This means there will be no new surge of young college graduates to remake the social and cultural outlook of the electorate like we've seen in Loudoun County or the Atlanta suburbs. The rise of the "professional class" and the "creative class" has already happened and it isn't large enough in numbers to overcome the gravitational pull of the non-college-educated majority in the country. What we're likely to have in the future is rough parity between people who have completed some postsecondary credential—with at most four in ten having received a bachelor's degree or higher, and one in ten who will have received an associate's degree—and those who haven't. And because people on both sides of this divide have freely chosen their path, political polarization by education will only increase as older voters who predominantly didn't go to college age out of the electorate. We aren't far from the day when all voters will have gone through this educational sorting machine. But both sides won't be equally matched. In an electorate polarized by education, those without a four-year diploma will endure as the majority and the share of college graduates is likely to go no higher than the low 40th percentile.

Figure 4.2: The College Graduate Minority

Percent with bachelor's degree or higher by race and five-year age cohorts

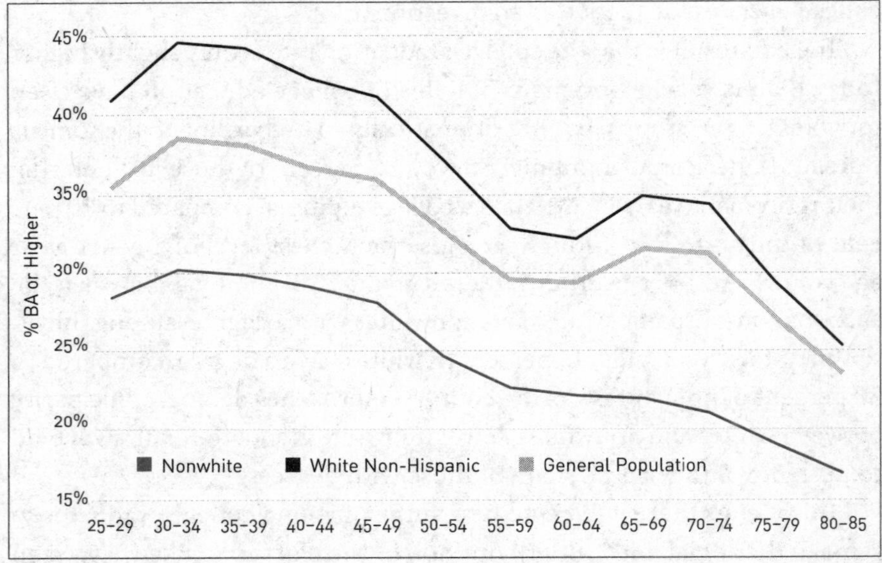

Source: American Community Survey, 2019 One-Year Estimates

What about the idea that the new crop of college graduates will be much more liberal than those in the past, pushing politics to the left? There's certainly much discussion today about "wokeness," cancel culture, speech codes, and ultra-left-wing student body politics on college campuses. At Harvard, Donald Trump received 6 percent of the vote in 2020—coming in third behind Green Party candidate Howie Hawkins at 7 percent. At the top twenty schools, the Trump vote averaged 10 percent. As you move down the college rankings, things do get a bit better for Republicans. Precincts at large state universities tended to give Trump between 20 and 30 percent of the vote. University politics as a whole leans left, and the more elite the school, the further left it is. But the fixation on the politics of elite universities paints a misleading picture of the politics most young people are encountering on campus (if they even attend college). America's college students are spread out across two thousand schools, many of them regional universities with student populations who commute while living at home. Everything about the average college experience, not just the politics, is very different from the milieu at Harvard or Yale.

The typical college experience in America happens at a school where only 61 percent of undergraduates will complete a degree, schools like the University of Nevada, Reno; Texas Tech; and West Virginia University. These are the places our Some College voter is more likely to have spent time at, and understanding the Some College voter is crucial to understanding the true nature of the electorate. Graduates of elite universities haven't personally encountered this reality. Just look at their graduation rates: Princeton, 98 percent; Yale, 97 percent; the University of Pennsylvania, 96 percent; Stanford, 94 percent. Graduates of most flagship state universities are also in a bit of a bubble: the University of Georgia, 87 percent; the University of Texas, 86 percent; Florida State, 83 percent.

Graduation rates are also a decent proxy for the prestige of an institution. They correlate strongly with test scores for newly admitted students and post-college incomes. The higher your school's graduation rate, the more rarefied a college experience you are likely to have had. Going to a school with a graduation rate of 80 percent or higher—a tier that includes many major state universities—positions you in the elite for people right out of college. Only one in eight people just old enough to have graduated college will have had an educational experience more prestigious. The following table shows how rare or common certain college experiences are, based on school graduation rates. I've tried to give illustrative examples of schools at each level, but you can see for yourself the graduation rate of your alma mater or current school at the U.S. Department of Education's College Scorecard at collegescorecard.ed.gov.

For those of you rising high school seniors stressing out about putting together the best application to a highly selective college: don't. The difference between attending an Ivy League institution or a state univer-

Table 4.1: The Country's Educated Elite Is Small and Unrepresentative

Odds of 2019 twenty-five- to twenty-nine-year-olds graduating from institutions, sorted by institution's graduation rate

Odds	Graduated from a school with a graduation rate at or above . . .
1 in 100	95%, like Harvard, Yale, Princeton, Columbia, or Stanford
1 in 50	92%, like Cal-Berkeley or the University of Michigan
1 in 20	85%, like the University of Illinois or Virginia Tech
1 in 10	81%, like the University of Delaware or Southern Methodist University
1 in 5	65%, like Ohio University or Kansas State
1 in 3	44%, like California State University–Dominguez Hills and the University of Louisiana–Monroe, and many smaller public universities or state university branch campuses

Sources: American Community Survey, 2019 One-Year Estimates and U.S. Department of Education College Scorecard graduation rates

sity flagship is small, and it won't make or break you. It's the difference between being in the top 1 percent and the top 5 percent of your peers, defined as all Americans your age. These small differences largely wash out when it's time to enter the workforce, where state school grads often outperform the Ivy Leaguers in the bunch. And yet, the obsession with hypercompetitive college admissions endures. In 2022, the *Wall Street Journal* featured the story of Kaitlyn Younger, an eighteen-year-old from Texas who scored 1550 on her SATs and graduated high school with a 3.95 grade point average. Harvard, Yale, Brown, Cornell, Stanford, and Northwestern all rejected her, so she ended up going to Arizona State University on a scholarship. While we are conditioned to view this as a step down, even a student attending ASU is breathing rare air, having an experience more prestigious than 90 or 95 percent of people their age.

Even those who graduated from a flagship state university with a more than 80 percent graduation rate are the elite in America. And combined with those who attended selective private universities, this makes up nearly everyone one encounters in politics and the media. Who you mostly don't encounter are people who dropped out of college or never went at all—the central protagonists in the political realignment of the last decade. Our focus on the politics of elite universities, the places where Donald Trump got less than 20 percent of the campus vote, are a fruitless distraction. The real numbers are elsewhere.

Discussions of higher-education policy are better focused instead on institutions where half or more of students drop out. This matters not only in terms of better understanding the all-important Some College voter, but to craft policy so that fewer people have frustrating college experiences that end in dropping out. And according to surveys, the reasons for leaving are not just financial—the obsession of policy wonks—but have just as much to do with family and lifestyle factors. According to a 2021 survey of college leavers, financial reasons are cited as the main reason by 42 percent, but also important are family commitments at 32 percent, "not the right fit" at 30 percent, and lack of time at 24 percent. Debunking some common misconceptions, it's not the students with the most student loan debt that leave, nor those in more challenging and competitive academic environments. Rather, the typical leaver is one whose commitment to higher education was more tenuous to begin with. Leaving is higher in schools with high admissions rates, lower test scores, and where students pay less in tuition. And it is much higher in schools with a two-year, rather than a four-year, commitment. This suggests a need to rethink the entire higher-education model. For those not philosophically bought into college life, even a two-year commitment can be too much. We desperately need better non-college pathways to avoid young people incurring crushing levels of debt only to drop out. And when we look at labor market dynamics, there's a clear reason why, for many, a full four-year degree no longer makes sense: the system is producing many more college graduates than the job market needs.

WORK

I wrote earlier that Jenn's job as a real estate title examiner is a profession that closely matches the educational profile of the American workforce. About half of title examiners have some credential after high school, be it a bachelor's or associate's degree, and half have none. It's also a white-collar job that pays a decent wage, defying the stereotype of non-graduates as working exclusively in "dead-end" blue-collar or service jobs. Other professions that do a good job of representing the educational mix of the workforce as a whole include teaching assistants, property managers, veterinary technicians, and door-to-door salespeople. In these jobs, it's possible to earn a decent living with or without a college degree.

Occupations like these are surprisingly common throughout the workforce. Overall, jobs that don't require a college degree make up the overwhelming majority of jobs in America. To see how, let's imagine a miniaturized American workforce of one hundred people. Forty-one of those people do white-collar work, typically in an office. Thirty-four of them work in a service job, with eleven of them working in health care. Twenty-five have a blue-collar job, working mostly with their hands instead of at a desk—the kinds of workers we typically think of when we think about the "working class."

Of the white-collar workers, just fourteen work in occupations where 70 percent or more of their colleagues have college diplomas. This includes four who work in professions where some kind of diploma or advanced degree is a hard requirement for entry—lawyers, teachers, scientists. Another ten work in jobs where a college degree is more or less a requirement—software developers, accountants, investment professionals, public relations specialists. That leaves twenty-seven white-collar workers where a college diploma is not necessarily a requirement. Nine are employed in professions like sales, human resources, and real estate, where between 50 to 70 percent have graduated college; here a diploma offers you a bit of a leg up, but it's not a be-all and end-all. And eighteen are in rank-and-file office jobs where less than a majority have a college degree, including customer service representatives, bookkeepers, bank tellers, and telemarketers.

Outside of health care, twenty-two of the one hundred workers are in the service sector. Sixteen are in rank-and-file roles, like fast-food workers, cashiers, warehouse workers, janitors, waitstaff, cooks, and childcare providers. In these lines of work, the most common educational credential is a high school diploma and less than one in ten have graduated college. Six of the twenty-two non–health care service workers can be classified as skilled workers; around a quarter have a college diploma; and about half have some college education. Their ranks include retail store workers, flight attendants, and post office workers. Health care has the most diverse educational mix: two of the eleven there are doctors or other roles requiring an advanced degree, three are nurses or other roles requiring at least an associate's degree, and six are support staff with minimal or modest educational requirements, from home health care aides to medical assistants.

Blue-collar jobs employ a quarter of our one hundred workers, and the vast majority of these—twenty-two—can be considered rank and file, including warehouse employees, truck drivers, and construction workers. No education beyond a high school diploma is required for these jobs. Three of the twenty-five are in skilled blue-collar jobs, where at least some education after high school is common; this small group include a motley of farmers, police officers, and firefighters.

When people talk about the "working class," they typically think of blue-collar workers in factories or on construction sites. Presidents give speeches in factories surrounded by heavy equipment and workers in hard hats to tout the benefits of their policies to working people. It's time to put this stereotype of the working class to rest. The working class is well represented across all sectors, with nearly two-thirds, or sixty-three out of one hundred, in rank-and-file jobs that you can mostly get with a high school diploma. By contrast, just sixteen have jobs where a college or graduate degree is a hard requirement or close to it—fourteen of them in white-collar work and two of them in the medical profession. (Nor are all of these sixteen jobs "prestigious." A significant share are teachers, who aren't very highly paid.) When we look at the educational credentials of our mini-workforce, there's a clear mismatch between the thirty-six who have college diplomas and the twenty-eight jobs in fields where the majority of workers are graduates. Four in ten college graduates currently work in fields where the majority of workers do not have degrees and the return on investment in a college education is likely to be low.

We can see this by visualizing every occupation by the share of people with a college degree or above. A majority of all jobs—60 percent—are in occupations where less than 30 percent have college diplomas. The largest group of jobs are those where less than 10 percent of all workers have college diplomas, at 25 percent of the workforce. The top end of the spectrum is not nearly as crowded; only 6 percent are in occupations where 90 percent or more have a college diploma or higher; only 16 percent are in those where that total is 70 percent or more; and 28 percent do work where a majority of their peers are college graduates.

This mismatch is why demand for a college diploma—especially in "middle skill" positions—is plummeting in a strong job market. Rather than an economy hungering for well-educated graduates, the job market is oversaturated with them. Other distortions in our understanding of the workforce were laid bare during the COVID-19 pandemic. Watching the

Figure 4.3: Most Workers Are in Fields with Few College Graduates

Employment by occupation in 2020, by percentage of workers with a bachelor's degree or higher

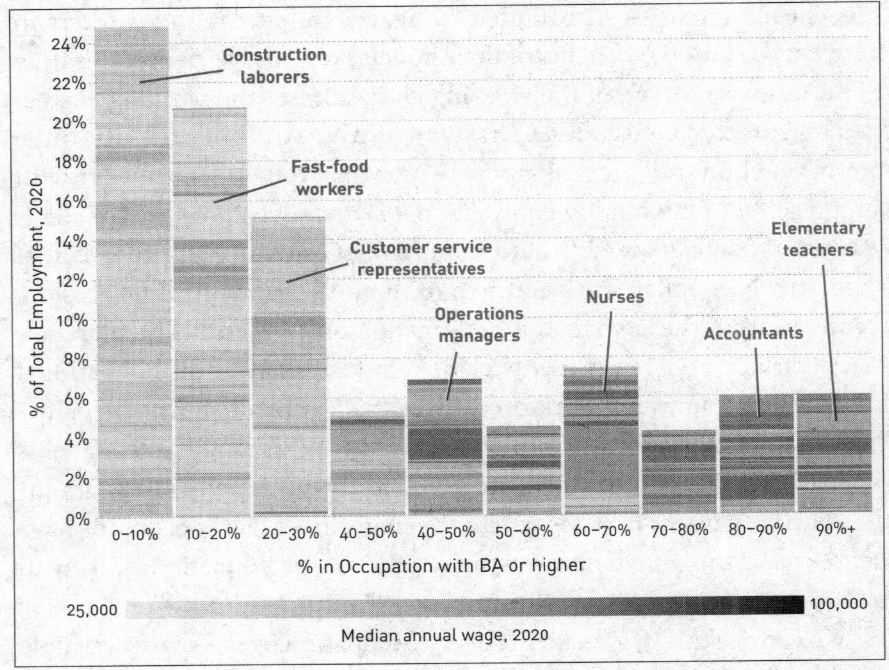

Source: Bureau of Labor Statistics Employment Projections

media coverage, you would think most people spent the pandemic working from home, contending with Zoom fatigue, with those in technology or finance plotting their escape from San Francisco or New York to greener, less expensive pastures. A whole new culture sprung up around Zoom work, including zany virtual backgrounds and the "Room Rater" Twitter account devoted to critiquing the home decor of TV pundits.

Most workers faced a different reality. Service workers bore the brunt of the early pandemic lockdowns and the resulting largest monthly job losses in history. When these workers returned to work, it was in person. Meanwhile, white-collar workers shifted effortlessly to working from home, seeing few job losses. Stark differences by job sector translated to differences by worker education levels. From May 2020 to April 2021, the average rate of teleworking measured by the Bureau of Labor Statistics was 24 percent. Rates were vastly different based on education: an average of 52 percent of those with graduate degrees worked from home, as did 38 percent of those with a bachelor's degree. The rate for high school graduates? Eight percent. Our median voters, those with some college education, more closely resemble high school graduates than college graduates, with a teleworking rate of 16 percent. These numbers manifest in racial disparities downstream from these educational divides, with an average remote work rate of 26 percent among whites, 20 percent among African Americans, and just 15 percent among Hispanics. Pandemic-era remote work was a substantial shift, but one that largely did not apply to the more than six in ten workers in rank-and-file jobs—or the six in seven who weren't knowledge workers.

A similar disconnect arises with the phenomenon of corporations taking a stand on social issues—as Major League Baseball did in moving the All-Star Game from Atlanta over a Georgia voting law or Disney did in opposing a Florida law banning the teaching of sexuality in elementary schools. On the one hand, it is not surprising that corporations would take these stands given the growing Democratic and progressive skew of their college-educated headquarters employees. On the other hand, the workplace dynamics they reflect are representative of only a tiny minority of American workers: the small fraction who are knowledge workers, and within this small group, the tiny elite with high-status jobs in corporate headquarters. This tiny minority is driving all the coverage you see about "woke capitalism." These high-status graduates are outliers in their socially progressive views compared to the public at large, supporting identity politics movements across race, gender, and sexual orientation all at once. They are also more politically engaged, and more likely to want to live out their politics at work as well as at home. The minority pushing these ideas is small, but hugely influential, deciding everything from the movies and TV shows that get made to which kinds of online speech are permitted. This is the group conservatives talk about when they argue that political power is downstream of cultural power.

Even if these well-educated knowledge workers make up a minority of all workers, aren't they growing quickly? No. Occupations with a majority of college graduates today are expected to increase by just one percentage point in the 2020s, from 28 to 29 percent. We will see at most a gradual change in the nature of the workforce over the remainder of the decade. That won't be enough to spark a new wave of college attenders and graduates who will adopt progressive ideologies and shift the country's center of political gravity.

The politics of America is the politics of the rank-and-file worker and the non-graduate. This doesn't just mean a blue-collar construction worker who voted for Obama and then Trump, but the supermajority of workers across white-collar, blue-collar, and service industries who hold positions where a college diploma is not a requirement, didn't work from home during the pandemic, and aren't agitating for their employer to take a stand politically. It includes millions of Democrats and Biden voters, but not of the progressive activist variety.

As for the other kind of politics we obsess over—that of campus speech codes, cancel culture, and woke corporations—that's a politics that's lived on a daily basis by no more than 15 to 20 percent of people, by those who graduated from selective colleges and are likely to be surrounded by fellow college graduates at work, forming a cohesively liberal political monoculture. This constituency is not even a majority of Democratic voters in elections, but they contribute the money, set the policy, and speak out on social media. This imbalance of power is what has created the opportunity for Republicans to win over more of the non-college, rank-and-file supermajority of voters whose views aren't represented by this elite.

In this chapter, I've focused squarely on the question of who this majority is: the basic background facts of their lives educationally and at work. They live in suburbs, not central cities or rural areas. They did not graduate college. They aren't knowledge workers. And these facts are unlikely to change anytime soon. If you want to understand the working-class majority in American politics, you need to understand what defines them. And you also need to understand something about their political views, and how these differ from the college-educated elite in both parties. That is the question I will turn to next.

5.

THE POLITICAL CENTER OF GRAVITY

In February 2019, former Starbucks CEO Howard Schultz announced that he was exploring an independent candidacy for president in 2020. Schultz's pitch was familiar enough for the CEO candidate: breaking through the logjam of partisan dysfunction to deliver the commonsense solutions Americans want, in polling at least. On immigration, Schultz sounded more like a Democrat—announcing that Starbucks would look to hire ten thousand refugees and criticizing Donald Trump's border wall. On the economy, Schultz drew a line in the sand against the progressives in the Democratic Party. He was especially critical of proposals for free college and free health care of the then-ascendant Bernie Sanders–Elizabeth Warren wing. His first political missive was classic "Corporate Dem": bemoaning the mistreatment of Amazon by left-wing activists when it announced plans to open a second headquarters in New York City. "Where has common sense gone?" asked Schultz.

Schultz's platform reflected the politics of centrist respectability in a region known colloquially as the Acela Corridor, for the slightly higher-speed intercity train that runs between Boston and Washington, D.C. That politics is fiscally conservative and socially progressive: pro-choice on abortion, for fiscal restraint, maybe for the occasional tax cut or two if we could afford it. Espousing these views, Republicans were routinely elected to Congress in places like New England, upstate New York, and the liberal Maryland suburbs of Washington, D.C. Except for Maine's Susan Collins or Alaska's Lisa Murkowski, the moderate Republican version of this ideology is all but extinct.

But their values live on at Schultz's Starbucks and most corporations. As publicly traded entities with a fiduciary responsibility to maximize shareholder profit, Fortune 500 companies are hardly manning the barricades of revolution. But they do want you to know that they care about things other than money and the way they do that is by embracing culturally progressive causes and the environmental, social, and governance (or ESG) criteria for attracting "socially responsible" investors. So on the wall at my local Starbucks I can find chalk-stenciled anti-racist quotes from Ibram X. Kendi alongside bulletin board missives on "how to be an ally." At the same time, Starbucks does right by shareholders by resisting efforts by its employees to unionize and closing down stores that do. Fiscally conservative, socially progressive: that's the politics of today's C-suite—and almost nowhere else.

When my Echelon Insights cofounder Kristen Soltis Anderson speaks before corporate leaders, she often asks how many in her audience would describe their politics as fiscally conservative and socially liberal. Nearly all the hands in the room shoot up. While this brand of politics is the default for the white-knight CEO candidate, it has fewer followers among real voters. In the lexicon of online "political compass" quizzes, this would be known as the libertarian quadrant. These quizzes visualize ideology as a two-dimensional space, with economic issues on one axis and cultural issues on the other. After the 2016 election, political scientist Lee Drutman applied this online-quiz rubric to survey data of voters. Hardly more than one in twenty Americans shared a mix of views that could be broadly characterized as keeping the government out of the bedroom and the boardroom.

At Echelon Insights, we test the strength of different ideological factions with biannual surveys asking Americans how they would vote in a hypothetical Western European–style multiparty democracy. In our multiparty America, voters can choose to align with a populist right or a traditional conservative right. They can choose between a working-class, a center-left, a socialist far-left, or a neoliberal Schultz-like party. That neoliberal party—sounding socially tolerant and fiscally responsible—consistently finishes last or next to last every time we ask it. In post-survey analysis, we've dubbed it the Acela Party.

What comes in first, consistently, is a working-class version of Democrats that broadly characterized the European and American left in the twentieth century: strong unions, health care and retirement benefits for the middle class, high taxes on the rich, and mostly silent on social issues. While the right is divided between its populist and Reaganite wings, an old-fashioned labor-left is far and away the most popular choice among Democratic voters. Asking only about party platforms—names and party leaders are added in analysis after the fact—we got the following result in October 2022:

Table 5.1:
Working-Class "Labor" Party Would Win in a Multiparty America

Party	Platform	Support
Labor (Joe Biden)	Put the middle class first, pass universal health insurance, strengthen labor unions, and raise taxes on the wealthy to support programs for those less well off.	29%
Nationalist (Donald Trump)	Stop illegal immigration, put America First, stand up to political correctness, and end unfair trade deals.	24%
Conservative (Mike Pence)	Defend the American system of free enterprise, promote traditional family values, and ensure a strong military.	18%
Acela (Mike Bloomberg)	Advance social progress including women's rights and LGBTQ rights, work with other countries through free trade and diplomacy, cut the deficit, and reform capitalism with sensible regulation.	12%
Green (Alexandria Ocasio-Cortez)	Pass a Green New Deal to build a carbon-free economy with jobs for all, break up big corporations, end systemic inequality, and promote social and economic justice.	8%

Source: Echelon Insights, November 2022

The failure of the Acelans is borne out not only in this theoretical multiparty experiment, but also in real life. Schultz's proto-candidacy was shouted down by anti-Trump online progressives and quickly shuttered.

Mike Bloomberg picked up the baton of the pro-business pragmatist against Sanders and Warren, spending $1 billion on a bid for the Democratic nomination and finishing a distant third or worse in most Super Tuesday states. There are deeper structural reasons for this, as a close examination of public opinion data will show. Most moderate voters—the kind that don't line up with Republicans or Democrats on every issue—look nothing like neoliberal urbanists or old-school moderate Republicans. In fact, they're the very opposite. They are fiscal *liberals* and social *conservatives.*

SECULAR POPULISM

In a crowded field of seventeen candidates in 2016, Donald Trump's politics stood out. He promised to build a border wall and stop the illegal immigrant "invasion" of the United States. But, in a break from the austerity politics of the Tea Party era, Trump promised he wouldn't touch Social Security and Medicare benefits, and had a paper trail of past statements in support of a single-payer, government-run health care system. He railed against globalization and free trade. Trump's GOP rivals quickly pounced, calling anyone with big-spending, isolationist views unfit to carry the mantle of the party of Ronald Reagan. The attacks fell on deaf ears. When former Nixon White House aide and political commentor Patrick J. Buchanan ran on a similar mix of views in the 1990s, his candidacies were eventually dispatched by the establishment, but not before he took 38 percent of the vote in the New Hampshire primary against an incumbent president and won the Granite State outright in 1996. As with the failed McGovern candidacy for the left, Buchananism would prove to be the shape of things to come on the right.

Lee Drutman's chart showed that Trump's populist revival worked, not just with primary voters, but in the general election.

Using public opinion data from the Voter Study Group following the 2016 election, Drutman mapped out the four quadrants in the American electorate. In the upper right and lower left, respectively, were conventional conservatives and progressives who held a consistent set of views on social and economic questions. Bisecting them diagonally were two groups of conflicted voters: populists who were left-leaning on economic issues, right-leaning on social ones, and the libertarian Acelans in the sparsely populated lower-right quadrant.

Drutman constructed detailed ideology scores for around five thousand Americans based on various issue questions in the Voter Study Group's survey of 2016 voters. An ardent proponent of a multiparty political system and of going beyond a static one-dimensional view of ideology, Drutman showed that substantial numbers of Americans are not consistently left, right, or even center, but quite literally all over the ideological map.

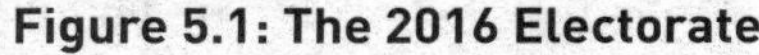
Figure 5.1: The 2016 Electorate

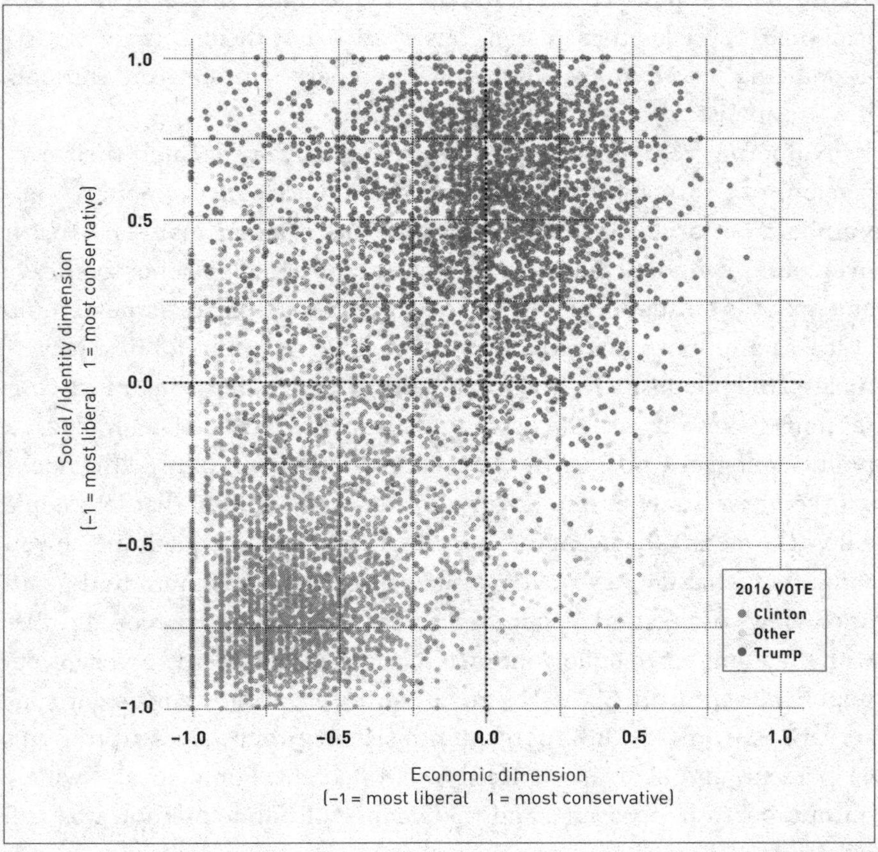

Source: Voter Study Group

Of those conflicted Americans who weren't consistently left or right, far more lived in the populist than in the libertarian quadrant. And because the same voters had been surveyed in 2012, Drutman could see that the majority of voters who flipped from Obama in 2012 to Trump in 2016 were also in the populist quadrant targeted by Trump. By Drutman's calculations, consistent conservatives were 23 percent of the electorate, consistent progressives were 39 percent, populists were 33 percent, and libertarians just 6 percent. Among those with conflicting sets of social and economic values, populists outnumbered libertarians in Drutman's map of public opinion by more than five to one. The quadrants find an overall balance of public opinion that is 72 percent to the left economically, 28 percent to the right, and 56 percent to the right on social and identity issues, and 44 percent to the left. The center of gravity in American politics was neither liberal, conservative, nor the corporate moderation being served up by Schultz or Bloomberg. Through and through, it was populist.

Numerous researchers, myself included, have re-created their own versions of Drutman's quadrants. In each of these efforts, populists outnumber libertarians. My own critique of the original analysis is that it overcounts economic liberals (and thus populists) by placing too heavy an emphasis on support for Social Security and Medicare, issues Trump at least temporarily removed from the field of partisan politics. Nevertheless, the populist advantage still holds when emphasizing more contentious issues that are the current focus of left-right debate. In 2021, a political blogger who goes by the pseudonym Xenocrypt used the open-source Voter Study Group data to create an online tool that let people adjust the factors that went into sorting Americans into quadrants. If you think that what defines an economic conservative has more to do with one's views of taxation as opposed to Social Security, you could tinker with the numbers to build your own scoring system. In my re-weighting, populists went from 33 to 21 percent of the electorate; consistent conservatives from 23 to 32 percent, consistent progressives from 39 to 41 percent, and libertarians from 6 to 8 percent. Populists still widely outnumbered libertarians, and the balance of public opinion was still economically liberal (62 to 38 percent), but culturally conservative (53 to 47 percent).

My colleagues at Echelon Insights collected their own survey data to construct similar quadrants in 2021 and 2022. On ten different issues across each of the economic and social dimensions, we asked respondents to choose whether a liberal or conservative statement better represented their beliefs. For instance, we might ask whether a respondent agrees more with the idea that "It is more important to control gun ownership" versus "It is more important to protect the right of Americans to own guns," or "I would rather have a bigger government providing more services" versus "I would rather have a smaller government providing fewer services."

What we found was an electorate that more often fit into traditional ideological camps, with consistently liberal and consistently conservative voters making up 43 and 36 percent of the electorate, respectively. Two in ten voters did not fit into these conventional groupings, and of those, populists outnumbered libertarians by more than three to one—17 percent to 5 percent. When looking at each of the two axes individually, cultural conservatives outnumbered cultural liberals by 53 to 47 percent. Economic liberals outnumbered economic conservatives by 60 to 40 percent. Between 2021 and 2022, public opinion turned in a more populist direction on the economy, with economic liberals increasing from 53 to 60 percent. This was especially evident in a sharp move to the left on raising the minimum wage, likely a reaction to growing inflation. It is notable, though, that this tide of economic populism did not add up to a Democratic political advantage, with the party's handling of the economy considered a weak point in the midterm campaign.

The right's advantage on social questions and the left's advantage on economic ones does not mean they will win consistently in those areas, regardless of the issue. Liberals win on some social issues, and conservatives win on some economic ones. The electorate is culturally liberal on the questions of whether gay and lesbian couples should be allowed to marry legally (with 62 percent siding with this position) and on whether abortion should be legal in all or most circumstances (56 percent). When the Supreme Court reversed *Roe v. Wade* in 2022, it was Democrats who campaigned on the issue, able to call attention to an unpopular conservative position. Mostly, though, conservatives win on culturally laden questions. Most agreed that America is the greatest country in the world (62 percent, juxtaposed against the idea that it isn't), that we should fully fund the budget of police departments (56 percent), and that the government should deal with illegal immigration by addressing border security and enforcement first (53 percent). On the economy, there is a liberal majority for raising taxes on people making $200,000 or more (60 percent) and seeing to it that everyone has health coverage (52 percent), and a conservative majority on positions like "Most people who want to get ahead can make it if they're willing to work hard" (57 percent) and "The fact that some people in the U.S. are rich and others are poor is an acceptable part of our economic system" (51 percent).

Conservatives are able to campaign and win on cultural issues because of how Trump and subsequent Republicans redefined them: away from a focus on issues of personal morality, like abortion and gay marriage, and toward a focus on quality-of-life issues like crime and illegal immigration. This was a brand of politics familiar to Trump from his days in New York City and a throwback to the culture war politics that realigned the white working class in the 1960s, when the right defined itself mainly in opposition to a counterculture of protest and drugs. In a big city like New York, examples of liberal excess were not hard to find. Trump's schtick was the same as the one he'd honed in 1980s New York, when he took out full-page newspaper ads against the Central Park Five and called for the withdrawal of U.S. troops from abroad if the host countries didn't pay their fair share for defense. It was also an echo of the tabloid politics that got Rudy Giuliani elected mayor: tough on crime and brash in his denunciations of political rivals. Nowhere in this was any trace of the fundamentalist or evangelical politics dominant in the South. Even those working-class New Yorkers that filled Catholic pews on Sunday were not those kinds of culture warriors.

By taking his New York politics national, Trump was able to execute a clever end run around the Moral Majority politics thought to hold veto power over the Republican nominating process. The idea that social conservatives were all-powerful in Republican primaries was held as an article of faith by the political press. Surely, a thrice-married playboy who seldom went to church, mangled Bible verses, and was on the record against late-term abortion bans would have trouble winning over a primary electorate dominated by evangelical Christians.

Trump solved this dilemma by dialing up the rhetoric and going where few other Republican candidates were prepared to go on cultural issues important to secular as well as religious conservatives. His candidacy also coincided with a shift in the Republican base, away from suburbs, where megachurches gathered their flock, and toward rural country back roads, where religious belief held sway but church attendance was atrophying. In *Alienated America*, Timothy P. Carney showed that low social capital, not just education, predicted Trump's early support in the primaries. Social capital is defined by high levels of social interconnectedness: by church attendance, volunteerism, marriage, and traditional two-parent families. These social ties have been fraying, especially in places that surged to Trump after shunning Republicans past. In the places where Trump ran strongest in the 2016 primaries, you had more people staying at home on Sunday, more out-of-wedlock births among whites, more males not in the labor force, and more deaths of despair. This led to unusual voter coalitions in the 2016 primaries: a cohort of highly organized movement conservatives and evangelicals battling not a moderate "Republican in Name Only," but a nationalist-populist raiding their base of alienated antiestablishment voters. The intersection of religious observance and education explained a lot about the 2016 primaries: the least religiously observant and least college-educated voters were the strongest for Trump, the most observant and most highly educated were the most likely to be against him. And the former group outnumbered the latter.

Nonetheless, evangelicals could not simply be ignored in a Republican primary, where they made upward of two-thirds of the electorate in states like South Carolina, and Trump knew better than to antagonize them. Without explanation, he flipped to a pro-life position. Trump finally neutralized any remaining evangelical skepticism with a pledge to nominate Supreme Court justices from a preapproved list developed by the conservative Federalist Society. In doing so, Trump was taking traditional social issues off the table while simultaneously laying the seeds for their return with the repeal of *Roe v. Wade*. He was now free to redefine cultural conservatism in ways that also animated the substantial number of Republicans who did not go to church: opposed to immigration, political correctness, and the denigration of working-class rural America by coastal elites. Trump's new right had no moral or religious test.

By shifting the emphasis toward nationalism, Trump built a stronger, more internally cohesive right than the old coalition of interest groups Ronald Reagan called "the three legs of the stool": economic conservatives, social conservatives, and national security conservatives. This understanding of conservatism had been thoroughly hollowed out by the time Trump rolled around, with conservative discourse in Washington, D.C., looking nothing like how an actual Republican voter would speak. An avid viewer of Fox News, Trump had a knack for channeling the sensibilities of the median Republican voter, one who could care less about corporate tax policy or the right number of exceptions to a ban on abortion. Hiding beneath Trump's abrasive rhetoric was a rawer form of culture war politics more popular with primary voters—and, it turns out, general election voters—than the strictures of movement conservatism. For instance, when Trump advocated a ban on Muslims entering the United States, this was denounced—and rightly so—as an unconstitutional violation of religious liberty. Trump's critics included conservatives like then Indiana governor Mike Pence, who would become his vice presidential running mate. But conservatives and others had to grapple with the fact that a temporary blanket ban on Muslims had something approaching majority public support, and that a ban on travel from specific countries designed to pass constitutional muster commanded an outright majority. Where others would not cross these rhetorical red lines, Trump felt no restraint.

It is worth understanding how Trump succeeded where populists like Pat Buchanan failed. Trump's success was partly the result of a changed Republican voting base since the 1990s, with wealthy *Wall Street Journal* readers replaced in the party by ex-Democrats with populist economics. But Trump's persona was also radically different than Buchanan's—or other would-be populist white knights like the anti-immigration congressman Tom Tancredo. Trump was a showman through and through, known to Americans through the tabloids, reality TV, and hip-hop lyrics, eliding ideological categorization. By contrast, Buchanan gladly cast himself as an ideological warrior, one focused on moral and religious issues. "There is a religious war going on in this country. It is a cultural war, as critical to the kind of nation we will be as the Cold War itself," Buchanan proclaimed in a prime-time speech at the 1992 Republican convention. For all that Trump was, he did not come across as a rigid ideologue or moralizing prude. For Republicans, what distinguished Trump was his willingness to *fight*. Contrasted with Trump, the avatars of the Republican establishment seemed like weaklings who wouldn't fight. Decent people perhaps, but easily shoved aside when someone came along who would.

Trump's repositioning of the party succeeded in winning over midwestern swing voters where other Republicans failed. His secular populism placed him close to the center of gravity of the American electorate, with surveys of voters rating him more moderate than Hillary Clinton. And the reason that Beltway elites didn't see it is that the worldview of the average voter was alien to college graduates like themselves.

IDEOLOGICAL WHITES, MODERATE NONWHITES

There is a group of Americans that is politically obsessed and bitterly divided: college graduates. And their views on any given issue are easily predicted by their choice of party. Those who are conservative on economic issues tend to be equally as conservative on cultural issues. This is reflected in the quadrant scores, showing where these voters stand on a 0–100 index of economic and cultural conservatism. For college graduates, the scores closely match. Public opinion among non-graduates isn't like this. The relationship between party affiliation and issue stances is looser, with lower-information moderates mixing and matching different left and right positions. Non-graduates also tend to be much more culturally conservative relative to their economic views—or more economically liberal relative to their cultural views, looked at another way. The overall electorate is more culturally conservative than it is economically, the working-class majority especially so.

Table 5.2:
Non-Graduates Are More Conservative Socially Than Economically
Social and economic conservatism scores from Echelon Insights' Political Quadrants survey

	Social	Economic	Gap
Whites, college degree	53.1	48.1	5.0
Nonwhites, college degree	46.3	44.2	2.1
Whites, no college degree	59.2	50.3	9.3
Nonwhites, no college degree	45.3	38.4	6.9
White	56.9	49.5	7.4
Black	40.4	37.0	3.4
Hispanic	37.8	40.7	7.1
Asian	51.7	42.1	9.6

Source: Echelon Insights, June 2022 Political Quadrants Survey

The quadrant exercise is inherently a bit reductive in the way that it groups voters into static conservative or liberal camps, either on social issues or economics. In real life, a voter who leans just slightly to the right on social issues is very different from a Moral Majority warrior at the 99th percentile on the social and cultural index. When you separate the rigid ideologues from those who are broadly speaking in the middle, a telling difference emerges. Those that congregate at the polarized extremes—holding conservative or liberal positions on almost every issue—are overwhelmingly likely to be white. Those in the middle are far more likely to be nonwhite. We can see this by scoring the sixty thousand interviewees in the 2020 Cooperative Election Study on an index based on whether they gave left- or right-leaning answers on more than fifty policy-related prompts, similar to the indices used in our political quadrants.

Being in agreement with either the left or the right more than 75 percent of the time turns out to be a key threshold for this analysis. Above the line you find Assad-like electoral majorities—98 percent—for the respective candidates of the right and left, Trump and Biden, in 2020. That's an even better predictor of vote choice than party identification, or even self-reported ideology crossed with party identification—of liberal Democrats or conservative Republicans. Below the 75 percent threshold, your vote quickly becomes up for grabs, progressing in logical fashion according to your issue score. There's a big difference between lockstep ideologues and the non-ideological in the middle; to the non-ideologues, a slight change in how you think about issues leads to better odds for supporting the candidate aligned with those views. Above the 75 percent threshold, your vote is locked in.

The majority of voters are in this ideological middle, and there are vast differences by race and education. Among Black Americans, 83 percent are non-ideological. Among Hispanics, 77 percent. Among Asian Americans, 69 percent. Among working-class whites, defined as those without a college degree, 58 percent fall in the ideological middle ground. There's one glaring demographic exception: whites with a college degree, where just 38 percent are non-ideological. Alone among demographic groups, white college graduates are polarized on both sides, with 34 percent taking strongly liberal positions and 28 percent taking strongly conservative positions. The image we have of ourselves as a country hopelessly divided, with private spaces endlessly polluted with partisan politics, is mostly only true of one demographic cul-de-sac: well-educated whites. They are 26 percent of registered voters, but majorities of cable news viewership, online news readership, and political Twitter.

This night-and-day difference between whites and nonwhites, and more to the point, the white college graduate and everyone else, becomes even clearer when we map exactly where on the ideological spectrum different groups of Americans fall. Visualized this way, the differences are even clearer. Both sets of white voters—graduates and non-graduates—have graphs unlike those of any other racial groups. White working-class voters cluster more on the ideological right, with few ideological liberals. White college graduates have twin ideological peaks, one each on the

Figure 5.2: Liberalism Is Strong Only among College Whites

Right-left ideological consistency scores by demographic group

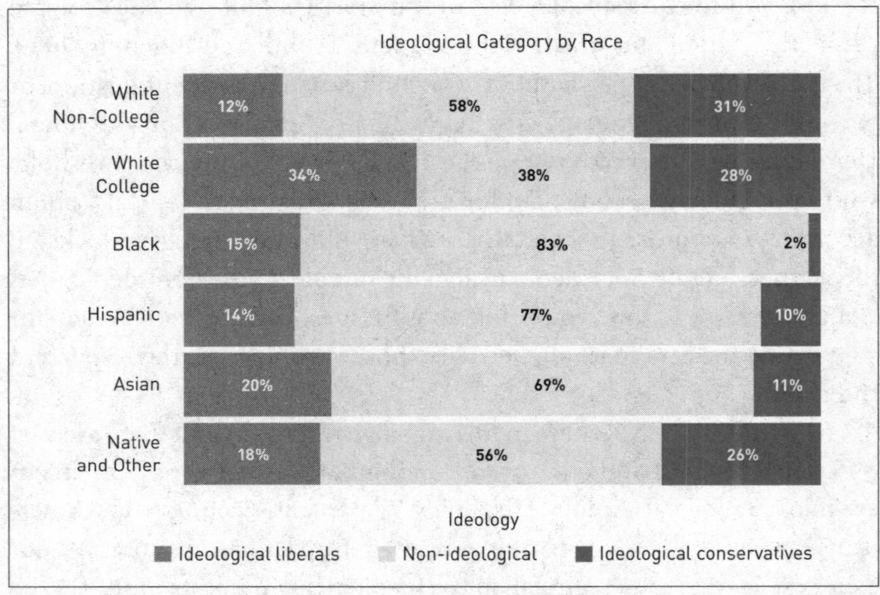

Source: Index calculated based on 2020 Cooperative Election Study

left and right, with a trough in the middle. And minority groups—Black, Hispanic, and Asian American voters—are just the opposite, voting for Democrats but with issue views overwhelmingly in the middle.

Ideologues in America look different than non-ideologues, quite literally. When we adjust our definition of the rigidly ideological to include only the hyperpolarized who agree with one side 90 percent of the time or more, these groups are 82 percent white on the left and 89 percent white on the right. Those closest to the middle, narrowed down to those in the 40th to 60th percentiles on the ideological spectrum, are 55 percent white and 45 percent nonwhite. Neither group of ideologues represent the racial and ethnic diversity of their party's voters, and it should be noted that Republicans are lower in diversity than Democrats. But the lack of diversity is especially conspicuous on the ideological left, given how much of liberal politics lately has centered on questions of

Figure 5.3:
White College Voters on the Extremes, Nonwhite Voters in the Middle
Right-left ideological consistency scores by demographic group

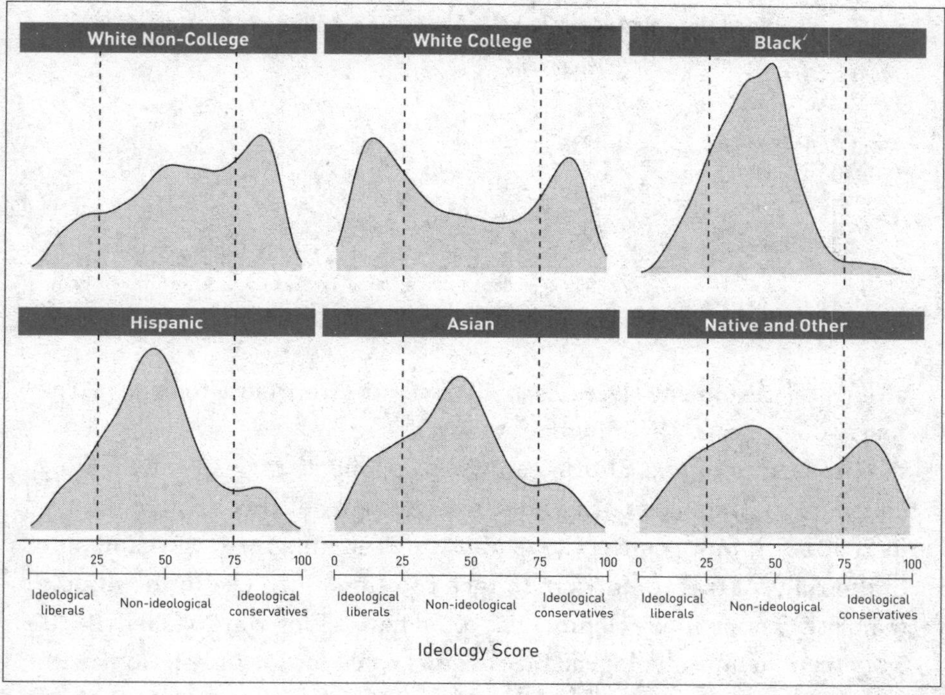

Source: Index calculated based on 2020 Cooperative Election Study

race. Black voters, who are more than 20 percent of Democrats, are just 3.1 percent of the most ideologically liberal. The most striking finding is just how thoroughly white college graduates dominate this most liberal group. They are 28 percent of the Democratic electorate, but 60 percent of hyperpolarized liberals.

Given that solid majorities of nonwhite moderates have continued to vote for Democrats, this data clarifies for us the nature of both party coalitions. The Republican coalition is a conservative ideological one. The Democratic coalition is ideological among whites—especially among college graduates—and group-interest based among nonwhites, able to encompass the lion's share of politically moderate members of all nonwhite

Table 5.3: Strong Liberals Are Mostly College Whites, Least Ideological Largely Nonwhite

Demographic makeup of 2020 voters grouped by ideological consistency

	White College	White Non-College	Nonwhite
Most Liberal (0–10 score)	60%	22%	18%
Most Conservative (90–100 score)	33%	56%	10%
Least Ideological (40–60 score)	18%	38%	45%

Source: Index calculated based on 2020 Cooperative Election Study

groups. In the Obama elections, the Democrats were close to being a true "party of everyone" in nonwhite America.

The Democratic coalition can work so long as race-specific factors continue to influence voting. But we saw signs of this breaking down in 2020, with more conservative nonwhites aligning with the candidate of the right. If this trend were to take root more broadly in the middle majority of nonwhites, Democrats would have a long way to fall. In 2020, 91 percent of non-ideological Black voters voted for Joe Biden, along with 70 percent of non-ideological Hispanics and Asian Americans. Non-ideological whites were fairly evenly divided between Biden and Trump, 51 to 44 percent. All things being equal, you would expect such voters to be equally divided, but for historical reasons that hasn't been true of nonwhite voters. Of course, Republicans can't simply hope to wave away these historical differences overnight, especially with Black voters. But they could make up ground by highlighting the wide gulf in values between nonwhite moderates and strong progressives. If Republicans pursue such a strategy, the data suggests they would have room to grow.

An analysis by Ruy Teixeira of our Echelon Insights quadrant data underscores just how large these differences are. He zeroes in on the similarity between Hispanics and working-class voters—defined as those without a college degree—and contrasts it with the values of the progressive left. In our study, we defined strong progressives as those who agreed with the liberal position both culturally and economically more than 80 percent of the time. Some of the Teixeira highlights are quite telling.

By 70 to 23 percent, Hispanics agreed that America was the greatest country in the world, and working-class voters agreed 69 to 23 percent. Strong progressives said America was not the greatest country in the world by 66 to 28 percent.

Hispanics were more likely to say that racism in America comes from individuals, rather than society or institutions, by a 58 to 36 percent margin. Working-class voters leaned toward individual explanations by 57 to 33 percent. Black voters leaned in the other direction, citing systemic racism by 58 to 35 percent. But this was nowhere near the consensus among strong progressives, where 94 percent favored a focus on structural or institutional racism.

On immigration, Hispanics were split down the middle—47 percent for easier legal immigration, 44 percent for tougher border enforcement. Black voters favored easier immigration by a similar 47 to 45 percent margin, while the working class favored more enforcement by a margin of 58 to 32 percent. Strong progressives were nowhere near as conflicted, with a 97 to 2 percent majority in favor of stronger legal immigration and against enforcement.

Hispanics and working-class voters also believe, with 55 percent support in both groups, that "most people who want to get ahead can make it if they're willing to work hard," contrasted with "hard work and determination are no guarantee of success for most people." Strong progressives disagreed, with 88 percent doubting that hard work was enough to get ahead. Many more examples abound of wide gaps between nonwhites and progressive ideologues, gaps that are especially apparent when we zoom in on the Democratic coalition itself.

DEMOCRATS DIVIDED

The ideologically split nature of the Democratic coalition creates vast ideological differences among voters of different races and educational backgrounds in the Democratic Party. We can see this by looking simply at data on self-reported ideology. The country is more conservative than liberal by a ten-point margin, according to the latest reading from Gallup. That makes liberalism weaker within the Democratic coalition than conservatism is within the Republican coalition, and most of the difference comes from nonwhite voters who don't readily embrace the liberal label. Among Democratic nonwhites, liberals are a bare majority—46 percent of Black Democrats, 51 percent of Hispanic Democrats, 63 percent of Asian American Democrats. Contrast this with 79 percent of white Democrats with a college degree who call themselves liberal, and 62 percent of white non-college Democrats who do.

Table 5.4:
White College Democrats Are Much More Liberal than Other Democrats
Ideological identification among Democrats

	Liberal	Moderate	Conservative
White College	79%	19%	2%
White Non-College	62%	29%	6%
Black	46%	36%	13%
Hispanic	51%	34%	9%
Asian American	63%	32%	4%

Source: Cooperative Election Study, 2020

Whites with a college degree are outliers within the Democratic Party, but they punch above their weight. Just as they dominate political discussion, they are also the majority of Democratic Party staff, donors, activists, and campaign operatives. Though there have been conscious efforts made to diversify the upper ranks of Democratic politics since then, liberal analyst Steve Phillips writes that of the $514 million Democrats spent on political consultants in the 2010 and 2012 cycles, 97 percent went to white-owned consultants and businesses.

While Democrats are making efforts to diversify—a worthy goal for both parties—they aren't doing so in a way that reflects the ideological beliefs of their diverse rank and file, who are moderate to conservative as much as they are liberal. Ideological stances from the focus on "systemic racism," to defunding the police, to the use of the word "Latinx" to describe Hispanics, are pursued in the name of justice for racial minorities, yet a conspicuous number of foot soldiers for them are college-educated whites. The "Latinx" debacle provides an obvious and extreme example. A 2020 Pew Research Center study found that the gender-neutral alternative to Latino or Latina is known by fewer than one in four U.S. Hispanics, and used by just 3 percent. When we asked in a 2022 survey what term was best to use to describe Hispanics or Latinos in America, 9 percent of white liberal Democrats said Latinx, but *zero* Hispanics did. Our results show that, at some level, progressive Democrats know that using Latinx is cringeworthy, yet the president of the United States continues to use it, as do brands from Starbucks to Nordstrom, renaming Hispanic Heritage Month to some variation of "Latinx Heritage Month." Democratic representative Ruben Gallego of Arizona has pleaded with the party's allies to stop. "To be clear my office is not allowed to use 'Latinx' in official communications," tweeted Representative Gallego in December 2021. "When Latino politicos use the term it is largely to appease white rich progressives who think that is the term we use."

This yawning gap in the ideology of various Democratic groups extends to the news media they consume. We think of Fox News as an exclusively Republican, conservative outpost, but another Pew Research Center study published in 2020 found that it was among the most read or watched news outlets for Black and Hispanic Democrats—at 36 percent for Black Democrats and 31 percent for Hispanic Democrats, as compared to 17 percent for white Democrats. Black Democrats are three times as likely to be getting their information from Fox News than media outlets like the *New York Times*, the *Washington Post*, and National Public Radio. On the flip side, liberal outlets like the *Times*, the *Post*, and NPR are all three times more likely to be consumed by white Democrats than Black or Hispanic Democrats. This comes at a time when coverage of racial issues has grown in national newspapers like the *Times* and the *Post*, with usage of the terms "racist" or "racism" increasing sixfold in the last decade, and the concept of "systemic" or "institutional" racism increasing roughly tenfold. As the readership data make clear, this explosion of race-centric coverage has mostly been for the benefit of a white audience.

The Manhattan Institute's Zach Goldberg argues that liberal media shining the spotlight on racial issues in the aftermath of the killings of Trayvon Martin and Michael Brown led to a sea change in public opinion among white liberals who disproportionately consume these news sources. Between 2012 and 2016, the share of white liberals believing that racial discrimination was the reason that African Americans couldn't get ahead jumped from less than 40 percent to over 70 percent. There was little to no change among white moderates and conservatives. Meanwhile, the share of Americans reporting that they knew someone they would consider a racist dropped or remained the same in every group from 2006 to 2015—except for white Democrats, where it increased nearly 20 points. Today, white Democrats are more liberal on most racial issues than their Black counterparts. The gap is especially noticeable on more abstract ideas popular in academia, like the idea of "systemic" racism or "implicit bias," as opposed to addressing tangible, day-to-day examples of discrimination.

In the following analysis of survey data, and throughout this book, I divide whites by educational attainment, but don't do the same for nonwhites. This may beg the question of whether the differences I'm highlighting are actually a function of education, not race. After all, whites are more likely to have college degrees, and those with college degrees are more liberal, especially on cultural issues. On all the issues I write about, the education divide makes a much bigger difference in the attitudes of whites than it does among nonwhites. While one may quibble with college-educated minorities being grouped with the multiracial working class, survey data finds that they are quite similar in their views to the working-class members of their race or ethnicity. The same is not true of whites.

Another reason for calling out white college graduates specifically is that, in the Trump era, their votes have become more vital to the

Democratic Party. To the extent that college graduates and whites are overrepresented in major institutions, they exert disproportionate influence in Democratic politics—and their views are far to the left of those of every other Democratic group. In important ways, white college-educated Democrats set the tone for the party, guiding campaigns and setting the policy agenda when Democrats win. For example, polls show wide gaps in the priority that graduates and non-graduates place on the environment and climate change. Black Democrats are less liberal on environmental issues relative to the rest of the Democratic Party, but are just as liberal in favor of social spending. Yet, when it came to fashioning the compromises necessary to pass the Democrats' "Inflation Reduction Act," the environmental spending remained in place and the social spending didn't make the cut.

The shift left has been so noticeable that white college Democrats now score lower on academic definitions of "racial resentment" than nonwhite Democrats do. One such statement that scholars have used as a marker for racial intolerance is that "Irish, Italians, Jewish and many other minorities overcame prejudice and worked their way up. Blacks should do the same without any special favors." In the 2020 Cooperative Election Study, a supermajority of 79 percent of white college-educated Democrats disagreed with this statement. Only 53 percent of Black Democrats did. Or, consider the question highlighted by Ruy Teixeira, about racism being baked into society and institutions as opposed to being mostly a personal failing. Most Black voters—Democrats or not—do agree with defining racism as institutional or systemic. But white Democrats go further, endorsing it with a 75 percent majority compared to 54 percent of Black Democrats. In the American National Election Studies' 2018 survey, white Democrats went further than any group of Democratic minorities in saying that diversity improves the U.S.—with 78 percent of white Democrats endorsing this view, compared to 57 percent of Black Democrats and 63 percent of Hispanic Democrats.

These dynamics extend also to views of the criminal justice system. A few weeks following the murder of George Floyd, activists in Minneapolis launched a campaign to defund the police, with the city council quickly advancing proposals to redirect police funding to social services and to disband the police department. The movement quickly went national, providing a rallying cry in the protests around the country. But it never caught on in the court of public opinion, polling badly, except among one group: white Democrats with a college degree. They favored reducing police budgets by a 50 to 17 percent margin, with a 14-point margin overall for reductions in the police budget among Democrats. It was a different story among Black voters: 42 percent of Black Democrats favored increasing budgets, compared to 24 percent who favored decreasing them—the mirror image of whites and the most support for the police of any racial group among Democrats. The activist cry to "defund the police" was only ever embraced by white college-educated liberals. It was never taken up by Black voters.

Zach Goldberg uses the term "luxury beliefs" to describe this dynamic around defunding the police. In a 2022 paper, Goldberg found that all forms of privilege—not just so-called white privilege, but higher education levels, higher income, and living in low-crime areas predicts stronger support for police defunding among Democrats. The Democrats with the lowest levels of support for police defunding are nonwhites who live in areas where crime levels are highest. One can posit that these are the same people most likely to have a negative encounter with the police—but also to benefit from police protection. In his 2021 mayoral campaign, New York City mayor Eric Adams, a former police captain, demonstrated that the politics of policing in the city's Black community was far removed from that of white racial progressives. Adams denounced police defunding and ran on a slogan of "safety and justice," winning the Democratic primary with overwhelming majorities in the city's Black precincts.

Hispanic Democrats exhibit the same pattern on immigration that we've seen with Black voters on race and criminal justice. The Democrats most opposed to Trump's immigration policies were highly educated whites, not Hispanics. According to the 2020 Cooperative Election Study, more Hispanic Democrats would have supported the declaration of a national emergency to build a border wall (12 percent) than white Democrats (7 percent) or white college Democrats (3 percent). On suspending the policy to allow some asylum seekers to remain in the U.S. (Trump's "remain in Mexico" policy), Hispanic Democrats were more likely to be in favor at 28 percent, compared to 18 percent support among white Democrats and 11 percent support among white college-educated Democrats. Many of these numbers are outdated given the ongoing crisis at the southern border, a crisis that increased support for border security measures across the board—including among Hispanics. And yet, driven by Democratic coalition politics, which saw primary candidates from Kamala Harris to Pete Buttigieg embrace decriminalizing border crossing during the 2020 primary debates, the Biden administration immediately reversed Trump's "remain in Mexico" policy, opening the floodgates of illegal migration. In a survey of Texas Hispanics my firm helped conduct for the Texas Latino Conservatives with help from veteran Republican pollster Lance Tarrance and Hispanic marketing expert Leslie Sanchez, the state's Hispanics most associated Republicans with "fixing the immigration system," and other surveys in 2022 showed they trusted the Republican Party more to handle immigration. Progressive assumptions that Hispanics would line up behind an activist, racialized narrative around immigration were proven wrong. As Ruy Teixeira writes:

> It is hard to avoid the conclusion that Democrats have seriously erred by lumping Hispanics in with "people of color" and assuming they embraced the activism around racial issues that dominated so much of the political scene in 2020, particularly in the summer. This was a flawed assumption. The reality of the Hispanic population is that they are, broadly speaking, an overwhelmingly working class, economically progressive, socially moderate constituency that cares, above all, about jobs, the economy and health care.

Cultural divides among Democrats extend to core social issues, like abortion and gay rights. Social issue views are closely linked to religiosity and nonwhite Democrats are far more religiously observant and far more likely to identify as evangelical or born-again Christians than white college-educated Democrats. America's political divide is also a religious divide, with Republicans far more likely to attend religious services or to identify as evangelical. The Black church stands out as a striking exception to this pattern. In the 2020 Cooperative Election Study, 57 percent of Black Democrats said that religion was very important to them and 49 percent said they were evangelical or born-again. Contrast this with just 18 percent of white Democrats who said that religion is very important, and 12 percent who say they are evangelical, a number that drops to 8 percent among those with a college diploma. Black Democrats rate religion as being just as important in their lives as white Republicans do; they are nearly four times as likely to say religion is important in their lives and six times as likely to be evangelical Christians as white college-educated Democrats. Hispanic Democrats land in between these two groups, at 32 percent saying religion is very important to them and 24 percent identifying as evangelicals.

Given this context, it's not surprising that some of the largest divides within the Democratic Party center around social issues like abortion rights, where the party's seeming unanimity and pro-choice litmus test for officeholders mask deeper divisions below the surface. Some of the survey data I am about to cite comes from the 2020 election, the last year available for the Cooperative Election Study's extensive sampling at this writing. The *Dobbs v. Jackson* ruling has since led to a shift of several points toward the pro-choice position, in a mirror image of the immigration data cited earlier. Nevertheless, there is little reason to believe that the distribution of support for abortion rights has changed by subgroup, even if overall views moved somewhat to the left. This was evident in the politics of the 2022 midterm elections, where abortion figured heavily in advertising in majority white swing districts, but not by the Democrats in the Georgia Senate race, who were fighting to mobilize the state's sizable Black electorate. A *New York Times* report in July 2022 reported that Democrats sought to downplay the use of the term "abortion" in campaign stops by Vice President Kamala Harris before Black audiences, instead raising it primarily in the context of other issues, like voting rights.

In 2020, the Cooperative Election Study found that 60 percent of voters in the country as a whole supported a ban on abortion after twenty weeks of pregnancy. That's similar to the margin of support for a fifteen-week ban that Echelon Insights found before the *Dobbs* decision, cut down to a much narrower majority of 53 to 47 percent in the months following the decision. In the CES data, 37 percent of Democrats also supported a twenty-week ban, but the number was less than half that—17 percent—among white college-educated Democrats. In the 2020 data, most other Democratic constituencies were closer to the political middle on this question, with 53 percent of Black Democrats, 51 percent of Hispanic Democrats, and 39 percent of white Democrats without a college degree favoring a twenty-week ban. Solid majorities of nonwhite Democrats support legal abortion in some form, but that support is far from unanimous or unconditional.

And yet, the voices of these socially moderate Democrats are seldom heard in national political debates. Sometimes, it seems like the only evidence we have that they exist is in election results themselves: in collapsing Hispanic support for Democrats or the election of moderates like Eric Adams. In the political day-to-day, it is the voice of the college-educated that is heard the loudest, loudly campaigning on social issues that don't excite large parts of the Democratic base. Doing so scratches the itch to oppose the right on the issues that get donors and the extremely online most excited, but it disregards the views of the party's nonwhite voters.

We might stop to ask exactly what the problem is with well-educated white Democrats going a bit overboard in embracing racialized narratives or taking left-wing social issue positions. These may not be the views that nonwhite Democrats would themselves prefer, but at the end of the day, most nonwhite voters still vote Democratic, and their views are generally closer to white liberals than they are to those of white conservatives.

A mass overnight defection of nonwhites from the Democratic Party may seem unlikely, but even a small defection could badly wound the party. Whereas Democrats used to frame their appeal to nonwhites in vague group interest terms, whether in terms of race or class, today their language is the more ideological one of the faculty lounge. And so long as Democrats talk in ideological terms to nonwhite voters, they lose. The proof is in their substantial losses among nonwhite conservatives in 2020—voters once considered a core part of their base, not a swing group vulnerable to defection. Much of the progressive signaling that year likely contributed to these losses. A prime example of this came when Planned Parenthood, a mainstay in the Democratic coalition, came out in favor of defunding the police, pointing to additional articles in its statement like "We Don't Need Nicer Cops, We Need Fewer Cops," and "Anti-Racism Resources for White People." No doubt, groups like this probably felt like they were taking the morally righteous position. Progressive groupthink also led them to calculate that doing so was necessary to shore up their anti-racist bona fides, for which they'd be rewarded by Black voters. But rather than rally the Black vote, a plurality of Black Democrats rejected defunding the police.

Democratic group divisions on social issues contrast with their unity on economic issues. On many economic issues, nonwhite Democrats are more progressive than college-educated whites, a group that likely includes some recent Republicans who retain a vestigial aversion to high taxes. In the Democracy Fund + UCLA Nationscape study from 2020, identical shares of all constituency groups within the Democratic Party favored raising the minimum wage to $15 an hour, with over 90 percent support in all groups. The survey also found that a federal jobs guarantee for all Americans has conspicuously less support among white college-educated Democrats (64 percent), than it did among Black or Hispanic Democrats (79 and 76 percent respectively). When it comes to *giving* benefits to the working class, nonwhite and working-class Democrats are the most progressive Democrats. But nonwhite Democrats also hesitate when it comes to *taking* money from the wealthy to pay for it, with Black and Hispanic Democrats showing less support overall for a proposal to raise taxes on families making over $600,000 a year. Tax increases on the wealthy are nevertheless smart politics for Democrats, garnering strong majority support among all Democratic constituency groups while dividing rank-and-file Republicans. This commitment to economic fairness has historically been at the core of the Democratic Party's appeal to workers, and is what voters have historically understood the Democratic Party to be about. Using American National Election Studies data, Michigan State University political scientist Matt Grossmann notes that the Democrats' identification as the party of the working class was the thing voters liked most about the party in every election from 1952 to 2004. The thing they liked least about the Republican Party in all of those elections? That they were the party of big business and the upper class.

Outwardly, curing economic injustice remains a core commitment of the Democratic Party. But lately, we've heard less and less talk about the middle and working classes in the Democratic Party, even in the soothing moderate voice of Bill Clinton "feeling your pain." And this may be in part due to changes in the party coalition. According to IRS data, Democrats in Congress now represent 65 percent of taxpayers making $500,000 a year or more. And Democrats are increasingly standing up for these wealthy constituents, lobbying to reverse the Trump-era elimination of the state and local tax deduction that hit affluent taxpayers in blue states hardest.

Looking ahead to 2024, Democrats seem to have heeded the warning. Joe Biden himself is a creature of the old-school Democratic Party, the one that oriented itself around delivering benefits for working-class families. And as he prepares for a reelection campaign, he has smartly emphasized the parts of his agenda that hew toward economic populism: the $1 trillion infrastructure bill, "Buy American" rules for building out these new roads and bridges, and new restrictions on the sale of semiconductors to China. Biden has also dialed up his attacks on Republicans on Social Security and Medicare, singling out a 2022 proposal made by Senator Rick Scott to sunset all federal programs, including entitlements, every five years. In this, he has drawn comparisons to the reelection strategy employed by Bill Clinton in 1996: branding Republicans as the enemy of working families for cutting popular entitlements, while also co-opting popular Trumpian themes, like infrastructure investment. Clinton's strategy was a wild success, resulting in an eight-point victory in the popular vote.

It is worth examining the difference between Biden's gambit today and Clinton's "triangulation" strategy in 1996, in which the Arkansan set himself apart both from a fire-breathing right represented by Newt Gingrich's Republican revolutionaries and the old liberal left. After his drubbing in the 1994 midterms, Clinton successfully placed the spotlight on popular programs, as Biden is trying to do now. The words "Medicare, Medicaid, education, and the environment" were used so often that they were shortened to M^2E^2. But it was Clinton's repeated high-profile breaks from the Democratic left and his overtures to the cultural right that made the strategy work. To a stunned House chamber, Clinton declared during the 1996 State of the Union that "the era of big government is over." He signed historic welfare reform legislation. He assented to the Defense of Marriage Act defining marriage as between a man and a woman and ran campaign ads about it. With the help of his ex-Republican adviser Dick Morris, he devised a series of micro-proposals to de-fang conservative culture war attacks, from school uniforms, "V-chips" built into TVs to block violence and smut, and the death penalty for drug kingpins. In his 1992 campaign, he had his famous "Sister Souljah" moment when he called out a rapper for her violent lyrics. He said that abortion should be "safe, legal, and rare."

Democrats may calculate that, simply by focusing on economic issues, they can keep cultural issues from eating into their base. But what Bill Clinton understood, and few Democrats have since, is that you need to firmly address both culture and economics. When voters' economic views and social views are in conflict, one's social stances more often drive voting behavior. Politicians already spend most of their time talking about the economy and other tangible problems their policies can affect. But this is not what the voters hear. Cultural divides are what voters vote on even if politicians don't talk about them. And they can be injected into the conversation, and politicians forced to comment on them, with every viral news story of an athlete kneeling for the national anthem or left-wing school curriculum. Simply ignoring them while gesticulating wildly in the direction of economic populism isn't a viable strategy. Only a hard pivot against the cultural left will be enough to get working-class voters to sit up and take notice.

6.

THE NEW AMERICAN MAINSTREAM

For the native-born Americans of the time, the 1840s were a period of rapid and unsettling demographic change. It all started with a potato famine in Ireland. Almost two million immigrated to an America that was twenty times smaller than it is now. The Irish quickly became the majority in Boston, and by 1850, just five years after the famine began, they were 26 percent of the population of New York City. They were not always welcomed, met by businesses with "No Irish Need Apply" signs. Religion was a key dividing line: the Irish were predominantly Catholic in a Protestant country. A row of classified ads appearing in the May 1, 1855, edition of the *New York Times* tells of the barriers Irish Catholic women faced in gaining employment: "Nurse wanted—To take charge of three children. A Protestant woman, Scotch preferred," "Clean, active girl wanted. . . . No Irish need apply," "Chambermaid and waiter wanted. . . . She must be a Protestant and with good recommendations," "Cook wanted—a Protestant cook," "A German Protestant preferred," "A Protestant woman wanted." The Protestant Irish already in the country took steps to distance themselves from the Catholic "wild Irish" new arrivals, henceforth calling themselves "Scots-Irish." Sectarian anti-immigrant sentiment spread nationally in the 1850s with the rise of the American, or Know-Nothing, Party.

When the Irish started to vote, their choice of party was an easy one. At home, the Irish had toiled—with many starving to death—under English colonial rule. The Democratic Party traced its origins back to Thomas Jefferson, who had sided with France over England and took up the banner of the farmer against pro-British mercantile interests. The

Democrats had all the right enemies, standing against the same kinds of people who had oppressed the Irish back home. And so the Irish in every city, save for Philadelphia, became Democrats. In politics, the Irish gained respect they could not find elsewhere. As a group, they were still working class, finding only limited success in business. Where they excelled was in fields where a backslapping, good-tempered sensibility gave one an advantage. This meant saloon keeping, banking, and politics. Hierarchical organization was also a particular skill of the Irish, who quickly built up the Roman Catholic Church in America and dominated the Church hierarchy long after new Italian arrivals filled the pews. Tammany Hall, a New York City political society that came to be dominated by the Irish, became synonymous with machine politics. In politics and religion, the Irish had built a society of their own standing apart from the American mainstream as it was then defined.

The migration from Italy had a different flavor to it, starting in the 1880s and reaching a peak at the turn of the century. It emerged from a particular kind of place—the Mezzogiorno, or Southern Italy—and it is almost a misnomer to call it *Italian* migration. It was Sicilian, Calabrian, Pugliese. More accurate still is to call this a migration of villages. The vista of a typical migrant extended not far beyond their family and village. Italy as a concept did not exist until the country was united in the 1860s, and even then, the Mezzogiorno was treated as an afterthought by the new country's northern rulers. Political participation was almost nonexistent, and to whatever extent nineteenth-century southern Italians thought about government, it was about *lo stato ladro*—the thief state. There was no national identity, no major institutions to re-create in the new country. These were temporary migrant workers—largely young men—with many returning back to their villages once they had made enough money, shuttling back and forth to America as the need arose.

Eventually, chain migration would take hold. Michael Barone writes about the story of Francesco Barone,* who was the first to make the jour-

* No direct family ties could be established, though Barone confirmed to me in an email that his ancestors also immigrated from Valledolmo.

ney from the Sicilian village of Valledolmo to Buffalo, New York. Fourteen others had joined him by 1905. By the mid-twentieth century, the Valledolmesi in America numbered eight thousand. The Italian immigrants had an entrepreneurial streak, starting businesses at a higher rate than native-born Americans or other immigrants. The pattern is reminiscent of the Hispanic immigration of the twentieth century—crossing back and forth across a porous border to work, providing for their extended families back home with remittances, sharing little in terms of a unifying ethnic identity, voting at low rates, and cynical or indifferent to politics.

Like the Irish, the Italians also faced discrimination in America. Their darker complexion made them a target of racial slurs. In the press, they were derided as "swarthy" and "kinky-haired." "There has never been since New York was founded so low and ignorant a class among the immigrants who poured in here as the Southern Italians who have been crowding our docks during the past year," proclaimed a *New York Times* editorial in 1882. Their children were not spared by the editorial writers, who declared them "utterly unfit—ragged, filthy, and verminous as they were—to be placed in the public primary schools among the decent children of American mechanics." The language used in an 1889 report on immigration from a Select Committee of the House of Representatives was no better:

> They are of a very low order of intelligence. They do not come here with the intention of becoming citizens; their whole purpose being to accumulate by parsimonious, rigid, and unhealthy economy a sum of money to return to their native land. They live in miserable sheds like beasts; the food they eat is so meager, scant, unwholesome, and revolting, that it would nauseate and disgust an American workman, and he would find it difficult to sustain life upon it. Their habits are vicious, their customs are disgusting, and the effect of their presence here upon our social condition is to be deplored.

In the South, Italians and other immigrants replaced the labor of former Black slaves in the aftermath of the Civil War. This became enough of a political issue that Alabama politician J. D. Ross campaigned on disenfranchising Greeks. While mistreatment of African Americans in the South was far more widespread, Italians also became the targets of lynching in New Orleans, with eleven killed on March 14, 1891, having been accused on flimsy evidence of the murder of the city's police chief.

The Irish and the Italians shared a common religion and were marginalized upon arriving in America, but they were not allies. A generation after the famine migration, the Irish had established a foothold in the Church, in politics, and in the civil service. A new wave of immigrants threatened their hard-won gains, undercutting the Irish working class with a willingness to work at lower pay, for longer hours. The animosity was such that in the 1910s, three decades after the Italians began migrating en masse to New York City, marrying a German Jew was a more common occurrence for the Irish than marrying an Italian.

Eventually, ethnic animosities cooled. I am here thanks to the marriage of my Irish grandfather and Italian grandmother in New York City in 1938, a relatively early product of lessened interethnic rivalries. Something not entirely of the old world, but not yet of the new, was being created. Immigrant groups were "transformed by influences of American society, stripped of their original attributes, they were re-created as something new, but still as identifiable groups," wrote Nathan Glazer and future senator Daniel Patrick Moynihan, in *Beyond the Melting Pot*, a 1963 study of New York City's ethnic communities.

War and suburbanization forged a new national mainstream. Millions of young men served on the front lines of World War II with others of diverse backgrounds, often fighting the armies of the countries their ancestors had left. On the home front, millions more left segregated communities, including the migration of Black workers to the war industries on the West Coast. That's not to say things were perfect: Japanese Americans were interned, and African Americans were still segregated within the armed forces, and in many other places. But the contrast between Black veterans' loyal war service and the Jim Crow laws at home was enough to spark an early move toward civil rights with the desegregation of the armed forces in 1948. After the war, the G.I. Bill of Rights helped Italians double their rate of college attendance in the years from 1940 to

1954. Urban white ethnics migrated in large numbers to freshly built suburbs like Long Island's Levittown, and there they found neighborhoods that weren't demarcated along ethnic lines—though this suburban melting pot notably did not include people of different skin colors. In these suburbs, the children of Ireland, Italy, Germany, Eastern Europe, and beyond mixed freely. Important aspects of their identity changed as a result. It was in the postwar years that interethnic marriages became the norm. Italians, who early on had eschewed the Irish-built Catholic Church hierarchy and adopted a highly localized version of the faith centered upon veneration of local saints, began to sit in the pews side by side with the Irish, sending their children to parochial schools at high rates. And they grew wealthier: by the 1960s, the Italians had reached the same income level as the average American and by 1990 they had incomes 17 percent above the national average and college graduation rates 50 percent higher. As sociologist Richard Alba put it, "Italian Americans have risen from ragpickers and ditchdiggers to virtual parity within three generations." Both the Italians and the Irish, the subjects of vicious invective upon their arrival on our shores, were now thoroughly embedded with the American mainstream.

A milestone in this immigrant coming-of-age came in 1928 when the Democratic Party nominated Al Smith, the governor of New York and an Irish Catholic, for the presidency. Smith was not successful in his race against Herbert Hoover; it's likely no Democrat would have been. The electorate divided along religious lines, even blurring North-South distinctions that served as the intractable dividing line of national politics. Suspicious of Catholicism, many parts of the Democratic "Solid South" went Republican, while Smith ran up huge margins in heavily Catholic northern cities. A generation later, another Catholic by the name of John F. Kennedy would pick up where Smith left off. The Kennedy camp hung its hat on the hope that much had changed since 1928. The Catholic children of immigrants were now more numerous, dominant in the key industrial battlegrounds. "Just remember, this country is not a private preserve for Protestants," advised Joseph P. Kennedy, the candidate's father. "There's a whole new generation out there and it's filled with the sons and daughters of immigrants from all over the world and those people are going to be mighty proud that one of their own is running for president. And that pride will be your spur, it will give your campaign an intensity we have never seen in public life."

Kennedy was elected the first Irish American and Catholic president with 78 percent of the Catholic vote, while 61 percent of white Protestants chose Republican Richard Nixon. The Catholic vote was concentrated in electorally significant northeastern and midwestern industrial heartlands, and Kennedy would win the ten biggest states except for Ohio and California. Electorally, the balance had shifted. If there was to be bloc voting on religious lines, it had now benefited the Catholic candidate.

Yet, Kennedy's triumph—short-lived and cut short by assassination—was the last hurrah of immigrant political unity under the Democratic banner. "On the day [Kennedy] died, the President of the United States, the Speaker of the House of Representatives, the Majority Leader of the United States Senate, the Chairman of the Democratic National Committee were all Irish, all Catholic, all Democrats," Moynihan wrote mournfully. "It will not come again." Yet the seeds of the Democratic white ethnic unraveling had sprouted a generation earlier. By 1932, Irish influence in the New York Democratic machine was already in decline. Four years earlier, they had nominated one of their own for president. But that year the party had snubbed Al Smith's comeback bid, nominating the patrician Franklin D. Roosevelt instead. Within the Irish community, a sort of "Never Roosevelt" movement grew. The Irish middle class tuned into the anti–New Deal radio fulminations of Father Charles Coughlin, and Smith would endorse Republican Alf Landon in the 1936 election. Tammany Hall was now but a shadow of its former self. More and more patronage jobs were going to Jews now numerically more dominant in the Democratic Party, and "reform" Democratic clubs sprung up to counter the influence of the old Irish machine. The Irish's diminished sway in the Democratic Party came partly because so many had left it. Many had cheered when one of their own, Republican Joe McCarthy, railed against communist infiltration in the country's establishmentarian, Protestant-dominated institutions. On McCarthy's staff was Robert F. Kennedy, brother of the future Democratic president. While McCarthyism was deplored by the country's elites, Peter Viereck, a 1940s and '50s popularizer of conservative thought, noted in a 1955 essay how it had seemed to displace other forms of social division. McCarthy's conspiracism largely steered clear of race-baiting or anti-Semitism as he trained his invective on a more general target: a subversive elite. "From these multiplying examples we may tentatively generalize: Manifestations of ethnic intolerance today tend to decrease in proportion as ideological intolerance increases," wrote Viereck. Anti-communist ideology, later refined by the likes of Richard Nixon and Ronald Reagan, served as the glue of a post-ethnic politics that shifted groups like the Irish into the Republican Party.

As such, Kennedy's 1960 campaign is more properly seen as a last hurrah for Irish Catholic political power than it was a sign of its emergence. Peaking at more than 70 percent in the 1960 election, Democratic identification among white Catholics began a steady downslide in the years following. Republicans reached near parity in the Reagan years and crossed the majority threshold, with a double-digit advantage over

Figure 6.1: White Catholics March to the GOP

Party identification among white Catholics, 1952–2019

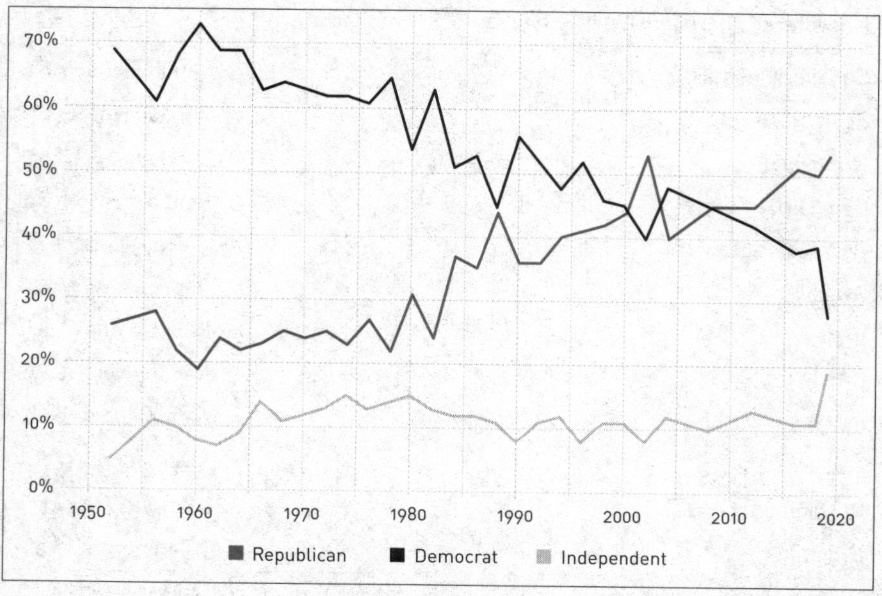

Source: Eric Kaufmann tabulations of American National Election Study data

Democrats, during the Trump era. From Kennedy's time to today, white Catholics went from being more Democratic than the country by double digits, to more Republican by double digits, as shown by data compiled by Eric Kaufmann. At around the turn of the millennium, white Catholics flipped from a Democratic to a Republican group.

Today, the ethnic people who migrated to the United States in the nineteenth and early twentieth centuries—not just Catholics, but Protestants, too—are more Republican than the nation as a whole. The most extensive data on partisanship we have come from voter registration records, and these records can be analyzed based on the voters' surnames. Generations of intermarriage limits the power of such an analysis, as someone carrying an Irish surname is no longer likely to be fully Irish. Nevertheless, those carrying the last names of groups that mostly came to America during the mass immigration of the nineteenth century lean Republican. This includes groups like the Irish and Italians, only a touch less Republican than those with "old stock" English and Scottish last names.

Table 6.1: Most Nineteenth-Century Immigrant Groups Now Match the White Average

Net voter file partisanship by ethnicity

Ethnicity	Net partisanship
English/Welsh	Republicans +7.8%
Scottish	Republicans +6.3%
Norwegian	Republicans +5.5%
German	Republicans +5.3%
White average	*Republicans +5.2%*
Swedish	Republicans +4.6%
Irish	Republicans +2.3%
Dutch	Republicans +0.9%
Italian	Republicans +0.8%
Polish	Democrats +1.0%
Russian	Democrats +3.8%
Greek	Democrats +5.5%

Source: L2 national voter file

These groups are disproportionately concentrated in northeastern blue states, but within those states, they tend to pull up the Republican average. In the 2016 Republican primary, heavily Italian neighborhoods in Staten Island or in Hempstead or Massapequa on Long Island stood out in their solid support for Trump.

Within a century or less of entering the United States, the European immigrants of the nineteenth century entered—and redefined—the American mainstream. As their populations grew in size, they did not aim to use their newfound power to overthrow the existing mainstream, a perennial fear voiced by immigration skeptics. They converged toward it. They started out living in poverty, gathering in discrete ethnic enclaves, facing suspicion from the native population. Over time, they assimilated with American norms, in turn imparting their own cultural influences. There is no reason to expect that today's new Americans will be any different.

MAKING IT IN AMERICA

In the last decade, Montgomery County, Texas, an exurb north of Houston, grew in population by 36 percent, or nearly 165,000 people. Much of this growth was fueled by Hispanics, whose share of the county population rose by six percentage points to 26 percent in the 2020 census. A vibrant Hispanic civil society is growing in Conroe, the county seat, with a Latino chamber of commerce, a Hispanic Baptist church, and a Hispanic branch of the local Republican Party. Hispanic Republicans are not an oxymoron in Conroe or other parts of the county: 57 percent of Hispanics in the county who vote in a primary pull a Republican ballot. Those Hispanics who do make it out to Montgomery County are more prosperous than those who still live in the urban neighborhoods of Houston, Dallas, and San Antonio. While Hispanics lag far behind the incomes of whites in Harris County, home of Houston, the gap is much less in Montgomery County.

Montgomery County is part of a Great Dispersal of Hispanics in America. The Hispanic population used to be concentrated predominantly in states along the U.S.-Mexico border; in Florida, acting as a receptacle from the Caribbean basin; and New York, a destination for Puerto Ricans and Dominicans. In recent decades, Hispanics have grown their share of the population the most in the places with the fewest Hispanics to start out with. Sunbelt states like Georgia and North Carolina far from any border now have significant Hispanic populations. Once concentrated along the border and in the cities, Hispanics in Texas are fanning out to the exurbs and rural areas. Farther-out suburbs of major cities like The Woodlands and Conroe in Montgomery County have seen particularly strong growth, along with Liberty County, where the Hispanic population share increased by 14 percentage points. Outside Austin, the Hispanic share of the population grew by 15 points in Caldwell County and 10 points in Bastrop County. Growth was particularly strong in the West Texas oil patch, as Hispanics filled jobs plentiful during the fracking boom of the last decade.

Meanwhile, the Hispanic population in those areas where they are an already high share of the population is either dropping or has stopped growing. In my analysis of the Houston metro area conducted with pollster Lance Tarrance, the Hispanic share of the population in the core central city dropped by 3.2 points from 2010 to 2020. The fastest growth was in the outer suburbs—with a 4.6-point increase in census tracts classified as outer suburbs and a 4.5-point increase in farther-out exurbs like Conroe and The Woodlands.

For Hispanics, as for generations of ethnic migrants before them, outward mobility equals upward mobility, with those in the suburbs making more than those in the cities. Suburbanization has coincided with a period of rising Hispanic prosperity nationally. In the five years from 2014 to 2019, Hispanic incomes grew by 22.8 percent, similar to the 21.3 percent growth for Asians, the other group with large numbers of first-generation immigrants. By contrast, income gains were lower for white and Black Americans, at 9.9 and 8.3 percent, respectively.

Extensive analysis of individual and household data by Harvard economist Raj Chetty and a team of researchers confirms that Hispanics and Asians are achieving the American dream by its most classic definition: moving up over generations—and in the case of Asians, leapfrogging native-born whites. Chetty's study marries individual census records with

Internal Revenue Service data for a complete view of what happened to a subset of Americans who were children between 1978 and 1983, comparing data on present-day Americans with that of their households growing up to quantify intergenerational mobility. And this data shows Hispanics rapidly closing the income gap with whites. The average Hispanic child growing up in a household at the 25th percentile of income, solidly within anyone's definition of working class, would end up with an income at the 43rd percentile in adulthood, just two points short of a white child's result in the 45th percentile. An Asian child growing up in the same financially pinched circumstances would end up even better, at the 56th percentile. The authors calculate what a "steady state" would eventually look like, once the effects of intergenerational mobility have had a chance to fully unfold. They find that the typical Hispanic will be on track to end up at the 48th percentile, two points shy of the national median and six points behind the typical white American.

Like the Italians of the early twentieth century, entrepreneurship has been an engine of upward mobility for Hispanics. One in eight Hispanics worked for their own business, making them 30 percent more likely than the population at large to do so. According to one report, the number of businesses owned by Hispanics grew by 34 percent in the 2010s, while the number of other businesses grew by just 1 percent. These statistics defy the stereotypes on the left and far-right of Hispanics as an economically downscale group, ready to be mobilized for leftist policies either on the basis of working-class solidarity or the promise of welfare benefits. Hispanics are entrepreneurial, increasingly suburban, and moving up the economic ladder, year after year, generation after generation. They are making it in America.

Upward movement into the economic mainstream has gone hand in hand with cultural assimilation, with more Hispanics identifying as Americans than by their ethnicity or country of origin. Our 2022 survey of Texas Hispanics found that "American" was by far the most common label these Hispanics gave themselves, at 48 percent, followed by 23 percent saying they identified as "a Texan," and 21 percent saying Hispanic or Latino. Just 13 percent said they would identify by their ancestry (such as "Mexican American"), a sentiment concentrated among the 16 percent of voters who were first-generation immigrants. While surveys of Hispanic adults can often find higher levels of identification with home countries, these surveys include first-generation immigrants who aren't yet citizens and can't vote. Those who can vote in U.S. elections and are the subject of the trends discussed in this book overwhelmingly consider themselves Americans first.

The typical Hispanic in the United States lives in much different circumstances than they did fifteen years ago, when illegal immigration across the U.S.-Mexico border reached record levels and the issue became a touchstone for the Republican voter. Despite an uptick after 2021, the number of border crossings have dropped from their mid-2000s highs, driven by improved economic circumstances in Latin America, combined with the 2008 recession and the slow recovery afterward that made the U.S. a less attractive destination for work. Today, the average Hispanic in the United States has been here for a longer period and is more likely to speak English. From 1998 to 2008, the number of foreign-born Hispanics in the labor force had increased by more than 50 percent over the previous decade, from 7.8 million to 11.8 million. In the decade since, it has increased at a much slower pace, to 13.4 million, roughly mirroring the overall growth of the labor force. Also in this period, the share of that foreign-born workforce here illegally dropped from 55 to 44 percent, while the share of Hispanic workers in the United States for more than twenty years grew from 36 to 50 percent. Increased longevity in the United States has coincided with a rapid rise in Hispanic incomes. And in turn, first- and second-generation Hispanic immigrants are increasingly seen as contributors to, not a drain on, the American economy.

THE NEW DEMOGRAPHICS OF MIXED IDENTITY

By around 2045, demographers expect the United States to become a majority-minority country, with racial and ethnic minorities making up a majority of the population. The march toward majority-minority status has been driven by the growth in recent decades first of Hispanics, then of Asians. A second-order effect of this new wave of immigrant growth has been the rise of children of mixed race—a trend that is further accelerating the advent of majority status for nonwhites, since demographers count children with one white and one minority parent as nonwhite. This majority-minority milestone is likely to be crossed regardless of what immigration policy changes are made in the near term. Already a near-majority of all births are nonwhite, while those dying in any given year are disproportionately white. That combined with even modest amounts of legal immigration will be enough to push the U.S. past the point where whites are no longer a majority of the population.

Figure 6.2: Nonwhites Near a Majority of U.S. Births

Racial and ethnic makeup of those born in the U.S., by age

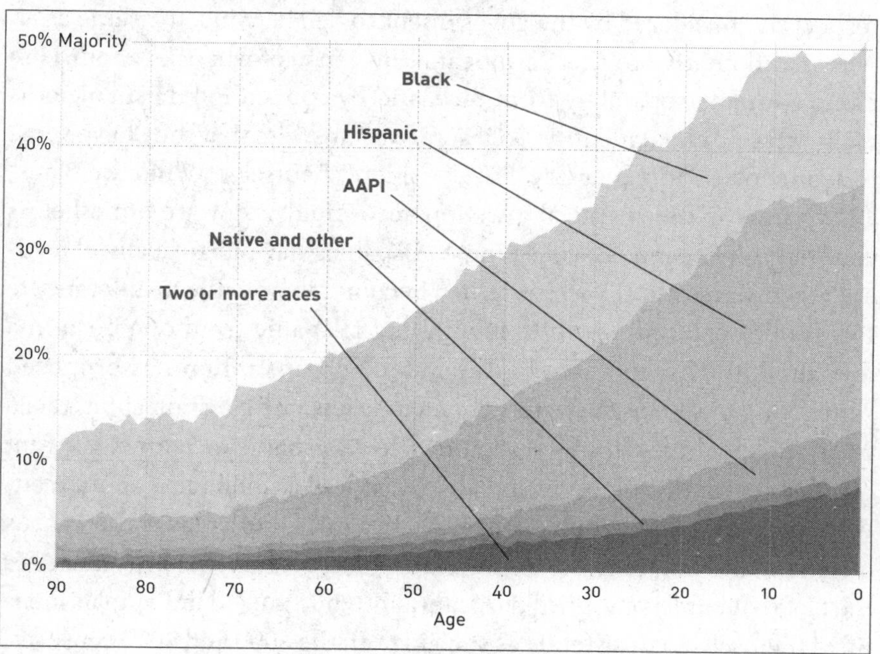

Source: American Community Survey, 2019 One-Year Estimates

As with other long-range forecasts, caveats abound. If immigration slows down further, the actual transition point may happen later than 2045. Nonwhite birth rates have also slowed considerably since 2008, when their current rough parity with whites was first achieved. The only subgroup of nonwhite births that are rising are interracial births, the majority of which will involve a white parent. This raises the question of how these mixed-white minority children will eventually identify: as white or nonwhite? There will be no one answer to this question but millions of individual ones. For the purposes of government statistics, though, they will count as nonwhite.

As law professor David Bernstein writes in his recent book, *Classified: The Untold Story of Racial Classification in America*, this treatment of mixed-race Americans is one of many examples of the arbitrariness of government-defined racial categories. A first-generation immigrant from Spain speaking high Castilian Spanish, a white European in every respect, is considered by the government to be Hispanic, the same as an Afro-Latino native to the Caribbean. The census form asks about Hispanic ethnicity separately from race, and by convention, Hispanic ethnicity trumps racial identity. So if someone answers that they have some Hispanic or Latino ancestry, but considers themselves white or Black, answering the census racial question accordingly, they are nonetheless counted as Hispanic. Because most Hispanics have historically considered themselves racially white, it then becomes impossible to differentiate this traditional kind of white-identifying Hispanic from one born in a mixed-white Hispanic family. The Biden administration has proposed simplifying the 2030 census form to include just one question about racial or ethnic identity, with the option to select Hispanic or Latino. Current confusion over the two-question format, as well as fluid ideas about identity, have led many people—not just Hispanics—to answer the census questionnaire differently over the course of a lifetime. Richard Alba cites the fact that barely one-third of Asian-and-white-mixed individuals identified themselves consistently as such in both the 2000 and 2010 censuses, while almost two-thirds switched identities, with more switching to and from fully white than to and from fully Asian.

Regardless of how the mixed-race population is counted, it is growing rapidly and becoming a fixture of mainstream American life. Its presence was not formally recognized until 2000, when Americans first had the opportunity on the census to check boxes for multiple races. And in 2020,

Figure 6.3: The Race Question on 2020 Census Questionnaire

7. What is this person's race?
Mark ☒ *one or more boxes* ***AND*** *print origins.*

☐ White – *Print, for example, German, Irish, English, Italian, Lebanese, Egyptian, etc.*

☐ Black or African Am. – *Print, for example, African American, Jamaican, Haitian, Nigerian, Ethiopian, Somali, etc.*

white and Black Americans were invited to write in their specific ethnic ancestry, information that was used to reclassify millions of Americans as mixed-race. For instance, a white person listing some Japanese ancestry could be classified as being of two or more races even if they did not also check the Asian box. Partly as a result of natural increase, and partly as a result of this change to the census form, the mixed-race share of the population doubled between 2010 and 2020.

The rise of the mixed-race population should temper predictions of the end of a white-majority America, with a new progressive era following in its wake. Obama-era books like Robert Jones's *The End of White Christian America* and Steve Phillips's *Brown Is the New White* confidently predicted a new politics resulting from new demographics. The far right doesn't exactly disagree with the left's analysis, as evidenced by the title of Ann Coulter's 2015 bestseller, *Adios, America: The Left's Plan to Turn Our Country into a Third World Hellhole.*

Both camps badly miss the mark. The white majority isn't being replaced; it is being blended into a new multiracial mainstream majority. As a country, we've been here before. A century ago, the mixing of the Anglo-Protestant elite with Irish, Italian, German, and other immigrant groups was also considered unthinkable—yet it happened. These newcomers were not simply a different flavor of European: many had a strange "Romanist" religion, a distinction that Americans back then took very seriously. Today, racial and ethnic mixing is taking hold faster than it did among the immigrant groups of the nineteenth century, when white interethnic marriages took almost a century to become commonplace. In 2015, 17 percent of new marriages were interracial or involved a marriage with one Hispanic partner, a number that has likely reached one in five today. It takes a few years for these marriages to produce children, so the rate of new interracial births lags marriages by a few points, but these numbers are on the rise, too. Standing at 14 percent in 2015, they are likely more than one in six today. If children of mixed race and ethnicity (including those with one Hispanic parent) were considered a racial category of their own, they'd count as the largest "minority" group among babies born in the U.S. today.

Hispanics and Asian Americans—the same fast-growing groups driving us toward the majority-minority future—are those most likely to intermarry and have children of mixed-race backgrounds. Of those newly married in 2015, 29 percent of Asians and 27 percent of Hispanics married someone of a different racial or ethnic background. The rate for African Americans was 18 percent, and for whites, members of a demographic majority more likely to be surrounded by others like themselves, 11 percent. Given Hispanics' larger share of the population, and their high rates of intermarriage, children of mixed Hispanic heritage made up around half of the mixed-race births in the United States in 2015. Of these mixed Hispanic births, around eight in ten involved a white co-parent. Yet, for reasons discussed earlier, these white-Hispanic children are hard to find in a conventional reading of census statistics. It is likely that these mixed Hispanic-white births represent around a third of the 22 percent of babies born as Hispanic each year—leaving 15 percent as Hispanic alone.

Conservatives fear that the politics of the future will resemble the group identity politics of today, with race-based voting patterns the norm for an ever-larger share of the electorate. The intermarriage numbers reveal hope for a more united future. Rather than the Balkanized future they fear, racial boundaries as they exist today will be unrecognizable for a growing share of the country. And even the 85 percent or so born with one clear racial identity are being born into a country where interracial relationships are universally accepted, racial groups are increasingly living side by side with one another in the same communities, and the economic fortunes of new immigrant groups are on the rise. This is not to say that our racial problems are fully behind us—far from it—but recent decades have brought significant progress.

In 1958, the Gallup poll found that just 4 percent of the public approved of marriages between Black and white partners. A decade later, and a year after the *Loving v. Virginia* ruling legalizing interracial marriage, just 20 percent approved, including 17 percent of whites and 56 percent of nonwhites. Today, support for interracial marriage stands at 94 percent, and the racial gap in attitudes has practically disappeared. Much of this increased acceptance is new. As recently as 2003, just 65 percent approved of Black-white unions. Interracial marriage has always been a lagging indicator of support for civil rights, with support for equality in employment and accommodations reaching a majority decades earlier. A form of discrimination that used to be commonplace even a decade or two ago has virtually vanished. Public acceptance has also risen hand in hand with the frequency of interracial marriage and relationships in practice. With this will come a new generation for whom the old racial lines will be blurrier than they are today. This is not wishful thinking for a color-blind future, but a statement of demographic fact.

It is also likely that the children of mixed-race families will not uniformly see themselves as members of minority groups as they exist today. In fact, they will not identify consistently as one thing at all, with racial identity existing on a spectrum. Generations from now, it could be that being purely of one race will be as common as being purely Irish or Italian in America today: a relative rarity. And with that, political differences between those defined today as white and nonwhite will diminish. Studies of mixed-race voters are hard to conduct due to their currently low numbers in the electorate, but they back up this conclusion. Mixed-white and minority voters end up somewhere in between the group averages of their respective parents' racial backgrounds. Some groups, like voters who were partly Black, lean closer to Black voting patterns, while white Asians landed right in the middle of the racial group averages in a 2015 Pew Research Center study. The crucial white-Hispanic group was not included in the analysis, since the study only looked at those of multiple *races*, stemming from the aforementioned difficulties demographers have in filtering mixed Hispanic-whites from Hispanics who answer the census as white.

Why dwell so much on the tiny percentage of the population that has a mixed-race background? Because it won't be tiny for long—and the rising proportion of mixed-race families changes how race is experienced not just for the children of those marriages, but for parents, grandparents, and other family members. An important fact about the majority-minority future is that a large part of this new majority won't be defined as any one single race at all.

HEALING OLD DIVIDES

Thirty miles southeast of Atlanta on I-75 lies the city of McDonough, a suburban boomtown emblematic of many on the periphery of fast-growing southern and western metropolises. Real estate is selling at a fast clip here. Zillow records nearly four thousand homes sold in the last twelve months as of this writing, almost a quarter of them new homes built within the last five years. When new housing construction ground to a standstill nationwide amid the supply chain disruptions of the pandemic, it continued apace in McDonough. Middle-class families are finding this rising community an appealing place to make a life, combining access to the amenities of metro Atlanta with reasonably priced housing with more square footage.

McDonough sounds like most outer suburbs throughout the country, but it defies the stereotype in one way: a majority of its new residents are Black, some of them exiles from Atlanta and its inner suburbs, others migrants from cities throughout the country. This migration is solidly middle- and upper-middle-class, with little difference in the incomes of Black and white residents. According to the American Community Survey, a Black household here earns $97,244 per year, 41 percent more than the Black Georgia average of $68,546. A white household makes $101,384, slightly less than the white statewide average of $107,248. Achievement gaps in local public schools remain, but they are strikingly lower than in the rest of the Atlanta metro. The typical white student in a Henry County public school is 1.2 times more likely to take advanced placement classes and is 0.9 grade levels ahead of their Black counterparts. Contrast this with the Atlanta city schools, where white students are twice as likely to take AP classes and are rated as being 4.6 grade levels ahead of their Black counterparts, or the Cobb County schools—a racially diverse inner suburb—where whites are 1.7 times as likely to try AP classes and are 2.4 grade levels ahead.

With a rising Black population, Henry County has undergone a political shift. It broke 51 to 48 percent for Mitt Romney over Barack Obama in 2012, but went 60 to 39 percent for Biden over Trump in 2020. Even the more rural and Republican parts of the county have not been immune to the shift. A precinct centered on the outlying community of Ola on the eastern edge of the county saw its Trump vote drop from 75 percent in 2016 to 65 percent in 2020, a net swing on par with Democratic gains elsewhere in the county. On a *New York Times* map plotting the precinct-level shifts in support in the 2020 election, a donut-like blue circle surrounds central Atlanta, showing Joe Biden's increased margins in the suburbs. This outer edge of the blue donut encompasses the boundaries of growth in the Atlanta metro area almost exactly, swinging from Dallas to the west, to Forsyth County to the north, to Locust Grove, just one town over from McDonough, to the south. This rapid blue shift over four years, which you see in Atlanta more prominently than anywhere else, is a function of the fastest-growing migration of African Americans to the suburbs anywhere in the country. Individual Black voters in the Atlanta metro area appeared to move a few points toward Trump in the last four years, as shown by the results in established Black precincts in Atlanta and neighboring Clayton County. But new movement of Black residents into previously white Republican areas was enough to turn these areas purple or even varying shades of blue. In Henry County, Democrats now control the county commission. And while race has become an issue in local politics, Henry County seems to have avoided the worst of these divisions. In 2018, a vote by the predominantly white Eagle's Landing community to secede from the majority Black city of Stockbridge failed.

A city like McDonough would have been unthinkable in the segregated South of fifty years ago. Then, residential segregation was an engine of inequality, the legacy of which persists to this day. The likes of George Wallace did not argue openly for inferior accommodations, merely for separation, but in practice, these two things turned out to be one and the same. Poverty became deeply entrenched in majority Black communities—mostly in the inner city—with the second-order effects of family breakdown and rising crime. The effects of "redlining"—of banks limiting loans to Black buyers—and restrictive covenants barring the sale of property to nonwhites continued to be felt long after the civil rights era. Like interracial marriage, fair housing was a lagging indicator of racial progress. Here, the legacy of discrimination does not go away overnight. Its undoing is a slow, grinding thing.

Yet the undoing is happening. Residential segregation has been steadily declining in the United States since the 1980s or before, and the 2020 census revealed this trend continuing in the 2010s. Oxford scholar Benjamin Elbers calculates that the rate of "racial residential segregation" has declined by 37 points since 1990, with all groups becoming less segregated vis-à-vis African Americans. Black-white segregation is down 23 points, Black-Hispanic segregation is down 36 points, and Black-Asian segregation is down 19 points. These calculations are based on an index where 100 is maximum segregation—different racial groups living entirely in different census tracts—and zero equates to a situation where all census tracts contain exactly the same share of different racial groups as the metropolitan area average.

Brookings Institution demographer William H. Frey has previously looked at changes in racial living patterns from 2000 through the mid-2010s, finding a drop in segregation across the vast majority of metropolitan areas, with notable regional differences. Sunbelt cities, more of which lived under the thumb of segregation, have on average done a better job at integrating members of different racial groups than have northern cities. In the mid-2010s, the most segregated cities on a Black-white basis were Milwaukee, New York City, Chicago, Detroit, and Cleveland. The least segregated were Las Vegas, Raleigh, Tucson, Riverside, and Virginia Beach. In the top fifty metro areas, forty-five saw declines in segregation over a fifteen-year period, with the steepest declines in the cities that were initially the most segregated. Faster growth tends to explain this disparity. High-growth South and West cities were largely built up since fair housing laws went into effect, compared to the North, with its older, more entrenched settlement patterns.

Even as the old lines of residential racial segregation are slowly fading away, we are still a ways away from Black economic parity. Raj Chetty's research team found that while Hispanics were on track to nearly match the household income of whites, African Americans are no longer progressing in their income levels across generations. The median Black person in the study universe landed at just the 35th percentile of income. Native Americans have a similar ranking, at the 36th percentile. At any given point of the parental income distribution, a Black child is likely to achieve a household income that is a full 13 percentile points below that of a white child. In important ways, the experiences of African Americans and Native Americans differ markedly from immigrant groups who are still making their way in America.

Different cuts on the data shed light on the reasons behind Black-white economic inequality. Family structure explains a lot of the difference, with African Americans less likely to grow up in families with two earners. While Black and white households are separated by 13 percentile points in income, the gap between Black and white individuals is just 5 points. And most of that shrunken gap is accounted for by gender differences: while Black women have fully closed the gap between their earnings and those of white women, Black men still lag 10 percentile points behind white men. Nor is this due to Black women working longer hours or second jobs to make up for reduced earnings of Black men; their wages and hours are also at parity with white women. For Black men, the story is very different, with both wages and hours lagging far behind their white counterparts. Here, the effects of mass incarceration have surely played a role.

What can be done to erase income gaps between Black and white Americans? Economic parity between Black and white women shows that this is an achievable goal, with remaining gaps concentrated among men. Chetty's researchers tested numerous variables to see what might predict better outcomes for young Black men in adulthood and found one that stood out above all others: the presence of Black fathers in a neighborhood. And this was not necessarily about the presence of one's own father. The mere presence of other Black male role models in a community was enough to improve outcomes for young men. Further studies by Chetty underscore the importance of social and family ties in reducing inequality, including a 2022 study that found that having friendships with those in a higher social class raised lower-class incomes later on. Sadly, too few communities today meet the conditions for fostering upward mobility for Black men. As the authors conclude, "Environment matters, but good environments are rare." If more diverse middle-class suburbs can produce such environments, they could remove important barriers to upward mobility for Black Americans.

THE POLITICS OF THE NEW AMERICAN MAINSTREAM

When a group moves from the margins and into the mainstream of American life, history provides ample proof that their politics change to match their newfound social station. After World War II, the children of nineteenth-century immigrants to the United States moved to the suburbs, married across ethnic lines, went to college, and saw their economic fortunes rise. In doing so, they joined a Republican Party many of them had formerly shunned. The lesson here is not that these voters were natural Republicans all along, but that they were natural *Americans*, voting and living more like the rest of their fellow citizens—about half Republican and half Democratic.

The path Hispanics in America are now following resembles that of this first wave of immigrants to the U.S. Alone among the country's racial and ethnic groups, Hispanics still adhere to the tradition of lower-income support for Democrats and higher-income support for Republicans. Everywhere else, this traditional pattern has been erased or reversed. And the reason it still holds is that, for Hispanics, prosperity is new, largely not secured by the self-perpetuating advantages conferred by a college diploma. A rise in taxes or environmental regulations targeting places like the West Texas oil patch might threaten these recent economic gains. On these and other issues, Republicans are more readily seen as defenders of Hispanic prosperity. As one moved up the income ladder, so, too, did Hispanic support for Donald Trump in 2020. This trend is strongest among the majority of Hispanics without college diplomas, who are more likely to work in blue-collar occupations.

Table 6.2:
Traditional Class-Based Voting Patterns Hold among Hispanics
2020 presidential vote among Hispanics by family income

	Among All Hispanics	Among Non-College Hispanics
Lower Income ($0–49,999)	Biden +36%	Biden +36%
Middle Income ($50,000–$119,999)	Biden +32%	Biden +24%
Higher Income ($120,000 and above)	Biden +23%	Biden +15%

Source: Cooperative Election Study, 2020

It is also the simple fact of being more *established* in the United States—of living here longer—that is shifting Hispanics right. In our survey of Hispanic political battlegrounds in Texas, new immigrants were far likelier to have voted for Biden than those whose family had been in the country for three generations or more. Among the new immigrants, Biden won by 23 points. Among those with families in the country for three generations or more, the two candidates tied. There is a corresponding divide in party preferences between English- and Spanish-dominant Hispanics, with those who prefer English less likely to vote Democratic.

Both high-income and longer-tenured Hispanics are growing as a share of the Hispanic population. Year after year, that places more Hispanic voters in demographic categories friendlier to Republicans. The conventional wisdom of a Hispanic electorate that's Spanish-dominant, extremely young, and made up mostly of recent immigrants does not necessarily hold true anymore. Among voters, longer-tenured Hispanics are already a supermajority: in our survey of Texas Hispanics, almost two-thirds of *voters* had families who had been here since their grandparents' generation or before. A corresponding majority of Hispanics who vote also prefer to speak mostly in English; fewer than one in ten Hispanics contacted will typically elect to take political surveys in Spanish when

Table 6.3:
Hispanics Grow Less Democratic the Longer They're in the U.S.
Recalled 2020 presidential vote among Texas Hispanics by immigrant generation

	Biden	Trump	Margin
Immigrated myself (1st generation)	54%	31%	Biden +23%
Parents immigrated (2nd generation)	49%	34%	Biden +15%
Grandparents immigrated (3rd generation)	44%	41%	Biden +3%
Family immigrated before (4th generation+)	41%	43%	Trump +2%

Source: Texas Latino Conservatives' Hispanic Realignment Survey

given the option; when one expands this to include the non-citizen population, this ratio typically goes no higher than one in four.

As with the first-wave immigrants, rising prosperity and longer tenure went hand in hand with a move out to the suburbs. Let's return for a moment to Houston. In our classification of different types of Houston-area communities, just 18.5 percent of Hispanic voters in the central city had any history of voting in a Republican primary. In the outer suburbs, it jumped to 37.1 percent. And in exurbs like Conroe and The Woodlands, it was 48.9 percent. The majority of Hispanics in Texas still live in cities and inner suburbs, which have a strongly Democratic tilt. But all the growth is in new suburbs, exurbs, and rural areas. The areas Hispanics are moving into tend to be whiter than the plurality-Hispanic city of Houston. Analytics on the voter file—a completely comprehensive view of all 207 million Americans eligible to cast ballots—helps us see this clearly. In states with party registration, the fewer Hispanics there are as a share of voters in a precinct, the more Hispanics in those areas register as Republican. The range is quite stark—from just 12 percent Republican in precincts that are 90 percent Hispanic or more to 40 percent in the least Hispanic precincts. Overall, the Hispanic population in America is tilted more toward neighborhoods without a Hispanic majority—which also happen to have the highest growth in their Hispanic populations. Miami-Dade County, Florida, is removed from this analysis, because its Cuban Republican neighborhoods single-handedly skew the national numbers, but everywhere else, the trend is in the opposite direction.

The same pattern holds among Black voters, though the share of the vote that is identifiably Republican is much lower—and positively microscopic in the most heavily Black precincts. Here, we must shift the analysis from states with party registration to southern states that are required to collect official data on race as a requirement of the Voting Rights Act, a necessary step since Black voters living outside heavily Black areas are more difficult to identify without hard data. The trend here is pretty much the same, though it's nothing for Republicans to write home about: the share of the Black vote that is either registered as Republican or has voted in Republican primaries goes from 2 percent in neighborhoods that are almost all Black to 11 percent in areas with the fewest Black voters. Actual Black voting for Republicans is higher than these numbers imply—12 percent nationally according to the 2020 exit poll—so we can speculate that Black voting ranges from less than 5 percent Republican in the most Black precincts—consistent with observed precinct results—to something like 20 percent among Black voters in the least Black precincts.

Alone, demographic shifts among Hispanics and other minority groups do not explain their shift to the right in the 2020 election. Persuasion—getting people to vote a different way—is always a better way to grow your vote share than waiting out the demographic tides, and this seems to be what happened in 2020. But demographic changes *within groups* has partly counteracted the effect of demographic shifts *between them*, changes that were supposed to usher in generational Democratic majorities. What I'm describing is a convergence toward a new mainstream—a convergence that's the inevitable consequence of nonwhites becoming the demographic majority of the country or something approaching it. Democrats cling to the hope that racial and ethnic minorities will vote exactly as they did when they were smaller groups, oppressed and marginalized within American society, needing protection from an organized political machinery. We celebrate all the ways in which this is not true anymore, both in law and in fact. But we don't necessarily pay heed

Figure 6.4:
Nonwhite GOP Registration Rises outside Majority-Minority Areas

Two-way Republican party registration among Hispanics by precinct-level percentage non-Hispanic, in states with party registration, excluding Miami-Dade County, FL

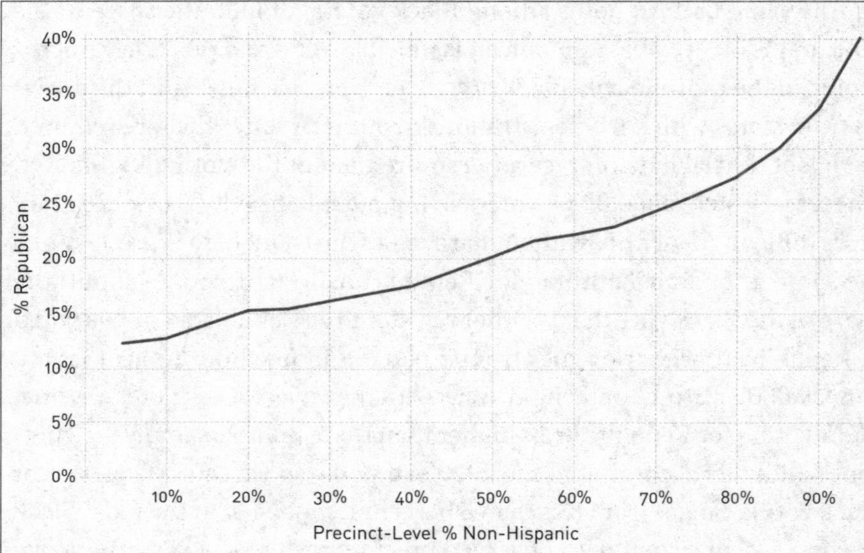

Two-way Republican registration among Black voters by precinct-level percentage non-Black, in Southern states subject to Voting Rights Act requirements

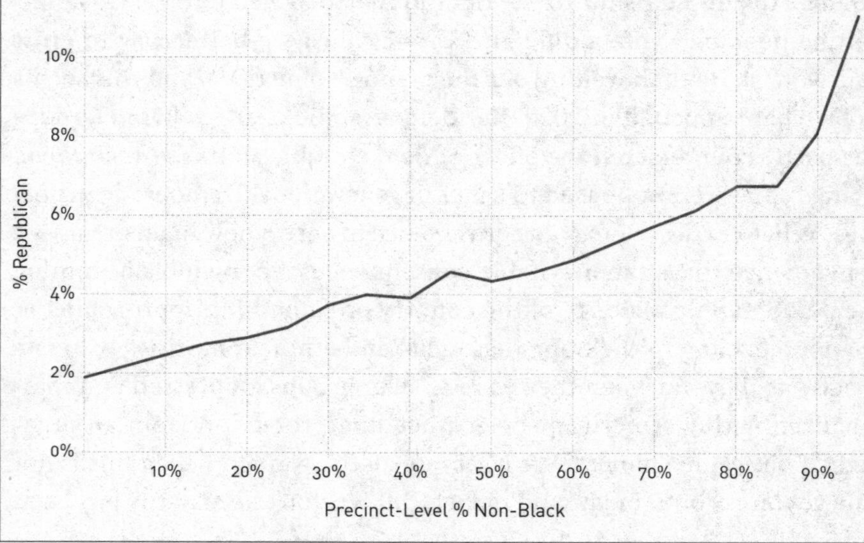

Source: L2 National Voter File

to what happens politically when a group stops thinking of itself as a disfavored minority. America has grown wealthier as it's become more diverse—not the "hellhole" of the far-right imagination—which means that nonwhites occupy the same place that the white working class did in postwar America: prime beneficiaries of a new prosperity not eager to see their hard-won gains taxed away.

To some, the invocation of the term "mainstream" will sound like a negation of group identity—with negative overtones of groups "becoming white." This is hard to square with the fact that this is coming about because of the voluntary choices *both* whites and nonwhites are making to live closer together, and in some cases, to find love and start families together. It also ignores our nation's history. White *Protestants* were once the American default, lording their privileged status over everyone else. Now such religious distinctions no longer matter; the mainstream simply absorbed Catholics and Jews. In the same way, a new multiracial mainstream majority will include members of groups once marginalized and discriminated against because of their race.

Can a future American mainstream plausibly include *everyone*, though? That can and should be the goal—but, no, it does not strictly need to be to qualify as multiracial and inclusive. Everyone living in a racially integrated middle-class community—a kind of community that basically didn't exist in postwar America—can be said to be living a "mainstream" existence today. Nevertheless, the country will keep welcoming new immigrants, who will take time to learn the language and become acculturated to our mores and customs. Large numbers of African Americans, Hispanics, and Native Americans also continue to live in racially segregated areas with incomes far below the national average. Whether they live in segregated communities or not, African Americans also have a unique politics that have mostly resisted any convergence toward two-party politics, one that will be discussed in depth later in this book. The experiences of these Americans should not be overlooked. But in the main, we are a less racially divided country than we were the last time working-class populism redrew the political map—and that's something to celebrate.

7.

HARDHAT CONSERVATIVES

In 1965, the main TV signal switched from black and white to color. But the images Americans would see in their living rooms were no more pleasing to the eye, consisting of more than the normal amount of war, riots, protest, and death. The country was still reeling from the assassination of John F. Kennedy a little more than a year earlier. In August, the Watts riots in Los Angeles unsettled the country. Not just in the United States, but throughout the world, social scientists began to notice a sustained drop in public confidence in institutions—national governments, political parties, and organized religion. At home, the postwar growth had begun to sputter and signs of inflation began popping up in 1966. Whatever the exact cause, the mood seemed to shift as the country entered the back half of the 1960s. The times they were a-changin'—and not for the better.

Politics was changing, too. Richard Scammon and Ben Wattenberg tracked this shift by examining the issues Americans said were "the most important problem facing the nation" in Gallup polling from 1958 to 1970. Through 1962, the top issues were exclusively ones of economics and foreign policy, mostly surrounding the Cold War. In 1963, racial issues began to creep into the mix. The election year of 1964 features a mix of racial problems and foreign policy, with Vietnam earning its first top ranking. From 1965 forward, socially polarizing issues are rarely outside of the top two issues as ranked by Americans, alternating between the Vietnam War, crime, and civil rights or race.

Scammon and Wattenberg dubbed this basket of concerns the Social

Issue, one that threatened to unmoor the working class from the Democratic Party. The Social Issue had four facets—crime, race, "kidlash," and "values." The first two are self-explanatory. Kidlash was the backlash against youth, in everything from sex to drug use to the protests against the Vietnam War. Values issues gained new prominence, with issues like pornography, sex education in schools, and abortion, which had never been the subject of public debate before. Before the mid-1960s, the big questions had been about money or security. Afterward, they reflected a growing national identity crisis—a battle over whether traditional American society as then constituted would continue or not. The sense of disorientation was profound. As Scammon and Wattenberg put it, "The man who works hard, pays his taxes, rears his children—the man who has always been the hero of the American folk mythology—now found himself living in an era where the glorified man is the antihero: morose, introspective, unconcerned with God, country, family, or tax bill."

Worry about the Social Issue was barely evident in the 1964 election, when conservative Barry Goldwater took on the Sisyphean task of challenging the successor to the martyred JFK, losing by 23 points. But his candidacy would have a lasting effect on the shape of the party coalitions for decades to come. Goldwater's candidacy ushered in the era of the ideological candidate, of voting for a party based on shared ideological belief, rather than out of ethnic, regional, or religious loyalty. Before Goldwater, the major parties had both liberal and conservative tendencies. Republicans had liberals like New York's Nelson A. Rockefeller and John V. Lindsay. There were the southern Democrats like Georgia's Richard Russell and Mississippi's James Eastland, virtually the only kind of southern politician with any power at the time, holding up progress on civil rights. Civil rights forced the Democratic Party to choose, casting its lot with the liberal reformist streak of its northern majority. Removing the taint of Jim Crow from the southern wing of the party was also a goal of an ambitious Texan, Lyndon Baines Johnson, who had designs on the presidency from his perch as the Democratic leader in the Senate, starting with a modest 1957 civil rights bill.

The important shifts in the 1964 election were not limited to the incipient realignment of the South. In the North, Goldwater's vote share collapsed in some of the GOP's most solid bastions, Yankee Protestant areas that had even held in Franklin D. Roosevelt's landslides. Statistics compiled by Nixon campaign aide Kevin Phillips in 1969's *The Emerging Republican Majority* chronicle the carnage. In Orange County, Vermont, Goldwater's vote share plummeted by 36 points from the level that Richard Nixon had achieved four years earlier. In Hancock County, Maine, the drop was 32 points. In Nantucket, Massachusetts, 31 points. His drop was nearly as steep in wealthy enclaves of New York and Boston, which could usually be counted on as Republican bulwarks against the ethnic urban Democratic masses. On Park and Fifth Avenues in Manhattan, Goldwater scored 29 points lower than Nixon, and on Beacon Hill in Boston, 25 points lower.

But Goldwater did not drop by nearly as much in working-class areas. In Italian North Boston, his vote share was just three points lower than Nixon's. In Throgs Neck in the Bronx, an Italian neighborhood, four points. In nearby Fordham, an Irish neighborhood, three points. Even with everything else going his way, Johnson could do little to further expand his party's Catholic support beyond Kennedy's breaking of the religious barrier. But there were signs the working-class shift was not purely sectarian in nature: Goldwater nearly matched Nixon in heavily Jewish neighborhoods as well, like the Grand Concourse in the Bronx and Borough Park in Brooklyn. When normalcy returned to the top of the Republican ticket in 1968 with the renomination of Richard Nixon, a muted version of these shifts endured. Eight years on, in an election nearly as close as 1960's, Nixon got fewer votes from silk-stocking urbanites and Yankee Brahmins, and more votes from middle-class ethnics.

The Goldwater moment and its aftereffects sets the stage for the story that Kevin Phillips would tell in *The Emerging Republican Majority*, a book that had stuck around in the political psyche so much that it served as the inspiration for 2002's *The Emerging Democratic Majority*. While Nixon's victory in 1968 was the first manifestation of what Phillips considered to be a durable Republican majority, Goldwater's 1964 campaign set the stage for this realignment by sounding the death knell of the northeastern liberal Republican, accelerating the cultural and ideological polarization of the parties. "Back in 1960, Richard Nixon had run for

President as the candidate of a Republican Party still partly controlled, as Henry Cabot Lodge's vice-presidential nomination bore witness, by its traditional Yankee bastion," Phillips explained. "By 1968, however, things had changed. Not only had the civil rights revolution cut the South adrift from its Democratic moorings and drawn the Northeast towards the Democrats, but it had increased the Southern and Western bias of the GOP to a point—the 1964 Goldwater nomination—where the party had decided to break with its formative antecedents and make an ideological bid for the anti–civil rights South."

This did not mean that every subsequent Republican nominee would be a fire-breathing conservative. Richard Nixon was a pragmatist careful to thread the needle between the party's traditional elite and its rising conservative wing. But it did mean that Republicans anywhere on the left side of the ideological spectrum, or solicitous toward it, no longer had a national future. The kind of Republican Party that once appealed to the cultural values and sensibilities of the upper class, on Park Avenue and Beacon Hill, had begun to die a long, slow death.

A TALE OF TWO BUCKLEYS

It was 1965, and Republicans liked their chances of winning the mayor's office in New York City.

Their candidate was John Vliet Lindsay, the liberal congressman representing what was known as the "silk-stocking district" on Manhattan's Upper East Side. Lindsay's campaign literature touted his Kennedy bona fides. The comparisons between the two did not end there. Even as a backbench congressman, national reporters had visions of him as a future president, JFK's natural heir in policy as well as style. Most savvy political operators did not bat an eye at the idea that he could be elected to that office as a Republican. The Democrat was the uninspiring Abe Beame, an accountant turned machine politician from Brooklyn. Within the city's dominant Democratic Party, politics was polarized between a "reform" wing—liberal urbanites and African Americans shut out of citywide office—and a "machine" wing of middle-class Irish, Italian, and Jewish voters. Lindsay versus Beame redrew the map of city politics with the most appealing possible "reform" archetype facing off against a middling "machine" candidate. In the city that year, the Republican ticket was to be the vehicle for liberal reform.

Things would not turn out that neat and simple. New York had a system of ideological minor parties that usually cross-endorsed ideologically allied major parties, but sometimes went off in unexpected directions. Typically aligned with Democrats, the city's Liberal Party endorsed Lindsay. Newer on the scene was the state's Conservative Party, founded in 1962 as the analog to the Liberals, with a mission to push the Republicans and state politics to the right. Having wrested control of the national nominating contest a year earlier, conservatives cast about for a high-profile alternative to Lindsay. They found one in the rakish editor in chief of the *National Review*, William F. Buckley Jr., whose candidacy seemed at first a prank. Asked what the first thing he would do if elected, Buckley quipped, "Demand a recount." Buckley's campaign for mayor is well remembered by conservatives to this day; a poster for the effort is displayed in this author's office. His policy papers were unusually detailed for a municipal candidate and often futuristic, envisioning an elevated bike path on Second Avenue. Buckley's wit dominated the press and stole the show in the debates, but his success as a politician fell far short of his skills as a public performer. He carried 13.4 percent of the vote, about par for third-party candidates in New York's "fusion" system of the time. Lindsay, the liberal running under the Republican banner, was elected by a four-point margin.

In some parts of the city, Buckley ran much stronger. In places like the Staten Island–based 64th Assembly District and the Queens-based 23rd and 27th, he ran second. In Throgs Neck, the Bronx neighborhood where Goldwater's numbers had nearly outrun Nixon, Buckley broke 28 percent. The Conservative standard-bearer may have looked more at ease on an English country estate than in the Bronx, but his strongest support came from the working- and middle-class white ethnics who had enthusiastically voted for their co-religionist JFK just five years earlier.

The year that followed, 1966, would see the national mood turn against the liberalism of LBJ's Great Society, with Republicans gaining forty-seven seats in the House of Representatives. Two elections that year carried added weight. In California, Ronald Reagan was running for governor, and student protests were the issue that trumped all others. In December 1964, more than one thousand student activists from Berkeley's Free Speech Movement occupied the school administration building. Around seven hundred were arrested, in what has been called the largest-ever mass arrest of middle- and upper-middle-class whites. California voters could hardly talk of anything else. As Reagan himself recalled, "Look, I don't care if I'm in the mountains, in the desert, the biggest cities of the state, the first question is 'What are you going to do about Berkeley?' and each time the question itself would get applause." Reagan won by a decisive 15-point margin. Back in New York City, Lindsay was off to a rocky start as mayor, with his plan to restructure the body tasked with investigating police misconduct running into a buzz saw of opposition from uniformed police officers and their supporters in the outer boroughs. A referendum was quickly placed on the November ballot to put the Civilian Complaint Review Board back under police control. It passed two to one, with Manhattan alone among the boroughs voting with Lindsay. More people voted in the referendum than in the 1964 presidential election.

The slow awakening of this reaction to liberalism—valiant but losing efforts in 1964 and 1965, victories in 1966—was fueled by the voter who was conservative, but not "*a* conservative," in the formulation used by 1970s conservative staffer and writer William Gavin. The child of immigrants, this voter was a working person squarely within the New Deal coalition who had been the strongest supporter of the Democratic ticket in 1960. They were not, however, part of the conservative *movement* that was then taking shape, of Bill Buckley's *National Review*, of Russell Kirk or the Mont Pelerin Society. But everything about how they lived their lives was small-*c* conservative: their religion, their support for the traditional family unit, their patriotism, and their reverence for the police and the military. The cultural issues that activated them for Reagan, for Buckley, for Republicans were not on the ballot in elections through the early sixties, when Republicans were still the party of the privileged elite and Democrats were still the party of the workingman. Things began to change with the social unrest that started in the mid-sixties, with the rise of what Gavin would dub the "street corner conservative"—the urban white ethnic straying from their Democratic roots.

When an embattled Lindsay ran for reelection in 1969, he lost the Republican primary to Staten Island state senator John Marchi. But he ran as a general election candidate on the Liberal line, winning reelection with 42 percent of the vote, thanks to the Italian American major-party nominees splitting the outer-borough vote. Third-party politics would again prove significant in 1970, with echoes of the 1965 mayor's race. This was the year of Kent State, the Cambodia incursion, and a rising anti-war protest movement. In lower Manhattan on May 8, construction workers in their hard hats descended from their posts at the World Trade Center site to confront a large anti-war demonstration in the days following the Kent State shootings, clashing violently with demonstrators throughout the day. Charles Goodell was the Republican U.S. senator appointed in the wake of Robert Kennedy's assassination, running for reelection that year. He opposed the Vietnam War and, like Lindsay, ran on the Liberal line. The Democrats nominated an upstate congressman, Richard Ottinger, also an opponent of the war. A clear lane was left for those on the right politically, a lane the upstart Conservatives would only too eagerly fill—and one that had seemed to grow much wider since 1965. Their nominee was James L. Buckley, Bill's brother.

Compared to his brother's mayoral effort five years earlier, Jim Buckley's campaign is seldom mythologized. But it was by far the more successful effort. In a state considered the mecca of the New Deal coalition, Buckley beat Ottinger by two points, 39 to 37 percent, with the Republican Goodell reduced to just 24 percent of the vote. Street corner conservatism had prevailed against a split liberal vote, a mirror image of the 1969 mayor's race. The city had traditionally provided the mass of votes Democrats needed to win statewide, but with traditional party lines taking a backseat to the new ideological alignment, there was only a modest difference between the city vote and the upstate vote. In the city, Buckley got 36 percent, just three points shy of his statewide total. Buckley's citywide number paled in comparison to the totals he posted in the city's Italian and Irish neighborhoods. His strongest showing came in the 69 percent he got in one Bay Ridge, Brooklyn, assembly district, 64 percent along Staten Island's South Shore, and the 64 and 60 percent he received respectively in Queens's Middle Village and Kew Gardens.

Buckley's victory sparked new talk of conservatism's newfound strength in the cities, where previously it seemed confined to the suburbs or rural areas. Social unrest was not only polarizing the electorate in new ways, specifically in the Republican vote that had emerged among those who had left the city for the suburbs. It was now cutting into the heart of the Democrats' white and Catholic working-class base in the cities, the party's strongest group at the beginning of the decade.

A NEW POLITICAL ALIGNMENT

The years between 1965 and 1970 had birthed a new alignment in American politics. Republicans established a beachhead with the working class, and conversely, the highly educated and affluent were finding themselves more at home within the Democratic Party. This was not yet the class role reversal we see today. In that period, the ideal of the Democratic Party as the home of the workingman—of the union man—was so ingrained that even the slightest sign of its weakening drew considerable notice. Signs of this were slight in the mid-1960s. They were something stronger than that in 1970 and 1972.

Democrats had solidified their image as the party of the working class during the New Deal. Running to extend the Democratic rule for a record fifth term, "Give 'em Hell Harry" Truman barnstormed the country as a progressive populist railing against Republicans in the back pocket of the rich. In his upset victory, Truman got nearly twice as much support among whites of lower socioeconomic status than he did among high-status white voters, a gap of 57 to 30 percent. Twelve years later, John F. Kennedy took 61 percent of lower-class whites and 38 percent in the upper class. By 1968, with issues of war, protest, and patriotism center stage, the class divide flattened and the historical edge Democrats had among working-class whites vanished. Hubert Humphrey received nearly identical shares of the vote among lower-, middle-, and upper-class whites—36, 39, and 38 percent, respectively. Much of this erosion came about as a result of George Wallace siphoning off lower-class southern white Democrats. But in a two-way contest four years later, they would not return. White voter support for Democrats dropped across the board with the nomination of George McGovern, with the party reduced to just 26 percent of the middle-class white vote. In the twelve years from 1960 to 1972, the Democrats had gone from reliably winning six in ten working-class white voters to winning barely half that number. A relative edge in support among lower-class whites of more than 20 points had disappeared in those twelve years. This shift roughly matched or exceeded the relative shift of white voters without a college degree that would elect Donald Trump.

These numbers were considered significant by political scientist Everett Carll Ladd, who compiled them in an influential 1976 journal article. This shift in American class politics, Ladd wrote, was not just a matter of a working class drawn to a Republican Party that campaigned openly against the counterculture. It was also a matter of relatively well-off Americans gravitating toward the increasingly liberal skew of the Democrats. These were the beginnings of an inversion in the well-established patterns of class politics—hence the title of Ladd's article, "Liberalism Upside Down."

Years before the term "yuppie" entered the lexicon, and a quarter century before David Brooks would lampoon the "bourgeois bohemians," Ladd noted the changing character of the nation's upper class. No longer defined by commercial success, a kind that might favor the party with a laissez-faire approach to business, the upper class was increasingly delineated by smarts in professions like medicine, the law, and engineering where a college education was the ticket to entry. This led them to a new set of cultural values centered on tolerance and the psychological trait of openness to experience. "The size of the upper classes is new," Ladd wrote, "as is the boldness of their assault on older values and life styles." What was once a clash on economic issues, which would place the elite on the same side as the right, was replaced by a clash on cultural issues that placed it more and more on the left. In this new political alignment, those at the top became much more likely to call themselves liberal than those at the bottom. In 1970, almost twice as many skilled professionals described themselves as liberals as did unskilled workers. The gap was just as wide by education in 1975: 41 percent of college graduates called themselves liberal, compared to 21 percent of high school graduates and 22 percent of those with less than a high school education. But the "inversion" that Ladd had predicted had not yet fully materialized. The late 1960s and early '70s were the crossroads of the class role reversal, where upper-class whites were now just as likely to vote Democratic as their lower-class counterparts. Democratic support in the white working class still far exceeded their adoption of the liberal label with which the party was becoming increasingly identified. With party and ideology increasingly aligned, this was a sign that the Democrats had more room to fall among working-class whites.

To trace the shift up to that point, we must delve deeper into the world of the white working class in the 1960s. Two decades of economic expansion after World War II lifted the working class from destitution to a better life. Government programs like the G.I. Bill made access to college and the American dream of owning a home available to millions of war veterans. Shared experiences in the trenches and on the home front also strengthened the social fabric. Churches saw an upsurge in attendance and civic associations thrived.

Just as confidence in traditional institutions began to wane in the mid-sixties, so did the American economy. Inflation—kept well under 2 percent throughout the 1960s—began creeping up in 1966 and peaked at 6 percent in 1970. This would prove to be a precursor to much worse bouts of inflation in 1974 and 1979–80. Economic growth slowed by more than half in 1967 and the country entered a period of slow growth it would not emerge from until 1972. The Dow Jones Industrial Average made a new high of 990 in January 1966. The drop that followed was unusually long-lasting, with the market not reaching its previous high until December 1982. Expanding vistas of economic opportunity that middle-class Americans had begun to take for granted gave way to a sense of narrowing possibilities. Zero-sum thinking became the norm.

High taxes further eroded the middle-class family's paycheck. Median-income families who had paid 11.7 percent of their income in taxes in 1953 were paying 22.7 percent by 1975. Taxes had also risen for the affluent, those at four times the median income, but the sticker shock was less, with the total tax burden growing from 20.2 percent to 29.7 percent. Rising homeownership meant that the working and middle classes also bore the brunt of paying property taxes, a form of taxation millions of new homeowners had never encountered before. Inflation also magnified the tax burden, with "bracket creep" pushing families into higher tax brackets year after year. The fact that they were no longer as poor as they were during the Great Depression was cold comfort in an economy where taxes and inflation rapidly eroded the value of a dollar.

The economy of the 1960s and '70s created a working class more economically conservative, more risk averse, more sensitive to what could be taken from them. This was the middle-income strata that self-proclaimed "radical" community activist Saul Alinsky described as "Have-a-Little, Want Mores," those who would not rock the boat because they had more to lose than to gain from revolution. They still organized within and supported labor unions, but the radicalism of the unions of old was no more. Far from joining the students at the barricades, they now stood on the other side. "Labor, to some extent, has become middle class," said AFL-CIO chief George Meany in a 1969 *New York Times* interview. "When you have no property, you have nothing to lose by these radical actions. But when you become a person who has a home and has property, to some extent you become conservative. And I would say to that extent labor has become conservative."

The old politics of the New Deal—the fight of the many against the few—was over. A new relationship between partisanship and social class took root. As Ladd wrote:

> Much of the working class has become *bourgeois* and behaves as the bourgeoisie has historically—anxious to protect a status achieved at considerable effort and often tenuously held. The thirst for change which characterized this stratum in the New Deal era has been quenched by the affluence of the last three decades. Many of the current pressures for equalitarian change, moreover, ask for sacrifices from the lower social strata. In contrast to the 1930s, when policy innovation often involved efforts by the working class to strengthen its position vis-à-vis the business strata, some of the most tension-laden areas where equalitarian change has been sought over the past decade have found the white working

> class (or lower middle class) and the black underclass confronting each other. More secure in their position, less threatened by such quests for societal transformation, typically residing some distance from the "front," the upper social strata have come easily to a more change-supportive posture.

Having achieved a decent standard of living—the home in the suburbs, a family car, new appliances that relieved the backbreaking toil of housework that was a grinding reality for their parents—the working class grew less interested in economic redistribution. Liberals hailed government's role in ensuring a rising middle-class standard of living, but this easily overlooked the pride that working Americans felt—from foreign battlefields to the home front—to secure a better world. *Their* hard work, *their* sacrifice, *their* willingness to follow the rules and abide by a moral code had built postwar America. And now it was all in jeopardy. "Everything I got I worked for," said one Brooklyn cop after an exchange with a group of anti–Vietnam War protesters. "It gets me sore when I see these kids, who been handed everything, pissing it away, talking like bums." What's more, anti-war politicians like John Lindsay seemed to be on the side of those fomenting disorder, or at least doing nothing to stop it.

The media had started to pick up on this frustration, "rediscovering" the white working class with extensive magazine features written about them. A cover spread in *Harper's* in August 1969 focused on the "'forgotten man,' perhaps the most alienated person in America." Words flowing forth from the page with effervescence, Pete Hamill would also capture the working-class gestalt in an April 1969 piece for *New York* magazine. "The working class earns its living with its hands or its backs; its members do not exist on welfare payments; they do not live in abject, swinish poverty, nor in safe, remote suburban comfort," wrote Hamill. "They earn between $5,000 and $10,000 a year. And they can no longer make it in New York." Eddie Cush, Hamill's ironworker friend, relayed an experience familiar today for workers whose paychecks are barely enough to cover even the basic essentials:

> I'm going out of my mind. I average about $8,500 a year, pretty good money. I work my ass off. But I can't make it. I come home at the end of the week, I start paying the bills, I give my wife some money for food. And there's nothing left. Maybe, if I work overtime, I get $15 or $20 to spend on myself. But most of the time, there's nothin.' They take $65 a week out of my pay. I have to come up with $90 a month rent. But every time I turn around, one of the kids needs shoes or a dress or something for school.

This was not the end of the quote. There's a more irate part of it directed at welfare recipients and campus rioters. While lawbreakers were being coddled by politicians, Eddie Cush worked hard and followed the rules. What good had it done him?

The contrast between a working class that goes to work, only to barely scratch out a living, and those living on the government dole comes up frequently. The racial overtones do not need to be drawn out by the liberal writer-anthropologist on safari through the working-class neighborhood. They are made known by Hamill's free-speaking subjects, who weren't bashful in their associations of Black New Yorkers with welfare and crime.

In previous decades, New York City and cities throughout the North had been a destination for the "Great Migration" of Black southerners escaping Jim Crow. Like newcomers to the city before, African Americans had started at the bottom of the economic ladder. This made them potential adversaries to the white workers, both as a lower-cost labor pool and in the fight for political power. Still, these Black newcomers had faced challenges the first wave of Irish and Italians had not. There were struggles with family formation, with a third of Black children born out of wedlock. That number seems unremarkable today, with four out of ten babies born out of wedlock, but it was distinctive for its time, when the rate of illegitimate births among whites stood well below one in ten. The net result was that Black families were more likely to end up as recipients of government aid programs targeted at mothers with children in poverty. Black economic fortunes lagged, Hamill noted, in part because of union rules barring Black workers from highly paid construction jobs.

Many white working-class New Yorkers did not see the contradictions in this. Where was the talk of affirmative action and reparations for groups like the Irish, who had also been discriminated against? "Compensate him?" asked one man. "Look, the English ruled Ireland for 700 years, that's hundreds of years longer than Negroes have been slaves. Why don't the British government compensate me? In Boston, they had signs like 'No Irish Need Apply' on the jobs, so why don't the American government compensate *me*?" Group stereotypes flowed freely. "At least the Puerto Ricans are working," said one carpenter. "They open a grocery store, they work from six in the mornin' till midnight. The P.R.'s are willin' to work for their money. The colored guys just don't wanna work." The then-young medium of television, Hamill wrote, fueled racially charged attitudes:

> In any conversation with working-class whites, you are struck by how the information explosion has hit them. Television has made an enormous impact on them, and because of the nature of that medium—its preference for the politics of theatre, its seeming inability to ever explain what is happening behind the photographed image—much of their understanding of what happens is superficial. Most of them have only a passing acquaintance with blacks, and very few have any black friends. So they see blacks in terms of militants with Afros and shades, or crushed people on welfare.

Though not the formalized legal oppression of the South, this casual racial stereotyping had lasting generational effects for Black economic empowerment. Many whites lived in fear of Black buyers moving into their neighborhoods, viewing it as a slippery slope to slum status. As a result, legal and de facto barriers were set up against affordable homeownership and suburbanization for African Americans—the very things that had built the postwar white middle class. It was also an early missed opportunity to build a cross-racial working-class coalition against the educated elite then coalescing in the universities. When hardhats clashed with student protesters in New York City, polling showed Black Americans siding with the white workers. A poll by Daniel Yankelovich found that one-third of Black New Yorkers considered themselves conservatives, a figure Gavin used to cite as evidence of a "mutuality of interests between many black families and urban conservatives." In *The Real Majority*, Scammon and Wattenberg, too, noted an overlap in the cultural concerns of the Black and white working classes that could have served as the foundation of a new political coalition, writing, "Blacks, too, are 'plain people'; they too, are 'forgotten Americans'; they, too, belong in the Silent Majority—and many, too, are unyoung and unpoor." Yet the racial animosity of the period overshadowed everything, preventing any rainbow coalition united by the Social Issue from taking shape.

The immigrant experience also shaped the worldview of New York's white ethnics. They loved their country with the zeal of the immigrant, appreciative of the many opportunities it offered to build a better life. Just twenty-five years earlier, a large percentage of them fought for it in a world war, in many cases against the armies of their ancestral homelands. Hamill filtered this through a slightly cynical lens for his elite readers, but did a good job conveying the simple, undistilled patriotism that ran through a place like Bay Ridge:

> Patriotism is very important to the working-class white man. Most of the time he is the son of an immigrant, and most immigrants sincerely believe that the Pledge of Allegiance, the Star-Spangled Banner, the American Flag are symbols of what it means to be Americans. They might not have become rich in America, but most of the time they were much better off than they were in the old country. On "I Am an American" Day they march in parades with a kind of religious fervor that can look absurd to the outsider (imagine marching through Copenhagen on "I Am a Dane" Day), but that can also be oddly touching.

War service was core to the workingman's identity and the bedrock of civil society in ethnic neighborhoods. "Walk through any working-class white neighborhood and you will see dozens of veterans' clubs, named after neighborhood men who were killed in World War Two or Korea," Hamill wrote. "There are not really orgies of jingoism going on inside;

most of the time the veterans' clubs serve as places in which to drink on Sunday morning before the bars open at 1 p.m., or as places in which to hold baptisms and wedding receptions." On an individual level, service meant something to the workingman. "And as he goes into his 30s and 40s, he resents those who don't serve, or bitch about the service the way he used to bitch," Hamill writes. "And he sees any form of antiwar protest as a denial of his own young manhood, and a form of spitting on the graves of the people he served with who died in his war."

The Vietnam War had not been a purely partisan issue. Presidents of both parties had borne the burdens of its prosecution and there were hawks and doves in both parties. It was, however, a class issue, as it was the working class doing most of the fighting. Figures compiled by David Paul Kuhn in his book *The Hardhat Riot* are striking: white college graduates made up just 7 percent of soldiers in Vietnam, well short of the 38 percent of young whites at that time who attended college. This was a workingman's war, not just for whites, but also for Black Americans and Hispanics, who served at rates in line with their share of the population. The draft system should have spread the burdens of service equally throughout society. Instead, it functioned as a class-based filtration system, with the upper middle class mostly spared the horrors of combat. Fifteen million young men avoided combat through a system of deferments mostly granted to full-time college students, including a host of future political leaders. Others availed themselves of medical deferments. And if that failed, there was always outright draft evasion, which usually went unpunished. Of the 210,000 evaders, Kuhn noted, barely 10,000 were convicted and only 3,200 served any jail time. For James Webb, a writer and veteran of Vietnam who would go on to serve as secretary of the navy and as a senator, the injustice of the draft reflected a country "afraid to ask the men of Harvard to stand alongside the men of Harlem, same uniform, same obligation, same country."

This was a far cry from the shared sacrifice of the Greatest Generation. At St. Paul's, the elite prep school attended by John Lindsay, 104 boys died in World War II, a war in which Lindsay himself served. In Vietnam, three from St. Paul's died. A young man of draft age growing up in ethnic South Boston was nearly twenty times as likely to be killed in Vietnam as a graduate of nearby Harvard or MIT. For the working-class veteran, it was easy to look upon these children of privilege with nothing but contempt.

The protest movement lacked self-awareness of this problem. Reflecting upon the rough treatment of protesters by police, leftist historian Todd Gitlin would write, "Part of the brutality . . . reflected a kind of class war [the Students for a Democratic Society] had not reckoned with: working-class cops' resentment of the children of privilege." The protesters had styled themselves a tribune for the working class, standing up *for* the working-class troops needlessly dying half a world away. But the working class itself did not see it this way. As Father Andrew Greeley, a sociologist and Catholic priest, would write:

> From the point of view of the Polish television watcher on Milwaukee Avenue in the northwest side of Chicago, the longhaired militants and their faculty patrons are every bit as much part of the Establishment as are the presidents of corporations. The peace movement is seen as very much of an Establishment movement, working against the values, the stability, and the patriotism of the American masses, which incidentally are seen as footing the bill for Establishment games and amusements.

The event known as the "hardhat riot" was the most symbolic manifestation to date of the emerging class and education divide. Taking place just days after the killing of four anti-war protesters at Kent State, the May 8, 1970, incident saw World Trade Center construction workers clashing with thousands of protesters who marched through lower Manhattan with the goal of shutting down Wall Street. The event marked the end of the anti-war movement's short-lived mainstream acceptance. The October 15, 1969, anti-war "moratorium" was the movement's apex, declared a holiday in numerous cities and towns, with virtually no organized pushback. Things would be different that day in lower Manhattan. Thousands of hardhats thronged City Hall Plaza, demanding that the American flag be raised to full staff, reversing the mayor's order to lower the flag to half-mast in the days following Kent State. A beleaguered city hall official grudgingly obliged, to the sounds of workers cheering their vindication. The police, who lived in the same neighborhoods and sat in the same church pews as the hardhats, barely acted to contain violent outbursts directed at the protesters.

Twelve days later, hardhats would organize a march of their own in lower Manhattan in support of the war. As many as 150,000 construction workers, teamsters, and longshoremen showed up, waving the American flag. It was dubbed the "Workers' Woodstock."

THE UNSILENT MAJORITY

Until May 1970, the frustration of the white working class had been primarily a sociological concern. With this working-class outpouring of anti-anti-war activism, it became political, and Richard Nixon's White House swung into action.

Before the hardhat demonstrations, Nixon had largely been a spectator to the working-class realignment. When Hamill's piece came out in 1969, Nixon scribbled a note to an aide in the margins asking what could be done about the workers' complaints. The Labor Department conducted studies on working-class alienation. But working-class voters were in flux, and their votes had not been fully for Nixon in 1968. A large number of white ethnics remained loyal to the then-party of the people, voting for Hubert Humphrey, though in diminished numbers compared to Kennedy and Johnson. Many defected to George Wallace. Nixon channeled the prevailing national mood with campaign ads about violent crime and disorder, but he had yet to fully exploit the emerging cultural divide.

Pat Buchanan, then a young Nixon aide, urged the president to go further. On the day after the Workers' Woodstock, he saw his opening, penning a memo to Nixon, writing, "[I]t should be our focus to constantly speak to, to assure, to win, to aid, to promote the president's natural constituency—which is now the working men and women of the country, the common man, the Roosevelt New Dealer. There is a great ferment in American politics; these, quite candidly, are our people now." Aide Steve Bull added, "This display of emotional activity from the hardhats provides an opportunity to forge a new alliance and perhaps result in the emergence of a 'new right.'" In a national address the previous November, Nixon himself had spoken of a "great silent majority of Americans," those that didn't want America to just declare defeat in Vietnam. Now the silent majority seemed silent no more. Within a week, Nixon hosted a dozen labor leaders whose men had marched in the streets of New York. As a gift, he was handed a flag-emblazoned hard hat with his name and an American flag on it. An American-flag hard hat would become a Nixon campaign emblem in 1972.

Nixon's team knew a political opportunity when it saw one. Of the hardhat workers, Buchanan wrote, "They were clearly coming unmoored from the great FDR coalition. These guys were alienated from an establishment, which was undermining the American war in Vietnam. They were alienated from these college kids, the revolt of the overprivileged. They were guys like the guys I grew up with." Soon, it would be time to convert this outpouring of opposition against the defeatist anti-war demonstrator into votes for the Republican Party. Though not himself a Republican, Jim Buckley's Senate race that fall would prove to be the test case for the power of a conservative coalition of hardhats and cops from Brooklyn, Queens, and Staten Island. Nixon refused to endorse the liberal Republican Goodell, signaling tacit support for Buckley.

The ultimate goal was Nixon's own reelection in 1972. There were two distinct schools of thought on the prospects for rallying the working class to Nixon's side, with much hinging on the question of what George Wallace's voters would do. Kevin Phillips, the 1968 campaign aide, stated the optimistic case in *The Emerging Republican Majority.* Wallace voters, Phillips wrote, were "an electorate in motion between major parties rather than a new, permanent entrant into the national presidential arena." Their willingness to vote for a third party in 1968 signaled a permanent break from the Democrats, on the way to their future home with the Republicans. In *The Real Majority*, Scammon and Wattenberg—who themselves hailed from the more conservative wing of the Democratic Party—expressed a different view: that the Wallace and Social Issue voter was up for grabs in the 1970s. Democrats, they wrote, still had a chance to redeem themselves with these voters by seizing on the Social Issue themselves. In the ideologically flexible two-party politics that still existed then, it was certainly a possibility, and one that Nixon himself took seriously. In a memo to the president, Buchanan wrote that the book "contains a credible and workable blueprint for our defeat in 1972," one that could be neutralized only by seizing on "drugs, demonstrations, pornography, disruptions, 'kidlash,' permissiveness, violence, riots, crime." Chief of Staff H. R. Haldeman noted Nixon's approval of the memo, echoing that the president wanted "to hit pornography, dope, bad kids."

The Democratic primary in 1972 was a close race between the anti-war senator George McGovern and both of Nixon's general election rivals from 1968, Hubert Humphrey and George Wallace. Had Wallace prevailed, the White House's plans would have gone out the window. Wallace was then working to broaden his appeal, venturing farther north than he had in 1968. It was during a campaign stop in Maryland, a border state, that he was shot by a would-be assassin, effectively ending his campaign. Nationally, he finished a close third in votes. Rules changes instituted after the contentious 1968 Chicago convention gave more power to the party's grassroots activists and primary voters in the selection of convention delegates. These rules, shepherded by a commission co-chaired by McGovern, were enough to give the South Dakotan the nomination. With this, Nixon's team got the campaign they had dreamed of in May 1970, a fight effectively between the anti-war protesters and the rest of America.

The final results were a mirror image of 1964. Nixon's 23.2-point margin in the popular vote had slightly outdone Johnson's 22.6-point margin against Goldwater eight years earlier. As in 1964, though, there were some places that had held up better for the loser. McGovern did relatively well along the West Coast, and especially in the San Francisco Bay Area, doing one point better than Humphrey in Alameda County (Oakland), California, and five points better in Santa Cruz County. McGovern's losses were buffeted anywhere with a major university, thanks to the Twenty-Sixth Amendment's expansion of the franchise to include eighteen-to-twenty-one-year-olds. Within New York City, McGovern only ran 4 points off Humphrey's vote share in Manhattan. In the ethnic outer boroughs, his losses were steeper: 12 points in Brooklyn and 11 points in Queens. They were worse in other working-class counties. These included McDowell County, West Virginia, the heart of coal country, with a drop of 25 points; Macomb County, Michigan, a drop of 20 points; Providence County, Rhode Island, a drop of 18 points; and Luzerne County, Pennsylvania, also a hub of coal production, with a drop of 17 points. McGovern only topped Humphrey's vote share in percentage terms in a smattering of counties along the West Coast, his home state of South Dakota, and those Deep South areas where Humphrey was barely a presence in 1968. The lion's share of Wallace's votes went to Nixon. In tiny George County, Mississippi, Nixon went from 4 percent of the vote in 1968 to 92 percent in 1972. Wallace had gotten 91 percent there four years earlier.

The 1972 results represented a decisive step forward in the southern realignment of the Republican Party, but the realignment would proceed unevenly from there. Four years following the McGovern disaster, Jimmy Carter would sweep his home region on his way to the White House, winning George Wallace's Alabama by 13 points. The progression in the Deep South was from Goldwater to Wallace to Nixon to Carter to Reagan. In the working-class North, it was a different story. Republicans activated a working-class electorate that would not be fully reawakened until 2016. Luzerne County, Pennsylvania, saw one of Nixon's strongest gains in 1972. It is the home of Wilkes-Barre, the sister city of the more Democratic Scranton, the hub of a region occupied with the extraction of anthracite coal. During the Kennedy-Johnson elections, it had run nearly 20 points to the left of the country as a whole. In 1972, it matched Nixon's national result, with a Republican margin of 23 points.

In most of the elections that followed, Luzerne reverted to its Democratic roots, the symbol of a Republican Party that perennially fell short in the electoral battleground of Pennsylvania. Luzerne would only come close to matching the national Republican performance in 1980 and 1992, two elections shaped by the presence of more populist candidates on the ballot. In 1980, this would be the candidacy of the conservative outsider, Ronald Reagan, and in 1992 the third-party candidacy of Ross Perot, siphoning off change-oriented voters from Bill Clinton. Only in 2008 and 2012 would it become clear that a different political wind was blowing in the Wyoming Valley when Barack Obama barely outperformed his margin nationally in the region. In 2016, the dam broke. Trump won the county by 19 points, outperforming his national margin by 21 points, the first time since the 1950s that Luzerne had been a net contributor to Republican margins nationally and statewide. Trump's support in the county mostly held in 2020, when he won the county by 14 points.

Both 1972 and 2016 were elections where Republicans shed any pretense of caring about the parts of the electorate that were trending left on the Social Issue and made a move to appeal directly to the heart of the working class. This was a bet that paid handsomely. They also paid the price with the college-educated voter they spurned: 1972 was the first year in which the Democratic candidate had performed better among college graduates than non-graduates, and college graduates also fled the party of Trump in 2016. The tiny number of graduates in the electorate in the early 1970s made it unambiguously a trade worth making then. Today, a strong version of a coalition based on college graduates can win a national election, but at the expense of being tilted so heavily to large states on the coasts that it must win the popular vote by several points to take the White House. In both years, the side of the candidate able to rally the working-class voter had the advantage.

8.

THE 2020 SURGE

The story in the 2020 presidential election was largely that of an electorate that had made up its mind on Donald Trump four years earlier, with just the right number of votes in just the right states turning a narrow victory into a narrow defeat—but with one crucial exception. In most of America's nonwhite communities—especially those filled with first- and second-generation immigrants—Trump did better than he had in 2016.

In many Hispanic and Asian communities, the shift was in double digits. Estimates from the Democratic data firm Catalist show that, nationally, the Hispanic vote shifted the most, by a net of 16 points on the margin. Between 2012 and 2020, a blend of available data sources shows Hispanics shifting a total of 19 points in a Republican direction, African Americans 11 points, and Asian Americans 5 points. The GOP's underwhelming performance in the 2022 midterms did not see a reversal of these trends. Republicans had their best midterm ever with Hispanic voters, and the Republican share of the Black vote for the House rose to at least 13 percent, which, while modest, also happened to be their best showing in a midterm election in recent memory. The fact that all racial and ethnic minority groups swung toward Trump is notable in light of the fact that the rest of America—and by this I mean white America—swung against him. Areas dominated by whites with college degrees swung several points against Trump, furthering the white educational divide, while the white working-class vote trended one or two points against him. The net result was a somewhat weaker Trump coalition, a bit more downscale than the one in 2016—but much more diverse.

Generations of immigration to the United States have created a multiethnic, multiracial patchwork that still dots the political landscape. Different groups of Europeans imparted their own politics wherever they settled. To take one example, Scandinavians settling in states like Minnesota and Wisconsin made those places more progressive than the rest of the Midwest, which saw mostly German migration. Yet, over time, these differences have started to fade, giving way to a mostly uniform pattern of partisan polarization among whites dictated by density and college education. In 2016, the last of the Democratic ancestral holdouts fell, with places like Minnesota's Iron Range, Ohio's Mahoning Valley, and southwest Wisconsin breaking down and joining the old Democratic strongholds of Appalachia that had swung over the last decade.

Exceptions to the polarization trend lived on in places that were more diverse. First established in the 1964 election, a pattern of nearly uniform Black support for Democrats endures, with only subtle partisan differences across urban, suburban, and rural communities. Rural Black communities continued to support the Democratic Party in large numbers, as had similar places with large Hispanic populations, like the Rio Grande Valley of Texas. The ideological polarization that would whittle away the remaining Democratic holdouts in the white working class in 2016 would also come for nonwhite voters in 2020.

This led to a remarkably consistent shift to the right in nonwhite-majority areas throughout the country. It was stronger among Hispanics and Asians than it was among Black voters. It was stronger in places populated by exiles from communism—places like Little Havana in Miami and Little Saigon in Orange County, California. But the trend was broad-reaching. The shift could be seen in Hispanic neighborhoods from Lawrence, Massachusetts, to Reading, Pennsylvania, to Las Vegas, Nevada. It reached Cubans, Mexicans, Colombians, Puerto Ricans, and Dominicans. It reached into Asian American enclaves as distinctive as Hmong Village in Saint Paul, Minnesota. There was an associated shift among groups of whites without a Western European, Christian background: from Orthodox Jews in Brooklyn's Williamsburg neighborhood, to the heavily Jewish community of Great Neck on Long Island, to the Persians of Los Angeles—Muslims, Jews, and people of other faiths—who swung heavily in Beverly Hills and the Westside neighborhood known as Tehrangeles. Far from the dying last gasp of white Christian America that the modern Republican Party was supposed to represent, the 2020 election saw almost everyone except for white Christians surge toward the Republican Party in numbers almost great enough to save Donald Trump from defeat.

After the election, the media dispatched feature writers to places like Little Havana and the Rio Grande to understand what they had missed, in a revival of the West Virginia diner-style of coverage after the 2016 election. Often, the theories revolved around issues specific to discrete regions or ethnicities, ignoring the fact that the shift was much broader than just a few ethnic groups or regions.

In Miami-Dade County, the center of the country's Cuban American population and home to a large contingent of Colombians and Venezuelans hostile to socialism in their homelands, the explanations centered around the renewed visibility of socialist leaders in the Democratic Party. These included Bernie Sanders and Alexandria Ocasio-Cortez, elected in 2018 along with other members of her "Squad."

Others conjectured that the Hispanic shift came because of an issue that mostly *wasn't* discussed in 2020, in stark contrast to 2016. That issue was immigration. "When Mexico sends its people, they're not sending their best," Donald Trump famously declared in his June 16, 2015, announcement speech, words that would echo throughout the entire 2016 campaign. "They're sending people that have lots of problems, and they're bringing those problems with us. They're bringing drugs. They're bringing crime. They're rapists. And some, I assume, are good people." Gone in 2020 was this sort of sweeping invective directed toward members of the largest Hispanic nationality group in the country, replaced by an immigration discourse that centered more on threats to public safety, particularly in border communities. One can add to this fact that the border security problem seemed to be more manageable after four years of wall building and enforcement—not to mention a pandemic that temporarily stopped global migration. The lack of a shift against Trump among Hispanics in 2016 followed by a large shift in 2020 could be interpreted as a sign that Hispanics were ready for the populist Republican Party of

Trump, only hesitating due to his hostile immigration rhetoric. When that rhetoric went away, pent-up demand was released.

Others look to Latin American political traditions for why Trump ultimately proved more successful among Hispanic voters than mild-mannered Republicans like John McCain or Mitt Romney. Trump's machismo, a "strongman" style common to the region, resonated. His blunt language, backers of this theory argue, was more in line with the way Hispanics (and working-class people in general) talk among themselves. The image of Trump as a brash, tough-talking businessman disrupting a corrupt establishment was appealing to those familiar with Latin American politics, where political corruption runs rampant.

Another explanation centers around the issue that replaced immigration at the center of cultural discourse in 2020: crime and policing. Hispanics in polling take a strong law-and-order position, and by the time the 2020 election came around, Hispanics were more unfavorable than they were favorable toward the Black Lives Matter movement. In Echelon Insights polling after the election, Hispanics were the swing group most concerned about defunding the police under a Democratic majority. To the extent the 2020 issue environment lent itself to a stronger Trump Hispanic performance, crime and policing may have contributed.

A more general theory is that a focus on cultural issues rather than economic issues in the Trump era sparked a shift among nonwhite voters who are more conservative culturally than they are economically. What made the Republican Party toxic for nonwhite voters in the Obama years was not the idea that the party was racist or xenophobic, but that it was run by out-of-touch country-club elites who looked out for their rich business buddies first. When these issues were taken off the table, by a different kind of ultrarich candidate who promised to blow up the system he had benefited from, Hispanics and other nonwhites felt freer to vote on the cultural issues on which they were to the right of the modern Democratic Party.

A competing explanation points to the economy itself, which was booming prior to the pandemic, with those groups more likely to be at the margins of the economy—Hispanic and Black voters—prospering more in relative terms. Incomes among Hispanics and Asian Americans had surged in the years leading up to 2020. Black poverty and unemployment rates reached new lows under Trump. And when it came to the pandemic itself, people working with their hands or in service industries—people whose jobs could not be done over Zoom—could get back to work a lot faster, thanks to red-state governors like Florida's Ron DeSantis and Texas's Greg Abbott quickly reopening their state's economies. In Texas, this meant a sizable group of people working in the oil and gas industry, where demand for the product was crushed by stay-at-home orders.

Alas, votes for president do not come with rationales attached. If they did, we could divine all the mysteries of the political universe. The only truly foolproof data source is the election results themselves, which tell us broadly which kinds of communities and demographics swung, and large-scale preelection surveys about the issue preferences of individual voters. The theories outlined pretty much all point in the same direction: toward a Hispanic and new-immigrant swing to Trump, but the exact role each issue played is and will remain an enigma.

What we do have clear evidence of is an ideological shift: Trump won many more nonwhite voters who call themselves conservatives in the 2020 election as compared to the 2016 election, with shifts of at least 36 points among conservatives who were either Black, Hispanic, or Asian American. In general elections, candidates are often advised to tread lightly on ideological rhetoric, lest they turn off swing voters. This advice applies first and foremost to white voters, where appearing more ideologically extreme serves to turn off moderate voters. But sharpening ideological contrasts serves a useful purpose with nonwhite voters, since so many who are in the middle still vote Democratic. Emphasizing the ideological stakes of the election—on crime, the economy, culture wars, and pandemic lockdowns—combined to produce a surge among ideological conservatives who agreed with Trump on these issues. And Republicans did not yet need to do a lot of persuading of voters in the middle to achieve these gains. They just needed to collect votes from already-aligned conservatives, votes previously unavailable to Republicans. As stated before, the erosion of racial voting patterns in favor of ideology presents a major opportunity for the Republican Party to realign nonwhite conservatives—and their fair share of moderates also. All of the bespoke explanations for the 2020 surge fit within this framework of ideological polarization. But numbers alone can only go so far. The stories of individual communities matter too.

NO AL CASTROCHAVISMO

Giancarlo Sopo is the embodiment of a younger generation of Cuban Americans, one taking Miami's politics in a new direction. Sopo's family was among the first wave of exiles fleeing Fidel Castro's communist revolution. His father fought at the Bay of Pigs, and was a fierce anti-communist, reflecting the politics of his generation of Cuban exiles. In Miami, this meant staunch support for Republicans, where the party routinely won the city's Cuban exile community by a margin of three to one or more, an urban island of support for the GOP virtually unmatched in any city in America. It wasn't always this way. Cuban Americans had divided their ballots evenly between Jimmy Carter and Gerald Ford in 1976. It was in 1980 that Cubans shifted right, with Ronald Reagan's promise of a more assertive foreign policy replacing the Cold War détente policies of Richard Nixon and Ford. So eager was the community for Reagan's strong stances against Castro's Cuba and communist guerilla movements in the Western Hemisphere that he received 86 percent of Cuban Miami's votes in 1980. During his pilgrimage to Little Havana in May 1983, thousands thronged the streets to give Reagan a hero's welcome. The front page of the *Miami Herald* the next day did not mince words: "Superstar Wows Little Havana; An Ebullient Reagan Scores More Than a Few Points in Miami."

The political climate had changed by the mid-2000s. The Cold War was long over. For a younger generation, the issues of war and recession moving other young Americans left seemed more pressing than the doings of an aging dictator to the south. Like others of his generation, Giancarlo Sopo opposed the Iraq War. He got involved in Democratic politics in 2004. When a young senator named Barack Obama announced his campaign for the presidency, Sopo immediately volunteered, later serving as a youth representative on the 2008 Democratic platform committee.

Sopo was part of a trend that saw a community that was once solidly Republican go fifty-fifty by Obama's reelection. Enthusiasm for Hillary Clinton ran nowhere near as high as for Obama, but precinct results from 2016 point to a near even split between Clinton and Trump in the Miami-area Cuban American strongholds of Little Havana and Hialeah. A generational divide was at play, and Sopo was part of it. Florida International University's survey of Miami's Cuban Americans found widespread disillusionment with both party nominees in 2016, with nearly a third reporting they wouldn't vote for either candidate or were unsure. But the race was close, a far cry from the Republican blowouts of the past. Clinton held a 9-point lead among Cuban Americans born in the United States and a staggering 27-point lead among younger migrants who came after 1995. Together, this "new" Cuban vote was the majority inside the community in Miami.

Things began to shift following Donald Trump's election. The defeat of Bernie Sanders in the 2016 Democratic primary should have marked the end for the party's socialist moment. Instead, Clinton's loss gave it a new lease on life, and a fresh new spokesperson, with the primary victory of Alexandria Ocasio-Cortez in New York's 14th district. An ideology under whose banner Fidel Castro and Che Guevara marched had not been heard from in U.S. politics since the early-twentieth century candidacies of Eugene Debs and Norman Thomas. It was now a factor in Democratic politics, attracting a vibrant following among young people and with high-profile victories by the so-called Squad. Suddenly, socialism was back in the conversation, to the delight of the White House, which gladly shone the spotlight in Trump's 2019 State of the Union address. "America will never be a socialist country," Trump vowed, in a line he would repeat twelve days later in Miami in a speech before exiles of the Venezuelan Chavista regime.

For Sopo, who considered himself a moderate Democrat, this newfound interest in socialism would prove to be a bridge too far. "One of the things that pushed me over the edge was [DNC chairman] Tom Perez going out there and saying that AOC is the future of our party," recalled Sopo. "And when I read that, I just thought to myself, 'Well, if she's the future of the party, then I may as well be just a part of the party's past.'" He began writing online articles about socialism, a few of which went viral. The staff on Trump's reelection campaign noticed. He would soon find himself with a job as the director of rapid response for Hispanic media for the campaign. Soon thereafter, Sopo was given responsibility for all Spanish-language advertising.

Most campaign advertising is rote and formulaic, from rat-tat-rat recitals of poll-tested policy positions, to the "bio" ads of candidates pushing their kids on a swing, to the black-and-white motif of negative ads as bits of opposition research flash across the screen. Sopo quickly understood that this approach would not work for his friends and family members. In Miami, the connection the Trump campaign needed to make was personal, signaling that it got younger Cuban voters, the ones the Republican Party was losing. To accomplish this objective, Sopo would sprinkle cultural cues liberally throughout his ads. Four years earlier, Trump's outreach to Florida Hispanics had been limited to the older generation of hardened anti-Castro partisans. It ignored the largest group of voters, those who had come over after 1995. "What we did differently in 2020 is that we held those people," said Sopo, referring to the older core, "and then we shifted the focus to newer arrivals." Trump's advertising deliberately featured spokespeople, slang, and accents familiar to the post-1995 majority.

The Trump campaign first waded into the Hispanic culture wars with an ad targeting left-wing activists for boycotting Goya Foods after the company's CEO had praised Trump. Narrating the ad was Susana Pérez, a well-known Cuban actress popular with the younger set. The ad's choice of words reflected a cultural literacy uncommon in political Spanish-language advertising, which usually offer warmed-over Spanish translations of ads made for an English-speaking audience. Instead of saying that Goya was being "canceled" by the left, the ad instead called it an *acto de repudio*—or act of repudiation—a term from communist Cuba referring to the orchestrated intimidation of political opponents by the regime.

While Pérez's support for Trump was loaded with generational significance, the reaction to it also offered a lesson about the politics of nationality. While in Cuba, Pérez had said complimentary things about the Castro regime, which she was forced to do as a high-profile figure.

Local Democrats trotted out a spokesperson to attack Pérez for these transgressions, but they erred in sending a Colombian, not a Cuban—a faux pas that overshadowed the Democrats' message. Florida's electorate is 7.2 percent Cuban American—and 18 percent non-Cuban Hispanic, with large contingents of Puerto Ricans, Colombians, and Dominicans. In Miami-Dade County, fully half of the county's Hispanic population is non-Cuban. For Sopo, cultural competency meant a deep knowledge of each nationality group, with specific appeals to each.

In early October, the Trump campaign released an ad titled "Castrochavismo." Using a term popularized by former Colombian president Álvaro Uribe, the ad linked the choice in the election to the fight against socialism in Latin America, starting with the endorsement of Biden by Gustavo Petro, a Colombian socialist and former member of the FARC guerrilla movement. Petro was narrowly elected Colombia's president in 2022, but underscoring his unpopularity among Colombian Americans, he received less than 20 percent of the U.S. overseas vote. Colombia did not have a socialist leader before 2022—but fear of the left-wing FARC spurred many Colombians to leave for the U.S. In their home country, these immigrants were mostly on the right. But in America, they voted for the party of the left. The "Castrochavismo" ad highlighted this disconnect, tying together Petro's endorsement, Biden's votes in the 1980s against the anti-communist Contras in Nicaragua, and footage of a friendly Biden handshake with Venezuela's Nicolás Maduro.

Sopo's final ad was his most recognizable. It would not address one nationality, but tied all of them together in a festive explosion of vibrant colors and salsa music. A pro-Trump salsa band played festive Cuban music, known as *timba*, as people danced and waved American flags alongside those of different Latin American countries. The creative inspiration for the ad had come from the Disney film *Coco*, which Sopo felt perfectly captured Latino culture for an American audience.

On Election Day 2020, Republican margins among Cuban Americans in South Florida had been restored to something approaching Reagan-era levels. Trump won by two to one throughout suburban Hialeah, the heart of Miami-Dade's Cuban community, with swings of 30 points or more. The pre-election FIU poll hinted at the demographic makeup of the shift:

it was not an older anti-Castro base coming home, but a breakthrough among younger Cubans and new arrivals—exactly those targeted by the Trump campaign. Instead of losing post-1995 immigrants by 22 points as in 2016, Trump won them by 31 points. Partisan allegiances among the most recent arrivals were even further to the right, with 76 percent identifying as Republicans. This is not at all how Democrats had expected things would work out when Obama pursued a policy of rapprochement toward Cuba, allowing these newer arrivals free travel back and forth to see their families. Instead, cynicism grew as the Obama policy failed to deliver the economic transformation promised on the island. The Trump administration reversed much of the Obama Cuba policy, but took care not to disrupt the parts of it that allowed for family travel and financial remittances to Cuba.

Trump also made breakthroughs in other parts of the Latin American diaspora in South Florida. The most Colombian-heavy precincts in Kendall trended between 25 and 30 points toward Trump. In Doral, home to a Trump golf course and so many Venezuelans it earned the nickname *Doralzuela,* the swing was an even more impressive 50 points. Colombian and Venezuelan voters started off more skeptical of Trump than Cubans, casting two-thirds of their ballots for Hillary Clinton in 2016. By 2020, the non-Cuban Hispanic vote in Miami was tied. There was a surge in support for Trump and Republicans across all of the Hispanic nationality groups in Florida, with an especially strong swing in the Cuban, Colombian, and Venezuelan communities, with socialism at the forefront.

BORICUA BREAKTHROUGH

Puerto Ricans are the second largest group among Hispanics in Florida, one which Democrats hoped would counter Republican strength among Cuban Americans. The Sunshine State's perennial status as a swing state has made winning over the state's diverse Hispanic communities a crucial task for strategists in both parties nationally. And no community was adding numbers at a faster clip than Puerto Ricans, who migrated to the Orlando area, on either side of the line between Orange and Osceola Counties. While the Cuban Adjustment Act grants immigrants from the

Figure 8.1: 2016–20 Precinct-Level to Trump, Miami-Dade County

Source: Voting and Election Science Team

island an unusually fast track to citizenship and voting, Puerto Ricans are U.S. citizens who can vote the minute they settle on the mainland.

Historically, Puerto Ricans who migrated to the U.S. mainland lived in New York City. They were one of the five great ethnic groups profiled by Nathan Glazer and Daniel Patrick Moynihan in *Beyond the Melting Pot* in 1963, with the population of Puerto Ricans in New York reaching close to one million by 1980. But in the next forty years, New York's Puerto Rican population would hardly grow, reaching a total of 1,080,631 in 2018. All of the Puerto Rican migration went elsewhere, mostly to Florida. Numbering just 98,780 in 1980, the community surpassed New York City's in 2018 with 1,171,637 people. Most of this growth has happened since the turn of the millennium.

Those looking for hints at how Puerto Ricans in Florida might behave politically looked naturally to their voting patterns in Gotham. Living in some of the poorest neighborhoods of the city, Puerto Ricans and their Dominican neighbors rivaled Black voters in their loyalty to the Democratic Party. The political context in which they settled governed their choice of party: New York City was a place where politics predominantly took place in the Democratic primary. In this, the Puerto Ricans of New York City were not unlike the Mexican Americans of California or the Chinese Americans of the San Francisco Bay Area, with lopsided support for Democrats a function of settlement in deep blue states and cities. By dint of the fact that these new-arrival migrants did not choose the big city, Florida's Puerto Rican community would be different. That the Sunshine State also attracted its share of Puerto Rican movers from New York, driven away by high taxes and high crime, was testament to this fact.

Also overlooked is the politics of Puerto Rico itself. "The dirty little secret is that Puerto Rico, if it were a state, would be a red state—red to purplish red," says Jorge Bonilla, a Hispanic media strategist who is Puerto Rican and lives in Osceola County. Bonilla describes the island's politics as "socially conservative and fiscally reckless," a reference to the island's fiscal crisis in the mid-2010s. This is a recurring theme in the politics of Latin America, says Giancarlo Sopo, where politics has been a dialectic between two main ideologies: nationalism and social democracy. Absent from the debate were free markets or limited government, the cornerstones of pre-Trump Republican economics.

In Puerto Rico proper, politicians often align with one of the two major U.S. parties, and Republican politicians have won their fair share of elections, including current resident commissioner Jenniffer González-Colón and former governor Luis Fortuño. Statehood for Puerto Rico has appeared as a plank in the Republican Party platform.

Despite the evenly divided politics on the island, Orlando's Puerto Ricans have leaned Democratic in American elections—not unlike Colombians, who voted for right-populists back home but for Democrats in the new country. These historic patterns made the mass migration sparked by Hurricane Maria in 2017 look like a gift for Florida Democrats. Progressive nonprofits sprung into action to register them to vote. In the next election, the 2018 midterms, the Democrats would be in for a surprise. It was Republicans, not Democrats, who gained most of these new voters.

The Republican candidate for Senate in that election was then-governor Rick Scott, considered an underdog to incumbent Democrat Bill Nelson in a Democratic year. Scott had made Puerto Rico recovery a central focus, shuttling back and forth to the island to aid in relief efforts and sending first responders and equipment in large quantities. His staff set up a welcome center for Puerto Rican arrivals at the Orlando airport. The state waived occupational licensing requirements so that a doctor or nurse certified in Puerto Rico could immediately find work in Florida. Puerto Rican natives in the area seemed to notice. Bonilla calculated that nearly all of Scott's razor-thin victory margin of 10,033 votes came from an overperformance of 9,800 votes in the Hispanic precincts in Orange and Osceola Counties.

In 2020, the Trump campaign was ready with its own set of tailored advertisements and colorful local references for the Boricuas—shorthand for Puerto Ricans. Radio ads were aired in the distinctive accents of younger arrivals, and TV ads took aim at Biden's old Senate votes against Puerto Rican interests. It appeared to work: Osceola, the county with the highest concentration of Puerto Ricans in the state, saw a 10-point swing toward Trump, cutting the county's Democrats' margin to 13 points. In his landslide reelection as Florida governor in 2022, Ron

DeSantis won Osceola County outright. Heavily Puerto Rican neighborhoods like Buena Ventura Lakes led the shift. There, the Republican share has gone from 18 percent for Trump in 2016, to 28 percent for Rick Scott and 22 percent for DeSantis in 2018, to 30 percent for Trump in 2020, to 41 percent for DeSantis in 2022—a doubling of the Republican vote. All of this added up to a Republican victory among Florida's Hispanic voters. The VoteCast exit poll showed DeSantis winning Hispanics by a 13-point margin and drawing even among Puerto Ricans. Even as he gained ground, Trump lost Florida Hispanics by nine points and Puerto Ricans by 32 points. And if you knew where to look, you could see signs of an impending shift, with detailed voter registration data showing the Hispanic shift in Florida and other states gathering steam in 2019 and 2020. In states with significant Hispanic populations where voters also register by party, there was a steady upward trend in the share of Hispanic voters registering Republican, a trend that accelerated in mid-2019, notably in Florida and Arizona. Heading into the 2020 election and continuing after it, Republicans made up a majority of new Hispanic registrants in Florida on a two-party basis, up from a base of 35 percent following the 2016 election.

Perhaps no county in America better represents the potential of this populist realignment than Osceola, where almost nine in ten voters belong to the multiracial populist coalition, the white working class and nonwhites. The county has a Hispanic plurality, roughly matching its population of working-class whites. Just one in ten voters are white with a college degree, one of the most notable underrepresentations of this group in a diverse suburban county in the country. It's a place where people come to achieve the American dream, with the nearby Disney and Universal complexes serving as magnets for jobs. Working- and middle-class visitors to Disney tend to stay in Osceola, and the streets at night have a touch of Las Vegas to them, from the carnival-style Old Town amusement park on the Irlo Bronson Memorial Highway to the Machine Gun America across the street.

Puerto Ricans historically leaned Democratic, and as a U.S. territory, people there had no reason to be concerned about a socialist takeover, as was true for Cubans, Venezuelans, and Colombians. But they, too, moved

Figure 8.2: Hispanic GOP Registration Surged Heading into 2020

Two-way Republican share of new voter registrations in selected states with party registration, 2016–2022

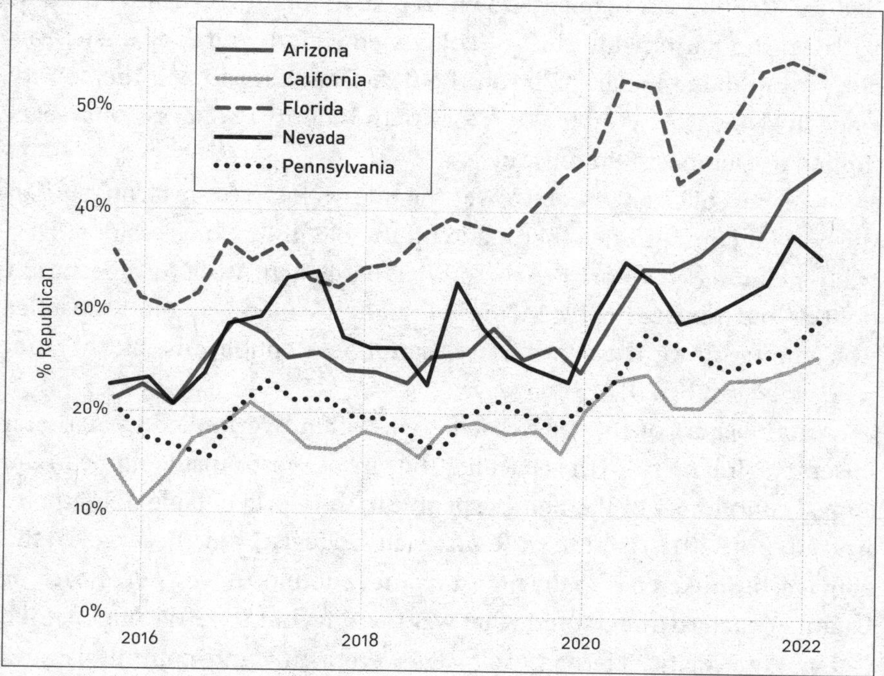

Source: L2 National Voter File

right, just like Hispanic voters in diverse communities across the country. More than the Cuban American shift right, it is the realignment of Orlando's Puerto Ricans that has taken Florida off the table for Democrats for the foreseeable future.

ASIAN AMERICA

Orange County, California, seemed to have been lost to the Republican Party for good.

Postwar, Orange County was synonymous with rock-ribbed conservatism, a land of aerospace industry workers and Okie transplants. The county gave Barry Goldwater a solid majority of its votes in 1964 and two years later launched Ronald Reagan to the California governorship, and then the presidency. By 2012, urban growth and diversity had whittled the Republican majority down to just six points for Mitt Romney. In 2016, the nationwide shift of college-educated whites against Donald Trump made Hillary Clinton the first Democrat to win the county since the New Deal. And in 2018, four of the county's congressional seats flipped to Democrats in unison.

In no part of Orange County was the tide against Trump stronger than the coastal communities that made up the old 48th Congressional District, including Newport Beach and Laguna Beach. With his libertarian politics and surfing hobby, incumbent congressman Dana Rohrabacher was a better fit for the community than most Republicans. But he, too, was wiped out by 2018's blue wave.

Another part of the 48th district was often overlooked by national observers. Inland from the coast lies the city of Westminster, home to the largest community of Vietnamese people in the world outside of Vietnam. And after the 2018 election, as Republican strategist Sam Oh surveyed the damage, he looked not to the high-income redoubts of Newport Beach or Laguna Beach to understand what went wrong, but to Little Saigon. Like Cuban Americans, Vietnamese exiles were firmly anti-communist and had found a home in the Republican Party following their arrival in the United States in the 1970s. Yet, like Cuban Americans, the Vietnamese vote was changing, with a younger generation more open to supporting Democrats.

Oh is the son of first-generation Korean immigrants to Philadelphia. He worked on Republican campaigns on both sides of the country, but quickly developed a taste for the kind of multiracial coalition building needed to win in Southern California. Orange County became his focus. Surveying the damage of the 2018 wave, he found a Republican machinery crippled by its lack of outreach to small-dollar donors or to minorities and independents. In the 48th, Oh calculated that Republicans had lost the independent voter by a staggering 50 points.

Running for Republicans in the 48th in 2020 was another second-generation Korean American, Michelle Steel. Oh signed on as her campaign consultant. While the loss of wealthy whites seemed like a foregone conclusion, the Vietnamese vote was not. Oh thought that if he could fix the party's problems in Little Saigon, Steel could win back a seat all but written off by the party in Washington, D.C. They had a steep hill to climb: Hillary Clinton had swept most of the precincts in Little Saigon with more than 60 percent of the vote.

Oh sent sixteen separate Vietnamese-language mailers into the community, followed up by continuous phone banking and text messaging in Vietnamese. The California voter file, with its detailed data on voters' language preferences, made this kind of targeting possible. Oh could tailor Steel's message for an older generation of exiles, with a different set of messages going to their American-born children. He intuited that while the older generation may have started out more Republican, they were more malleable, apt to switch from election to election. This was a dynamic he recognized in his own immigrant family. "There are people like myself—I grew up in Philly, English is my first language, I speak Korean—but to mix me in with someone like my parents would be a huge mistake, because I'm much more partisan than my parents would be," he explained. Data from the California voter file shows a large split by language preference in the community. Among Vietnamese voters whose primary language is Vietnamese, Republicans led Democrats in party registration by a more than two-to-one margin. These voters also tended to turn out less, with the upside for Republicans who could bring them out. Among the English-dominant Vietnamese, Democrats held a narrow advantage.

Table 8.1: Vietnamese Speakers Vote Republican

Party registration among Vietnamese in Orange County, CA, by language preference

	Republican	Democrat	Independent & Other
Vietnamese total	39,423	34,699	37,143
English preference	22,925	28,044	27,651
Vietnamese preference	16,316	6,498	9,272

Source: L2 national voter file

That summer, Oh started to notice comments about China coming up with increasing frequency in his Vietnamese-language phone banks. There was no love lost for China and its Communist Party rulers in Little Saigon, whom residents blamed for the loss of their homeland. And now the issue of China was more prominent than ever thanks to its role in the COVID-19 pandemic. Voters on the other end of the line voiced support for Trump's more confrontational approach to China, and wanted to know where Steel stood.

Oh also managed the campaign for Young Kim, a Korean American thought to be even more of a long shot in the nearby 39th district than Steel was in the 48th. Encompassing Buena Park, Fullerton, and Yorba Linda, the 39th was a majority-minority district, with a population that was 33 percent Hispanic and 33 percent Asian American. Kim's race attracted almost no help from national Republicans, who spent just $16,117 on her behalf.

After all the votes were counted, among the biggest surprises were the results out of Orange County. Steel won by 8,376 votes and Kim by 4,109, retaking two districts thought to be demographically unreachable for Republicans. Little Saigon had swung more decisively toward Trump than virtually any urban neighborhood in the country save for the Hasidic Jewish precincts of Williamsburg, Brooklyn. A 60–40 deficit in Little Saigon had turned into a 60–40 advantage for Trump—and Steel had performed even better.

Much of the post-election focus on Trump's surprising gains in nonwhite communities dissipated as the narrative shifted to his attempt to overturn the election results. Though California was such a shade of midnight blue that the election was not challenged there, the state was a poster child of all that Trump's allies said was wrong about the 2020 vote count. Nearly all of its ballots were cast by mail, which took weeks to fully count. Ballot harvesting—campaign workers collecting voters' absentee ballots—was commonplace. While widespread mail voting was new throughout the country in 2020, it was not new in California, where upward of two in three votes in past elections had been cast absentee. Both parties in the Golden State were used to competing aggressively for absentee voters, including elaborate ballot harvesting operations on both sides.

After 2020, many Republican voters followed Trump's lead and eschewed voting by mail. Oh promoted it extensively and considered the pandemic rules making it easier to vote by mail a secret weapon in Steel's victory, having mobilized an overlooked working-class minority community for Trump and the other Republicans on the ballot. "I was constantly fixated on who I could find that hasn't heard from anyone except for us," Oh recalled. "Some of these people had no history of ever voting, and we wanted to live or die by the fact that we could turn these people out, because the California voting system had changed. The hurdle for an immigrant voter was at an all-time low. The fact that you didn't have to put a stamp on a mail ballot to actually get it back to the registrar of voters—knowing all that helped us touch people who had never voted before."

Republicans' unwillingness to embrace new voting alternatives was also ignorant of the voter coalition that sent Trump to 1600 Pennsylvania Avenue in the first place. That coalition relied less on wealthier white voters, who were certain to vote in every election, and more on non-college-educated voters, who voted more sporadically. The idea that higher turnout helped Democrats, one that Trump traded on, was no longer axiomatic. The electorate expanded from 136 million to 158 million from 2016 to 2020. Many of those new votes would come from the multiracial populist coalition. Among new 2020 voters, Trump held his own: the Pew Research Center estimated that Trump only lost voters who hadn't voted in 2016 or 2018 by two points, less than his margin of defeat nationally. And specifically, his gains *among nonwhites* came disproportionately from new voters. By definition, new voters had no loyalty to either party, and this blank slate gave Republicans an opportunity to close the gap in nonwhite communities. Democratic super-analyst David Shor has been trying to get the message through to Democrats who think that all will be well if only they can turn out enough voters. "New voters are, in relative terms, a positive force for Democrats among white people and a negative force for nonwhite people," Shor says. "Working-class nonwhite voters really do not agree with us on a very meaningful set of things. If Democrats ignore that, they will vote for someone else. It's not like the old African American super voters. These people have very weak ties to the Democratic Party and it won't take much to turn them off."

Shor's warning would play out in the turnout surge in Little Saigon, where Oh estimates the electorate doubled from 2018, and where voters swung by 40 points toward Trump. A postmortem by the Democratic firm Equis Labs found that the strongest gains in Trump's job-approval rating among Hispanics between 2019 and 2020 happened among the lowest-turnout voters. We also see this in voter file data showing a sharp rise in Republican registration among new Hispanic voters in Florida and other states starting after the 2016 election. In Texas, our surveys have found a reverse age gap among Hispanics, where voters over the age of sixty-five remain the most loyally Democratic, while younger baby boomers, Gen Xers, and even millennials express more openness toward Republicans. Among Black voters, relative turnout increased the most from 2016 among young Black men, age eighteen to forty-four. Their support for Trump approached 20 percent, about double that of the Black community as a whole, and nearly triple that of the oldest Black voters who came of age in the civil rights era. The new voter coalitions Trump brought about mean that high-turnout elections don't necessarily hurt Republicans, and they might even help. This trend confounds years of work and hundreds of millions of dollars invested by progressive advocacy organizations in voter registration efforts designed to mint millions of automatic Democrats. Michelle Obama spearheaded a "When We All Vote" campaign that had this premise at its core. In 2020, it turned out that "when we all vote," new voters defy the assumptions of political prognosticators: Michelle Steel and Young Kim overcame the leftward shift of wealthy Orange County whites to win, and Donald Trump was nearly reelected. And running under newly redrawn district lines in 2022, both Steel and Kim won reelection in Biden-voting districts.

No region in the country is more stereotypically Democratic than Northern California, anchored by the San Francisco Bay Area. It, too, has a Little Saigon, based in San Jose, that shifted just as strongly to the right as its counterpart to the south. But in Northern California, the Chinese are the largest subgroup of Asian voters. Despite the rhetoric surrounding China during the campaign, they moved in a more Republican direction, too, albeit by less than the Vietnamese. Within the city of San Francisco, Chinese population centers like the Sunset District and the city's southern tier saw Trump cut into the normal Democratic margin by around ten points.

In San Francisco, Asian Americans are the main counterweight to the far left in city politics, a fact that might surprise some progressives who think that opposition to their ideas are mainly rooted in "whiteness." This was on vivid display in the February 2022 recalls of three city left-wing school board members. Citywide, the recalls succeeded with at least 68 percent of the vote. In Asian American precincts, the recall vote was upward of 80 percent. At issue in the election were the lengthy pandemic school closures, and the school board's attempts to end merit-based admissions at the city's elite Lowell High School, where Asian students were the majority of the student body. During these school closures, the board prioritized the renaming of almost fifty city schools—including one named after the great emancipator Abraham Lincoln—in the name of racial "equity." In the year following the end of merit-based admissions at Lowell, the percentage of the student body getting Ds and Fs skyrocketed from less than 8 percent to 25 percent. Following the school board recalls, random lottery admissions were reversed and merit-based admissions restored. But San Francisco–style education politics would prove harder to uproot elsewhere. In Fairfax County, Virginia, the school board also moved to water down merit-based admissions to Thomas Jefferson High School for Science and Technology, ranked the top public high school in the country (a parent lawsuit against the change is still pending at this writing). In both cases, the proponents of these changes put forth a disingenuous diversity argument. A more random admissions process might result in the admission of more African American and Hispanic students, but also of more white students—and fewer Asian students of color. Most important, it would degrade the high academic standards that made these schools engines of upward mobility, helping first-generation immigrants make the leap from poverty to prosperity in a generation.

Asian voters were also instrumental in San Francisco's turn away from progressive crime policy. Four months after the school board recalls, voters also threw out the progressive district attorney Chesa Boudin by a margin of 55 to 45 percent. A precinct's Asian American population was the strongest predictor of support for the recall, pointing to a 70 percent–

plus Asian vote against Boudin. Asian American neighborhoods in San Francisco are hardly breaking out the MAGA flags. Trump barely broke 20 percent anywhere in the city, though the places that he did tended to have more Asian Americans. In places like San Francisco with no conservative base to speak of, Asian American voters are applying a pragmatic, commonsense brake on the worst excesses of the progressive left. This is often the case in Asian city neighborhoods from coast-to-coast. In the Queens-based 6th Congressional District, represented by Democrat Grace Meng, Republican gubernatorial candidate Lee Zeldin came within 4 points of victory in a district Biden carried two years earlier by 25 points.

Taken as a whole, the Asian American electorate nationwide might not seem a likely candidate for inclusion in a multiracial populist coalition. A majority of Asian American voters are college-educated and the population is concentrated in left-leaning states and metropolitan areas, California especially, which is home to 36 percent of the country's Asian American vote. Outside of the Little Saigons, Asian voting patterns are quite Democratic to start with, and more reflective of the leftward trends among white college-educated professionals. The Asian American vote is as yet small—4 percent—with college-educated Asian voters making up 2 percent of the country. But it is the fastest growing in the electorate, outpacing Hispanics.

Despite this concentration of college-educated voters in leftward-trending metropolitan areas, Asian Americans nationally appeared to trend toward Trump in 2020. Though not closely contested, the Asian American plurality in Hawaii moved significantly in Trump's direction, with parts of Honolulu shifting thirty points or more. For the first time, an education gap opened up: non-college Asian voters trended Republican and those with college degrees held steady. These numbers are borne out in the precinct data from immigrant-heavy neighborhoods like Little Saigon, the Sunset District, and Flushing in Queens.

But as they revel in their gains in the working-class precincts of Little Saigon, Hmong Village, or Honolulu, Republicans should work equally hard to win over the Asian American college graduate. And they have just the issue to do it: a progressive "equity" agenda in education that explicitly discriminates against Asian students. This is the central issue in the attacks on Lowell and Thomas Jefferson High Schools. It is also the issue in the Supreme Court case about admissions at Harvard. And it's why many colleges and universities are working to remove the SAT as a criterion of admission, so they can have more discretion to turn down high-scoring Asian students who make up, in their view, an uncomfortably high percentage of the student body. The growth of college graduates and their geographic compartmentalization from the rest of the country made it possible for the Democratic Party to openly champion the progressive values of high-achieving graduates, but Asian Americans are being excluded from this new progressive order.

So often, policies advanced by progressives in the name of marginalized minorities have caused factional strife instead, from the war on merit in education to defunding the police. Often, these policies make the underlying problems that they purport to solve even worse. Relaxing grading standards in schools doesn't help underserved communities who need a quality education to overcome economic barriers. Decreasing the police presence doesn't protect Black communities, but makes it more likely that they and others will be victims of crime. Using the terms "Latinx" or "Latine" does nothing tangible at all for Hispanics, except signal inattentiveness to the tangible quality of life issues Hispanics care about. Race-conscious policies might make sense as a Democratic campaigning strategy if members of racial and ethnic minorities thought of themselves first and foremost as members of identity groups, rather than as normal citizens who want safer streets, better schools, and more job opportunities. Because Democrats have lost sight of the things that Americans across racial lines share in common, they've lost precious ground among the nonwhite voters once considered the indispensable core of their base.

9.

REALIGNMENT ON THE RIO GRANDE

Looked at in statistical terms only, the Rio Grande Valley at the southern tip of Texas is a land of outliers: the most Hispanic region in the country, the poorest and, until recently, one of the most Democratic. In 2020, the area made headlines for its sudden Republican shift. Just twenty-eight counties in the United States swung 15 points or more toward Donald Trump from 2016 to 2020. All but seven were in Texas, mostly along the Rio Grande River, where the vast majority of the population is Hispanic. Many of the others were heavily Hispanic, most notably Miami-Dade County in Florida, and a handful of counties close to the border in Arizona and California. A region that was once solidly Democratic by margins of two to one or more was now becoming something close to competitive.

Along the Rio Grande, every large urban county swung to Trump by 20 points or more. Outside the region's urban centers—McAllen, Brownsville, and Harlingen, the shift was about double that: 55 points in Starr County and 39 points in Zapata County just up the river, a county that Trump became the first Republican to win since Warren G. Harding in 1920. Just like the Upper Midwest in 2016, rural counties that had previously bucked the Republican trend suddenly fell into place, with the difference this time being that the counties were nearly all Hispanic rather than nearly all white. Competitive two-party politics had now come to the Rio Grande Valley. Heading into the 2022 midterms, Republicans were eager to capitalize, with designs on all three of the region's congressional seats and a number of local offices.

Figure 9.1: The Rio Grande Valley's Red Shift

Precinct-level swing to Trump in the Rio Grande Valley, 2016–2020

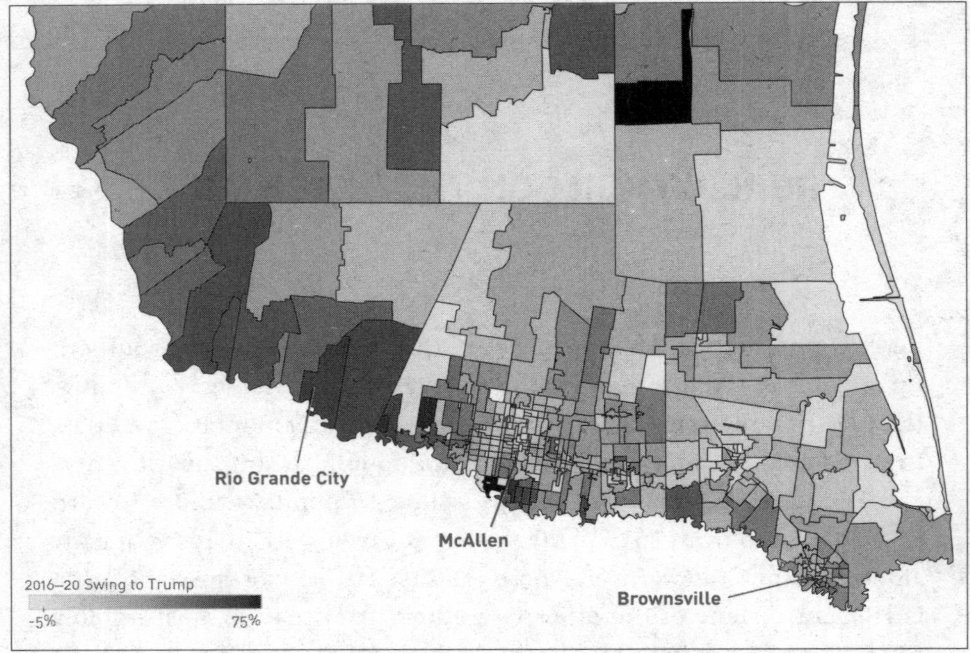

Source: Voting and Election Science Team

For more than a year, I pored over South Texas precinct data in search of answers. The data itself was contradictory. Voter file and survey data revealed an existing Hispanic Republican base in Texas, one that was higher-income, suburban, male, married, between the ages of forty-five and sixty-four. Except for the fact that Hispanic seniors remained staunchly loyal to the Democratic Party, and leaving aside ethnicity itself, this was the demographic profile you'd expect of the more established Republican voter of 2012, not the kind you saw materialize almost out of thin air in 2020. Outside some pockets in urban McAllen, there was virtually no Republican base in the Valley to speak of. Republicans were vilified as the party of the white person and of the rich, and, in some counties, barely more than a dozen people showed up to vote in Republican primaries. The South Texas shift in 2020 came from the kind of Hispanic voter that had passed over the Republican Party previously: lower-income, younger and, according to some Democratic postmortems, more female. I came to the Valley toward the end of the 2022 election season in search of answers that data alone couldn't provide.

The Rio Grande Valley has long been a distinctive place. This has fed negative stereotypes of the region as a poverty-stricken backwater resembling Mexico more than it does the United States, overrun by illegal immigration and the drugs and crime that come with it. An old WPA guide from the mid-twentieth century paints a picture of a border region that stood apart from the country that was its home:

> Mexicans here cling to the customs of their homeland across the river. One- and two-room *jacales* made of willow branches, daubed with mud or thatch, make rooms for the humbler folk; milk goats, dogs and cats, chickens and children swarm over these *casitas*. The border in those days was a porous thing, with no patrolling or border stations to speak of; and the Valley was kind of a border zone between the underdeveloped Mexican economy and the advanced economy of the United States.

In the colonias on the outskirts of the major cities, places settled by previous generations of cross-border migrants, you will find outward signs of economic destitution, in the modest cinder-block homes or oftentimes more ramshackle forms of construction. It is here that the region bears more of a resemblance to underdeveloped Latin America than to the United States, with the only English-language signs to be found on the front of government buildings. Many of the residents lack legal status, though their children born in the U.S. may have it. The illegal population lives the entirety of their lives in a corridor bordered by the Rio Grande River to the south and a series of Border Patrol checkpoints fifty miles to the north. These are often referred to as "the true border wall," one that serves to cordon the porous border region off from the rest of the United States.

A few minutes away from the colonias, however, are scenes of Middle American suburban normalcy, with spacious homes, big-box stores, and luxury-car dealerships. Many of the customers for these establishments come from across the border: retail tourism from Mexico makes up between 30 to 40 percent of the region's retail sales. Between 2019 and 2021, few metropolitan areas in the country saw faster income growth than the McAllen and Brownsville metros, where the large majority of the Rio Grande Valley population lives. And while the average income is the lowest in the country, people here are quick to note that the cost of living is, too. One can't help but be struck by the varied landscape in the Valley, part American suburbia, part Latin American, and part Western frontier. No place better embodies this Texas frontier archetype than my first stop, Rio Grande City, the seat of Starr County.

BATTLEGROUND: STARR COUNTY

Politically, Starr County is one of the most distinctive counties in America. In the 1996 presidential election, it ranked as the most Democratic in the country. Through the Republican landslides of 1972 and 1984, when the urban counties in the Rio Grande voted for Republican presidents, Starr remained solidly Democratic. And it remained so well into the last decade: Barack Obama got 86 percent of the vote here in 2012 and Hillary Clinton got 79 percent in 2016. Among those casting a straight-ticket ballot in 2016, 82 percent voted Democratic and just 16 percent voted Republican.

In 2020, the Democratic margin in Starr County collapsed to just five points, a hair more Democratic than the country. To put this in perspective, a shift of a similar magnitude in Brooklyn in the next election would place Republicans on a level footing with Democrats. If anything, the previous Democratic margins in general elections in Starr County understated their dominance of local politics. In 2018, just fifteen people voted in the Republican primary in a county with more than thirty thousand registered voters. This is a place where one did not have to think of one's party affiliation: one simply was a Democrat.

In the twentieth century, one-party rule along the border was enforced by political machines, none more formidable than that led by Archie Parr of Duval County. The "Duke of Duval" consolidated his power in a fateful

1906 sheriff's race that saw a judge sent to monitor the election murdered in his sleep, armed gangs occupying the Rio Grande City courthouse, and the Republican candidate gunned down in a bar on Main Street.

Parr's son, George, inherited his father's mantle, playing a pivotal role in the famous 1948 Democratic Senate primary between Lyndon B. Johnson and Coke Stevenson. Johnson trailed Stevenson in the initial runoff count by the thinnest of margins. Then, 202 ballots suddenly appeared in Box 13 in nearby Jim Wells County, the names in the pollbook signed in alphabetical order in the same ink and handwriting. Late in his life, election judge Luis Salas would admit to fabricating the votes that sent Johnson to the Senate—and eventually, the White House. "We had the law to ourselves there," Salas said. "We had iron control. If a man was opposed to us, we'd put him out of business. Parr was the Godfather. He had life or death control. We could tell any election judge: 'Give us 50 percent of the vote, the other guy 20 percent.' We had it made in every election."

George Parr died by his own hand in 1975, but the South Texas political machine lived on. When Ross Barrera, a retired army colonel, took on the job of resurrecting the local Republican Party in 2017, he was laboring against a long history of one-party rule, not to mention the social stigma attached to being a Republican. Democrats had won by large margins throughout the Valley, but at least in urban centers like Hidalgo County, home of McAllen, there had been some semblance of a Republican organization. In Starr County, by contrast, practically no one bothered to cast a Republican ballot in the primary, because hardly any Republicans ever bothered to run for local office. That a high-profile governor's race or a presidential race was on the ballot didn't matter. The local offices are what the residents of Rio Grande City really cared about, as I gathered quickly from the campaign signs on my drive into town. There were signs for school board, county judge, county attorney, and state representative plastered on every available surface—and comparatively fewer for gubernatorial candidates Greg Abbott and Beto O'Rourke, or even Henry Cuellar, the region's nine-term House representative.

To the extent that people in Rio Grande City debated the parties or national politics, they were rooted in what Barrera calls "our own form of racism." If you said you were a Republican, you were summarily dismissed as a toady for "the party of white people, the party of the rich." That was typically the end of the discussion.

And so, in October 2020, when a seventy car and truck convoy with Trump flags journeyed from Roma fifteen miles up the road to Rio Grande City, it was a display of Republican support unlike any the county's residents had ever seen. Stunned onlookers came out from their homes to watch. To Barrera's surprise, many started applauding. The first step to establishing a viable party was simply one of waving the flag.

On Election Day, Trump got 47 percent of the vote in Starr County, nearly tripling his support from four years earlier. Barrera himself put up a strong fight for the Rio Grande City mayor's office. The existence of Republicans in the county was now undeniable. Next came the task of organizing a slate of candidates for the 2022 midterm elections.

The job was made easier when State Representative Ryan Guillen of Rio Grande City switched parties from the Democrats to the Republicans in 2021. In the 2022 primary, Guillen single-handedly expanded the Republican electorate in Starr County from fifteen people four years earlier to the 1,402 who voted in his 2022 primary contest, the highest number of ballots cast on the Republican side for any office in the county.

With the primary approaching, Barrera was bombarded with questions about how voting in the Republican primary worked, previously a rarity for the local population. Could one vote for Guillen in the Republican primary and also for their favorite Democrat in the other primary? The answer was a straightforward no: one had to choose one party or the other, as it is in most places throughout the country with partisan primaries. The Democratic primary voting norm was so automatic that Alberto, a friend of Barrera's doing work on his property that day, told me that in a previous primary an election officer simply handed him a Democratic ballot without asking. When he told her he wanted a Republican one instead, the poll worker simply told him no.

I asked Barrera about the plethora of signs for the local school board races. At this he grew animated, rising out of his chair and sketching it out at the whiteboard for me like a head coach. Yes, there were two political parties now in Rio Grande City, drawing two circles. But this wasn't what mattered to local citizens. Instead, the power lay in *the factions*, rival political machines guiding voters in the nonpartisan races for school board and other local offices. And when candidates ran with party labels attached, the factions could and did endorse across party lines. The factions are where the real political power in Rio Grande City lay.

Barrera and I drove over to the county courthouse, where early voting was underway. The two rival camps ringed the courthouse, each with their own tent, with volunteers cooking up chicken dishes for voters. The camp a voter passed through signaled their loyalty. When a voter thought to be loyal to one camp passed through a rival's, colorful arguments ensued. (There were reports of chicken pieces flying, but I didn't witness any.) All of this was overseen by what are known here as *politiqueras*, the precinct workers hired to deliver votes for the machine.

School board races carry more weight with voters in South Texas than they do practically anywhere else, especially in poorer communities. The reasons have little to do with education policy and a lot to do with something more basic: jobs. Urban centers like McAllen have substantially diversified their economy from the predominantly agricultural one of the

Signs for faction-endorsed candidates outside Rio Grande City

past. But within this new service-based economy, local government work makes up a large share of the employment base. One in four workers are employed either in education or government, and the public schools are usually the largest single employer. Outside of the cities, the local job market boils down to agriculture and the school district—and the school jobs are the plums: a non-college graduate can land a position paying $60,000 a year in a place where the median income is below $30,000. Politics dictates who gets these jobs.

This dynamic was explained to me by Oscar Rosa, who ran for state representative from rural Hidalgo County in 2022. Rosa was a third-generation immigrant who grew up working in the fields, who then went on to finish college and start a successful pharmacy business. Rosa's classic American success story was still not the norm for many in the Valley. "There's not many jobs out here other than agriculture—the people who are here illegally are the ones who do those jobs," he explained. "If you can vote, you either work for the school district, or the drainage district, all of the municipal jobs, that's all there is. And if the boss sees you didn't vote, you will get fired."

School board elections are run under the auspices of the independent school districts, with little state or county oversight. When I visited him, Barrera was busy unearthing voting irregularities in the city school board races. The incumbent school board members included a currently serving municipal judge, two city attorneys, and one individual who simultaneously served as police chief and acting city manager. The school superintendent oversaw the counting of early votes in the last election. In Hidalgo County, the machine offers rides to the polls, and using the curbside voting option, the driver can monitor who the voter has voted for. This is an updated version of the absentee ballot fraud that resulted in high-profile indictments of Rio Grande Valley *politiqueras* a decade ago. Even when the machine doesn't know who a given voter has voted for, the voter rolls are rigorously checked for whether or not a job seeker has voted. The school board slates are so well oiled a machine that candidates for state offices will forgo traditional yard signs and door-to-door campaigning, instead paying the school board candidates to turn out voters for them.

Despite the continued influence of machine politics, competitive two-party democracy established a strong foothold in 2022 in the Rio Grande Valley. The Valley elected its first Republican to Congress in 151 years with the special election victory of Mayra Flores in the Brownsville-based 34th district. While she did not win the November election under more Democratic district lines, fellow Republican Monica De La Cruz won her race in the McAllen-based 15th district, outperforming Trump's vote from two years earlier. In places, the Valley's Republican trend ran up against pro-incumbent machine politics of a kind that's disappeared practically everywhere else. Where there were races for open seats, or two incumbents running against each other, Republicans outperformed Trump's numbers from two years earlier. Where incumbents ran against newcomers, the mostly Democratic incumbents retained an advantage. In Starr County, both the Democratic congressman, Henry Cuellar, and the Republican state representative, Ryan Guillen, won with about 70 percent of the vote. Republicans made headway in the other Starr County races, coming within four points of unseating the twenty-four-year incumbent county judge, the equivalent of county executive, and within two points of winning the county attorney's office. And in Rio Grande City, one of the reform candidates for the school board backed by Barrera won—by four votes. Barrera is optimistic about what comes next. "We already have candidates lining up to run in the Republican ticket," he said. "2024 will show that Starr County is no longer a Democrat stronghold."

FROM POVERTY TO PROSPERITY

Between 2014 and 2019, Hispanic incomes in the United States rose by 23 percent, faster than any other racial or ethnic group. In the two years from 2019 to 2021, a period spanning the COVID-19 pandemic, the McAllen metro area saw the fourth-fastest income growth in the country, rising 24.7 percent. The Brownsville-Harlingen metro area next door ranked eighth, at 22.1 percent growth. Many of the other fast-growing metros were in Hispanic-majority regions that resemble the Rio Grande Valley, such as California's Central Valley and the city of El Centro close to the Mexican border. The main South Texas metros rank as among the poorest in the nation, but recent economic advances represent a meaningful closing of the economic gap with the rest of Texas and America. As the 2020 election approached, voters in the Rio Grande Valley had every reason to feel optimistic about recent economic progress.

Javier Villalobos, McAllen's mayor, sees this recent growth as an opportunity to debunk old myths about the region. When we meet in his city hall office, he is eager to stress that McAllen ranks as among the safest cities in America—the third safest in fact. The pandemic, Villalobos believes, sparked an economic reawakening. When the border shut down, international trade continued, but the casual trips back and forth that powered McAllen's retail sector stopped. To the surprise of many, the local economy proved resilient. "We realized we were not dependent on Mexico," Villalobos tells me. "We realized we are self-sufficient like never before, and ever since, our sales taxes keep going up month after month."

The pandemic supply-chain shock has a lot to do with why. In recent years, many of the *maquiladoras*—factories in northern Mexico serving cross-border trade—had relocated to cheaper Asian markets. Pandemic shutdowns and a massive spike in the cost of transpacific shipping caused multinational firms to reconsider, moving their production capacity closer once again to the border. Ground has recently been broken on an expansion of the McAllen-Hidalgo International Bridge to accommodate this new growth.

In 2016, Donald Trump promised huge policy disruption in two areas: trade and immigration. The Rio Grande Valley sat at the nexus of both. As a result, people here were wary: of the economic dislocation of a trade war with Mexico and of a border wall that might disrupt cross-border travel. But as the 2020 election approached, the calamities predicted were nowhere in sight. Trump had successfully negotiated a new U.S.-Mexico-Canada (USMCA) trade agreement, forging strong ties with the left-wing populist Mexican president, Andrés Manuel López Obrador. The migrant influx eased, thanks to an agreement with Mexico to keep asylum seekers on the Mexican side—an action reversed by Joe Biden on the first day of his administration. Those sections of the border wall that have been built outside McAllen haven't proven to be hugely disruptive, mostly built along the side of existing roads, with open gates guarded by the Border Patrol for farm equipment to make its way across.

Villalobos's election was evidence of the region's political shift. Prior to serving on the city council, Villalobos had been the county Republican Party chairman. When he won in May 2021, his victory was hailed by Abbott and national Republicans as a sign of the region's shift to the right.

You won't find Trump-like culture war bombast from Villalobos and other local Republicans. "Here in McAllen, we're concentrating more on the economy, economic development, and that's what resonates with the Hispanic community," Villalobos explains. "Most people are concerned with their immediate family, how they provide for their families, how they put food on the table, more than anything else."

Oscar Rosa, the state House candidate, sees himself as an exemplar of an earlier wave of Valley Republicans. He came of age during Ronald Reagan's presidency, when the reasons for joining the GOP were rooted just as often in one's conservative religious values as they were in economics. Today, Rosa sees a new wave of Republicans. They are younger and hungrier, able to see a way out of the poverty of their parents' and grandparents' generations. Social issues have little to do with their rightward shift. This new wave came to the fore during the fracking boom of the last decade, when young men in the region found good-paying jobs in the oil and gas industry. Explains Rosa:

> The son who's working away at the oil rigs, who's making $150,000 but only keeping $100,000 after taxes, is like, I'm a freaking Republican. I am a Republican. I don't want to pay taxes. Now that you're making money, do you want government assistance? Hell no, I want to keep my job in oil and gas, making a ton of money. I can help my parents, I can help my younger siblings go to college, and I'm a Republican and my wife is a Republican. And it's not even the social issues, it's that I don't want to pay income tax because I'm getting killed. I'm killing myself on the oil rigs, and I'm keeping a small part of my income. That's a different Republican.

For decades, the Democrats won in the Rio Grande Valley as the champion of the impoverished. "'The Democrat is the party of the poor,'" Villalobos recalls being told at the family dinner table. "And I'm like, 'We don't have to be poor.'" For a long time, rising above poverty—rendering obsolete the need for a "party of the poor"—was a distant dream for many in the Valley. But in the last few years, it's become a reality for a younger generation. And this thinking extends to their parents, who don't want to see their children fall into the same trap of intergenerational poverty and government dependence.

Rosa talks of encountering illegal immigrants campaigning door to door. Naturally, they could not vote for him, but what he heard from many of them surprised him. "So, will you vote Republican?" Rosa recalls these conversations. "I can't but my kids are eighteen and I'll tell them to vote Republican because the other guys, the Democrats, just want to keep them on government assistance."

These words echo in the results of a survey of Texas Hispanics I helped conduct for the Texas Latino Conservatives in the summer of 2022. Looking forward to the midterm elections, the survey aimed to provide deeper answers to the realignment of Texas Hispanics in 2020. One question asked what bothered them the most about the Democratic Party of today. As it turned out, the main point of contention was not socialism, not the fact that the Democrats were "woke," not that they were out of step with the community's religious and family values—all of the points most discussed in the media. It was that the Democrats are a party "that supports government welfare handouts for people who don't work." This anti-welfare sentiment was more common in the Rio Grande Valley than among Hispanics elsewhere in the state.

By calling out the Democrats as the party of welfare handouts, Texas Hispanics are not leveling a blanket indictment against safety net programs. One is reminded of this by the storefronts in Rio Grande City doing a brisk business signing people up for government health care benefits, including Medicare, Medicaid, and Obamacare, with some advertising the latter with the signature *O*. Like most middle- and working-class people, residents along the Rio Grande draw a sharp distinction between programs like Social Security and Medicare they've paid into all their

Table 9.1:
Texas Hispanics See Democrats as the Party of Welfare Handouts

Q. I'm now going to read you a list of things some people have said they don't like about today's Democratic Party. Which one of the following things bothers you the most, if any, about the Democratic Party today? That they are a party that . . .

	Overall	South Texas / Rio Grande Valley
Supports government welfare handouts for people who don't work	18%	21%
Supports socialism	14%	13%
Focuses mainly on race and gender issues	12%	11%
Is out of touch	11%	10%
Doesn't support religion or the traditional family	7%	4%
Total Bothered by Democratic Party	**61%**	**59%**

Source: Texas Latino Conservatives' Hispanic Realignment Survey

lives—and are often the only retirement savings or benefits they have—and welfare programs that one can stay on for an extended period in lieu of working. Support for broadly based entitlements and short-term assistance for the jobless, or children and the disabled, coexists with suspicion of those who game the system. This feeling is palpable in the rural border counties, where the informal cash economy is used to augment low-reported incomes that are often used to fraudulently claim benefits. On Facebook, around the time of my visit, a picture was making the rounds of a Tesla parked in front of the food stamp office.

This nuanced thought process was evident in our survey. When we asked how people thought they could best provide for their family, far more people said that they could do so through their own hard work than said they could do so through government benefits. But a healthy percentage, around a third, volunteered that both were important, even though this was not explicitly offered as an option for most survey respondents.

Leslie Sanchez, one of my partners in this research and the author of 2007's *Los Republicanos*, a portrait of Hispanics in America that predicted today's political shift, sees a twofold explanation for these nuanced views of the safety net. The first is that Hispanic families, more than other families, stand ready to catch their own members when they fall. The second stems from a natural suspicion of government rooted in experiences with the rampant corruption that characterized the Latin American countries they arrived from.

"If I went and earned a college degree, my entire family earned that degree, because nobody did anything in a vacuum, and that is distinctly different from a Protestant white kind of Americanized culture, which thinks that you go off at eighteen and you do things for yourself and you become this incredible success," Sanchez explains. She adds that in Latino culture, "the child that does get out of that is beholden to the family, and has a responsibility to pay, not just pay it forward, but pay it back into the family. They pay it back by buying their family their homes, their automobiles, and their health insurance." One also sees it in the $131 billion in remittances Latin America received from abroad in 2021, many from relatives in the United States.

Just like those among my Italian ancestors suspicious of *lo stato ladro*, the thief state, these new Americans have tended to see the government more as predator than benefactor. As Sanchez puts it:

> Many Latinos have experienced or been in a community that has been touched by corruption. They have leaders who failed them for various reasons, and also elected officials who failed them—who failed to help get them their veterans' benefits or Social Security checks or any other benefits they were entitled to. They would also hear stories of other people who were scamming the system and, they felt, denying them the right to get what they earned. This feeling that there's a corrupt system that people take advantage of has been around for decades and most people will know somebody who did that, or went to jail for doing something like that. And a lot of that were echoes of things and the types of corruption they saw in Mexico, or different parts of Central and South America. Two things always came up. One is fear of corruption invading this more respectable, more pristine U.S. system, and the second was

the devaluation of the currency. They feared that banking in the U.S. could one day look like banking in Venezuela or somewhere else, where they would lose their money overnight.

With ingrained fears of financial collapse, people gravitate toward political leaders who will take strong, decisive action to keep them safe. The concept of the honest public servant, the goody-two-shoes grad from the Ivy League or Wellesley reforming the system from within is almost completely foreign to the Hispanic voter. This kind of candidate, one who might send the hearts of wonky fans of *The West Wing* racing, scans as weak to Hispanic voters, who judge them as unable to stand up to the bad people cheating them. Trump's 2020 Spanish-language ads got right to the point: "*Biden es débil*"— Biden is weak. Whatever Trump was, he did not come across as weak, his tough-guy persona an upgrade from generations of country-club Republicans. "They like the way Trump spoke because it was a very simple kind of brutish language that was confrontational but [one] they could understand and that they appreciated," explains Sanchez. "And not like the kinds of softer, genteel mannerisms of Republican politics."

Hispanics have rallied to political leaders they feel will offer them protection, which partly explains the dominance of machine politics in the Valley. These voters are not just trying to protect themselves but their children. And now that they have tasted prosperity, there's a stronger sense of hope for the next generation, and a desire to leave the poverty of the past behind. "I'm fifty-five, and some people my age will say it's too late for me, but I have a kid who's twenty-two, twenty-three, and the American dream can't be lost on him," says Oscar Rosa. "I need him to have a good education, I need him to start his own company, I need him to break that cycle of poverty." The longer that one's family is in the country, the more likely one is to cultivate the habits and experiences that pave a path to success. "It's not that I'm smarter," Rosa says, reflecting on his own path in life. "I was third generation. I didn't have the language barrier. We were poor, but I had an uncle who was an attorney, so I could see that it can be done. I kind of had a little path: this is what you do your senior year in high school, this is what you do your first year in college, and so forth."

Rosa's experience reflects that of the Hispanic community in America as a whole, which is now weighted more heavily toward the third generation or earlier, with fewer recent arrivals in the last decade. Among those who have gotten U.S. citizenship and can vote in elections, the skew is much heavier toward older generations: six in ten Texas Hispanic voters report being third generation or earlier. And the longer your family has been in America, the more likely you are to vote Republican. In our survey, those Texas Hispanics who immigrated to the United States themselves reported voting for Joe Biden by 23 points in the last election, those in the second generation by 15 points, those in the third generation by just three points, and among those with a family history in the U.S. that dates back further, Trump won by two points. But this immigrant experience does not automatically translate to support for unrestricted new immigration. Economically, the Rio Grande Valley is starting to thrive as the people there become more established. Many people are wary of an influx of new arrivals upending this delicate balance.

THE BORDER CRISIS

In recent years, the border between the United States and Mexico has been in a state of crisis. The end of the "Remain in Mexico" policy—requiring asylum seekers to stay in Mexico until their court date in the U.S.—sent a signal that any migrant looking to cross was now likely to succeed in staying. And so they came, by the millions. In total, there were 2.37 million migrant encounters at the border in fiscal year 2022, an increase from 1.73 million in 2021, a number that ticked up immediately following Biden's inauguration. That's the equivalent of a population greater than that of Los Angeles crossing the border illegally in just two years.

The vast majority of Hispanics in the Rio Grande Valley came from Mexico—or lived there when it *was* Mexico. Those crossing now come mostly from farther afield—Venezuela, Cuba, Nicaragua, and also from non-Spanish-speaking countries. In October 2021, the country was shocked by images of thousands of Haitians camping in squalid conditions under the International Bridge in Del Rio farther upriver.

If the Biden White House thought it could gain political support from Hispanics from its reversal of the Trump-era border policies, it appears to have badly miscalculated. The interests of the established Hispanic community of the Rio Grande Valley and those crossing the border are not the same. Republicans openly campaign on stronger border security in the Valley just as they would campaign on the issue to the most hardened primary voters. "We back the green" are words often heard around the Rio Grande, signaling support for the Border Patrol, a major employer in the region.

By a more than two-to-one margin, Hispanics surveyed in Texas sided with increasing border security measures to stop migrants from crossing. The margin was even higher in the border counties. By some estimates, four hundred thousand migrants have passed through Hidalgo County during the current crisis. And in a preelection rally for Republican candidates in the county, a speaker derisively contrasted that fact with the "humanitarian crisis" declared by Martha's Vineyard residents when forty or so migrants were flown there by Florida governor Ron DeSantis.

"A lot of people think that the Hispanic community is for open borders, and that is so far from the truth," says Javier Villalobos. "Down here in the Valley, we see the issues that are happening." Migrants can be seen daily crossing Main Street in Rio Grande City, where there is no border wall. Ross Barrera had a fence on his property torn down by one. "When that happens, who pays for that?" he asks.

In the current asylum crisis, a large majority of applicants have legally left the region, having free movement in the U.S. until their asylum claim is heard, a hearing they will more than likely skip. Getting north of the Border Patrol checkpoints allows them greater freedom of movement—and a bipartisan set of elected officials, from the Republican governor to the Democratic mayor of El Paso, have been only too happy to arrange for their travel out of Texas.

But many from older generations here illegally did not get north of the checkpoints. Today, an estimated one in eight people in Hidalgo County are illegal immigrants. For them, the Rio Grande Valley is a place they can never leave, creating difficult dilemmas for families with undocumented residents. This could include the threat of deportation for an undocumented member of the high school track team traveling to a meet in Corpus Christi. It has also served to tether many legal U.S. citizen children to the region, as they know their parents will never be able to follow them anywhere else. And in the Valley, family matters above all.

In his campaign, Oscar Rosa would listen to the challenges faced by these immigrants, even if they could not vote for him. And though there are now two public universities in the region, as well as a medical school, the checkpoints serve as a psychological barrier to leaving the region for a college education for their U.S.-born children. "Their kids are somewhat constrained even though they're U.S. citizens," explains Rosa. "You can send them up north, but you can't attend their graduation. As a Republican, I tell them I'm familiar with these stories, so I tell them, 'Why don't we try to get a law school here? I can talk to people up north to try to get more stuff down here because I understand your situation.'"

There is sympathy in the Rio Grande Valley, and throughout the country, for the longtime illegal immigrant with children born in the United States. There is also bipartisan support for dealing with the situation faced by "Dreamers," those who were brought in illegally as children, many of whom attended college and live normal American lives. Theirs is a tragic dilemma. What does not follow from that is placing millions more in these tragic circumstances by relaxing control of the border. Polls have long shown a duality of thinking about immigration: favoring legal status for those who have been in the country illegally for a long period, while at the same time supporting tougher border policies to prevent the growth of a new undocumented population. Hispanics think about the issue largely in the same way. Polls show them to be somewhat liberal on immigration issues, but the difference from other Americans is not a night-and-day one. And in the current border crisis, attitudes both among Hispanics and in the country at large have been moving right, as current conditions make clear the need for enforcement.

The 2013 Republican autopsy leaned more heavily on immigration reform as the party's strategy for winning more Hispanic votes. The party's harsh stance toward illegal immigration was thought to be a disqualifier for further growth in the party's Hispanic support. But instead of softening, the party's stance got harsher in 2016—and its Hispanic support stayed steady. The shift away from Trump's 2016 rhetoric on immigration in the 2020 election would make clear that Republicans paid some penalty for these tough stances; it was in the form of delayed future gains, rather than outright losses in support. By 2022, Republican strategists like Giancarlo Sopo were making ads in Spanish about the border crisis with the same tough rhetoric as those in English. The establishment in both parties mistakenly thought of Hispanic voters as soft, with an imperative to strike only compassionate or humane notes when talking of issues from immigration to social welfare. The 2020 and 2022 elections showed the Hispanic voter in the Rio Grande Valley and elsewhere to be otherwise: tough-minded, pragmatic, and up for grabs for both parties.

10.

BLACK POLITICS

Black voters had already been trending toward the Democratic Party at the time of the passage of the Civil Rights Act of 1964. But the law accelerated the shift, cementing the nine-to-one Democratic majority we see today. Ironically, the shift went in the opposite direction of the partisan split in Congress on the bill. On a percentage basis, more Republicans voted for the bill than did Democrats, a result of overwhelming opposition from southern Democrats. But this did not matter. What did matter was where the candidates in that fall's election stood: President Lyndon B. Johnson, one of the lone southern Democrats in favor, and Barry Goldwater, one of just six Republicans in the Senate against. Both candidates were outliers in the then-existing partisan and regional alignments, but their stances were a harbinger of the new racial politics. The Democrats would be the party that delivered civil rights, and the Republicans, eager to welcome into the fold white southerners, embraced gradual, slower-going enforcement. Polls showed there was a broad market for the Republican approach. Americans by and large supported the new law, but when Gallup asked them shortly after the civil rights bill's passage which approach to enforcement they preferred, 23 percent said strict enforcement, and 62 percent said a gradual persuasive approach. The resulting realignment of white southerners and Black voters shapes our politics to this day. Since 1980, no Republican candidate for president has won more than 12 percent of the Black vote.

The Democratic advantage among Black voters has not only been exceptionally large but also remarkably stable. Political scientists call this type of voting behavior "inelastic"— meaning that it doesn't change much from election to election. With so much of the Black vote locked in for Democrats, support for Republican candidates tends to trade in a very narrow range around 10 percent of the vote. This level of political cohesiveness has almost no parallel anywhere else in the American electorate. It can only be understood in the context of Black history, in four centuries of slavery and Jim Crow, and in the extraordinary collective struggle to achieve civil rights. Once Democrats signaled they would no longer be the party of the "Solid South," white voters in the Deep South bounced around as a bloc in search for a new home: first to Strom Thurmond's "Dixiecrats" in 1948, then back to the Democrats, then to Barry Goldwater's Republicans, then to George Wallace's third-party candidacy in 1968, before arriving, with a few detours along the way, in the Republican fold. If the white southerners of the 1960s were willing to vote as a bloc, the thinking among the new Black electorate in the South was that they had better, too.

It is not too surprising that bloc voting among African Americans emerged in the cauldron of the civil rights era. What is surprising is how long it's lasted. Ismail K. White and Chryl N. Laird, two experts on Black political participation, tackle this question in their 2020 book *Steadfast Democrats*. They framed the question as follows:

> [I]n the years since the civil rights gains that supposedly defined black partisanship as Democratic, black Americans have grown more politically and economically diverse. This has surely provided new incentives to abandon the centrality of civil-rights-defined group interest in party identification in favor of some other form of self-interest, ideological, or alternate group position as the basis for partisan defection. That such defection has not occurred, we argue, should be seen as a bit of a puzzle.

Black partisanship has proven largely immune to many of the trends discussed elsewhere in this book: closer social ties between the races and the emergence of a middle-class bourgeoisie rejecting high taxes and redistributive economic policies. Trends that have especially seemed to make Hispanics and Asian Americans less of a Democratic group have hardly moved Black voters.

Black Americans are the missing piece in the Republicans' multiracial populist coalition. The party made significant progress among Hispanics in the last election, but not Black voters. As a party founded in opposition to slavery, one that calls itself the Party of Lincoln, this absence is conspicuous. The party allowed itself to relinquish this mantle in the civil rights era, becoming the party of white former Democrats in the South. Populist realignment—representing the cultural values and economic aspirations of working-class voters of all races—now gives them the chance to reclaim it. Their ability to do so is a moral question as opposed to a political one: only being able to earn one in ten Black votes is something that should bother us as Republicans. Even without the impetus of the GOP's anti-slavery history, the ability of all parties to compete for and win large numbers of voters of all races is a worthy goal, a sign of a well-functioning multiracial democracy.

Republicans have been making major inroads everywhere in the nonwhite working class, but why have they made only modest progress among Black voters? What would they need to do to make further inroads? First, we need to understand the backstory. The barriers to a Republican breakthrough are not what you might assume them to be.

THE MATH

The conventional view of the Black electorate as immovable is a deceptive one. It is true that Black vote shares are relatively "inelastic," shifting only modestly from election to election. But because Democratic margins are so large, voter turnout enters into the equation in a way it does not for more closely divided groups. When a group delivers big margins, as Black voters do, the absolute size of that margin matters a lot. And these margins have varied greatly over the years. Before 2008, Black voters had low turnout rates, making up less of the national electorate than their share of the population. This changed during Barack Obama's campaigns for the White House: Black turnout and Democratic support surged, with turnout rates rising above the national average. In the aftermath of Obama,

Democratic margins and turnout have receded, but the Black share of the electorate is higher than it was before Obama.

Black voter influence in general elections is best understood by the net contribution the community makes to the Democratic margin nationally. This is a simple formula multiplying the Black share of the electorate by the Democratic margin in the Black vote. When Barack Obama won Black voters in 2008 by 95 to 4 percent, or 91 points, this, multiplied by their 13 percent share of the electorate, contributed 11.8 points to the Democratic margin, before votes from any other groups were factored in. Four years earlier, John Kerry's 77-point margin multiplied by the 11 percent Black share of the electorate translated to a net Democratic margin contribution of 8.5 points. This difference between these two numbers equals a 3.3-point shift in the national popular vote margin attributable to Black support—about a third of Obama's total gain. To use an old Joe

Figure 10.1: The Surge and Decline of Black Democratic Strength

Black net margin contribution to Democratic presidential margin, 1976–2020

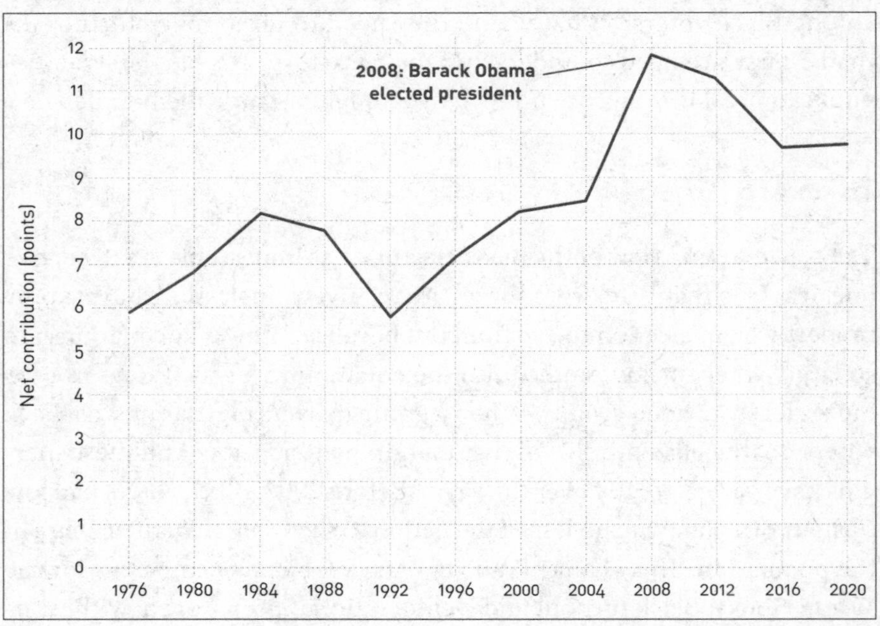

Source: VNS/NEP Exit Polls, 1976–2020

Biden–ism, shifts like this are a "BFD." An enthused Black electorate can make a big difference for Democrats in victory. An uninspired one will likely yield defeat.

To see how, we need only look to the 2016 election. Though Hillary Clinton was not expected to do as well in the Black community as Barack Obama, her campaign held out at least some hope that Donald Trump's history of racially charged comments would keep Black voters highly engaged. Clinton's actual performance would prove to be a bitter disappointment. She won Black voters by eight points less than Obama had, translating to the loss of about a point in the national popular vote margin. Black turnout was also down by around 9 percent, relative to 2012 benchmarks, cutting into Democratic margins further. In combination, these forces reduced the Black net contribution to the Democratic margin from 11.3 points during Obama's 2012 election to 9.7 points, for a total shift of 1.6 points right in the national popular vote, undoing half of Obama's 2008 gains. These shifts definitively cost Clinton Michigan and were responsible for nearly all of her margins of defeat in North Carolina, Pennsylvania, and Wisconsin. In Philadelphia, the city with the largest Black population in any swing state, Clinton netted almost 26,000 fewer votes than Obama in precincts that had voted 95 percent or more for Obama, a reliable indicator of Black majority areas. These precincts went from a margin of 290,444 for Obama to 264,783 for Clinton. At a first approximation, these areas were still overwhelmingly blue, with Donald Trump receiving scarce support. Yet the shifts in these precincts alone accounted for more than half of Clinton's margin of defeat in the state of Pennsylvania.

The steepest turnout declines in 2016 were among Black men, whose turnout was down a full 11 percent, compared to estimates modeled on the 2012 turnout. At the same time, every other racial group exceeded its pre-election turnout benchmarks, so this 11 percent decline understates the extent to which the electorate became less Black in 2016.

Among young Black men, the turnout drop was even steeper. In Nevada, Black men under the age of thirty reached barely 60 percent of their modeled turnout using 2012 as a baseline. In North Carolina, they barely cracked 70 percent. It was not a coincidence that younger Black men

Table 10.1: Black Turnout Fell in 2016

Difference between actual and expected turnout by race and gender in 2016

Race/Ethnicity	Female	Male
White	+2.8%	+2.9%
Black	−7.2	−11.3
Hispanic	+6.1	+5.5
Asian	+4.7	+6.7
Other	+6.0	+5.7

Sources: Echelon Insights, L2 Inc.

were also the group of Black voters with the least support for Clinton. According to the 2016 Cooperative Election Study, Trump got 17 percent of the vote among Black men age eighteen to twenty-nine, and 16 percent of those age thirty to forty-four. This stronger performance among young Black men is an inversion of the expected generational divides in the electorate, where younger voters are expected to vote more Democratic. Just 6 percent of Black men over the age of sixty-five voted for Trump in 2020. Among those age eighteen to twenty-nine, 21 percent did. If not reversed, this generational turnover stands to make Black voters slightly less Democratic over time. One silver lining for Democrats is that they retain strong support among Black women, regardless of age: Trump in 2020 won less than 6 percent of the vote among Black women in every age group.

Declines in Black turnout are striking in light of the growing activism around race in the Democratic Party tied to the rise of the Black Lives Matter movement. Repeated instances of police mistreatment of African American suspects, often captured on video, triggered public outrage. This new activism extended beyond the immediate issue of police misconduct. A shared goal of racial equality has given way to the language of "equity," defined as equality of outcomes over traditional ideas about equality of opportunity. Institutions from public schools to large corporations are embroiled in daily culture war skirmishes over critical race theory and "diversity, equity, and inclusion," or DEI, programs.

Table 10.2:
Republicans' Black Support Is Strongest among Younger Men
Trump 2020 vote share among Black voters, by gender and age

	Men	Women	Overall
18–29	21%	6%	13%
30–44	18%	6%	11%
45–64	15%	6%	10%
65 or older	8%	4%	6%

Source: Cooperative Election Study, 2020

Democratic politicians have reflected this shifting tone on race, starting with Hillary Clinton in 2016. As the Democratic nominee, Clinton became the first presidential nominee to utter the words "systemic racism," both in her nomination acceptance speech and in the general election debates. In doing so, the *New York Times* would note, she was "adopting the lexicon that has been embraced by a new generation of young black activists and liberal whites." Clinton was trying to address twin vulnerabilities. The first was her weakness with Black voters relative to Barack Obama. The second was activist pressure against her past comments labeling young gang members "superpredators" while campaigning for her husband's crime bill in the 1990s, legislation Joe Biden shepherded through the Senate. These activists blamed the crime bill's tough sentencing requirements for exacerbating the mass incarceration of young Black men. For a period of time, the politics of crime had also shifted for Republicans. Even as he used tough "law and order" rhetoric, Donald Trump advocated for and signed the First Step Act, bipartisan legislation aimed at curbing long prison sentences and reintegrating offenders into society.

Clinton's overt focus on racial and gender disparities contrasted with Obama's more subtle approach. Progressives had criticized Obama for not using the presidential bully pulpit to speak out forcefully enough on race. But there was a certain logic to this: what Obama represented for African Americans did not need to be spoken—and a more heavy-handed approach could backfire. When he did speak directly about race, his words resonated because they were rooted in personal experience and not the abstract academic language of today's left. Such an example came when he walked into the White House press briefing room to address the 2013 not-guilty verdict in the killing of Trayvon Martin:

> There are very few African American men in this country who haven't had the experience of being followed when they were shopping in a department store. That includes me. There are very few African American men who haven't had the experience of walking across the street and hearing the locks click on the doors of cars. That happens to me—at least before I was a senator. There are very few African Americans who haven't had the experience of getting on an elevator and a woman clutching her purse nervously and holding her breath until she had a chance to get off. That happens often.

The balance Obama struck gave Democrats the best of both worlds. He was able to inspire historic levels of Black political participation and support for the Democratic Party. At the same time, he won over working-class whites in the Midwest that Clinton and Biden would later lose. Obama would acknowledge the tradeoffs involved after leaving office, telling Ezra Klein in 2021, "Is it more important for me to tell a basic, historical truth, let's say about racism in America right now? Or is it more important for me to get a bill passed that provides a lot of people with health care that didn't have it before?"

In the end, the hope of electing and reelecting the first Black president proved more inspiring as a form of political mobilization than the more abstract racial rhetoric in Clinton's speeches. Obama connected in personal ways that subsequent Democratic standard-bearers have not. This remained the case in the 2020 election, even after Trump's widely acknowledged mishandling of the George Floyd protests. The traditional exit poll showed a basically stable picture between 2016 and 2020, with lower Black voter margins in 2020 but higher turnout, and net contribution staying unchanged at 9.7 points. Meanwhile, the VoteCast exit poll pointed to a slightly smaller margin contribution of 9.2 points. Precinct data throughout the country showed Trump gaining a few points in Black communities from 2016, and the Cooperative Election Study showed a large shift in his direction among Black conservatives, alongside similar shifts among Hispanics and Asian Americans. The signals are mixed, but the portrait of Biden's 2020 performance painted by these sources is one of weakness more than strength.

More surprising still were the results of the 2022 midterms, with the traditional exit poll and the VoteCast survey showing a Republican vote for the U.S. House of 13 and 14 percent, respectively. While these numbers are still woefully low for the GOP, they are higher than the numbers the party got in every midterm election going back at least until 2002, including its 2010 and 2014 romps. Combined with traditionally lower Black turnout in midterm elections, the net contribution to the Democratic margin declined almost two points further from 2020, to 7.6 points in the VoteCast survey and 8 points in the traditional exit poll—four points off the Obama pace.

And yet, Biden was able to win in 2020 and Democrats able to outperform in 2022 despite weaker showings among Black voters. The key was adding enough support from white voters—especially those with degrees—to offset losses among nonwhites. For now, Democrats are learning to win with a whiter coalition. Such was the case in the 2022 Pennsylvania Senate race, where the hoodie-wearing John Fetterman won rather comfortably with a playbook ripped out of Obama 2012, disqualifying daytime TV show host Mehmet Oz as aloof, wealthy, and out of touch. The patterns of support for Fetterman were telling. Base Democratic turnout from African Americans in Philadelphia was weak, even by the standards of previous midterms. But Fetterman was able to run several points ahead of Biden in largely white and Trump-voting central and western Pennsylvania. Fetterman is an example of the success Democrats can have with a candidate who appeals to the sensibilities of the white working class. But other Democrats elsewhere have relied on running up margins with whites with college degrees. This means highlighting the particular concerns of these voters, a postmaterialist cocktail of high-minded rhetoric about "democracy" and progressive rhetoric on social issues like abortion. As we'll see, these are not the priorities of Black working-class voters.

Is this a disconnect Republicans could potentially capitalize on? Those answering "Yes" would point to the large, 43-point shift to Trump among Black conservatives, slowly rising Republican numbers across the last few election cycles, and rising suburbanization, all trends reflected to an even greater extent among other nonwhite groups. But there's a strong "No" argument, too: the Black experience in America is unique, and it's one that can't be compared to Hispanics or Asian Americans. Shaped by the common bonds of slavery and Jim Crow, Black America is much more cohesive as a group than the disparate nationality groups that immigrated here after 1965. A Democratic supermajority among Black voters developed for very specific historical reasons. Debate rages about whether conditions are now different enough from the 1960s to warrant a change in political alignment, a debate that will ultimately be resolved by Black voters themselves. The best those on the outside can do is try to understand the forces shaping this alignment.

SOCIAL FORCES

"Barack Obama plans to win South Carolina—by a hair," quipped a news report touting the candidate's latest strategy for reaching voters in the crucial early primary state. The year was 2008 and Obama campaign staffers fanned out to nine hundred or so Black barbershops and beauty salons throughout the Palmetto State, registering voters, handing out rally tickets, and answering questions about the candidate. This idea had a long pedigree: in 1957, Dr. Martin Luther King visited a convention of Black beauticians as part of an organizing push for voting rights. The "B&Bs" have long been a social hub of Black America, a place to spread the word about matters of politics or other issues of public importance. "The rise of Jim Crow laws limited spaces where Blacks could gather, and the barbershop filled this void, similar to Black churches but on a smaller scale," write Joyce Balls-Berry, Lea Dacy, and James Balls. Barbers and beauticians were political influencers in the truest sense, selecting reading materials for patrons and proselytizing for the captive audience in their chairs.

Obama ended up winning the South Carolina primary going away, in what would become the decisive victory setting him on a path to the Democratic nomination and the presidency. His 80 percent among the Black majority of the state's Democrats was a key reason why, but this result was not foreordained due to his race. The previous fall, when Hillary Clinton led in the national polls, she also led by 24 points among Black Democrats. That's reflective of a pragmatic streak in the Black community, which has been with every winning Democratic nominee since backing Bill Clinton in 1992. It was only after Obama's surprise 2008 victory in Iowa, showing that a Black candidate could win over a largely white electorate, that things began to shift. In South Carolina, the "B&B" strategy helped nudge things along.

The B&Bs are just one small element of a larger web of Black social ties, one that includes Black churches, historically Black colleges and universities, and other institutions that emerged during the Jim Crow era, acting as a support structure for Black Americans with limited opportunities. It was not only the institutions themselves that could help one advance but also one's individual ties within Black social networks. As Chryl Laird put it to me, "And so what then becomes very imperative for a Black individual is that the resources that you are going to be able to get more than likely to gain economically or socially or politically, are going to be ones that are going to be garnered through the social capital that you can get from the Black community itself." When one is resource-constrained or faces challenges accessing opportunities, it is other Black people they will turn to most. And maintaining strong social ties is essential. "Why do social ties matter?" Laird asks rhetorically. "Because my survival in a lot of ways relies on the social ties that I have and those Black social ties will often be the ones that lift me out of a circumstance when I'm dealing with challenges from this systemic types of practices that can keep me from being able to achieve the things that I want to achieve in my life."

These social ties turn out to be the hidden key to explaining Black politics, and specifically why, sixty years after the passage of the Civil Rights Act, Black voters remain so fiercely loyal to the Democratic Party.

Laird's study of this phenomenon along with Ismail K. White is a clarifying portrait. White and Laird show Black voters started out in the civil rights period by taking very liberal positions on the key issues of the day. Over time, their positions moderated. But their Democratic allegiance remained. In the early 1970s, almost 80 percent of Black respondents expressed support for a government guarantee of jobs and income, a share that dropped to just over 50 percent in the last decade. Conservative ideological identification rose from under 10 percent in the 1970s to more than 40 percent shortly after Obama's election, dropping to around 30 percent more recently. These numbers are not consistent with a nine-to-one majority for the party of the left.

White and Laird stress that the initial consolidation behind Democrats had a practical calculus: a concentration of votes in one party meant that the Black electorate could more efficiently translate votes into political power. With legislation promoting the creation of majority-minority districts, Black membership in the House grew from just five in the 1963–64 Congress to fifteen in 1973–74 to forty-one by 1995–96. By 2021, there were fifty-seven Black voting members of the House, with a majority elected from districts where voters of another race, usually white, are the plurality. On one hand, the election of Black candidates in white majority districts, as well as the election of an African American president, can be taken as a sign of racial progress. Nonetheless, Black voters remain vigilant that any dilution in Democratic voting strength could jeopardize their representation in the halls of power.

"Linked fate" is one explanation for Black political unity, advanced by political scientist Michael Dawson. The linked fate hypothesis holds that individual Blacks will subordinate their own behavior to what is best for the group. If political unity in the Democratic Party is deemed best for advancing Black interests, individual Blacks will gladly set aside their oftentimes conservative views for the good of the group by voting for the more liberal candidate.

This explanation is appealing, tracking closely with the extraordinary political support Black voters give Democrats. But White and Laird find that social pressure is the active ingredient holding Democratic loyalty in place. Deeper social ties to other Black people, not conceptual support for the "linked fate" idea, more readily predicts Democratic loyalty. This is systematically true across different social domains: Black church attendance, living in majority Black neighborhoods, having friends that are mostly Black. The key "tell" is how differently Black conservatives behave in contexts where they are surrounded by others of their own race versus when their surroundings are largely non-Black.

Specifically, in heavily Black social spaces, Black conservatives support Democrats at a rate approaching or equal to that of Black liberals. To take one example, nearly all Black respondents who reported having mostly Black friends *and* also supported gun rights identified with the Democratic Party in a 2013 Public Religion Research Institute study. Among pro–Second Amendment Black respondents with mostly non-Black social networks, almost no one identified as a Democrat.

White and Laird use the term "racialized social constraints" to describe this phenomenon, arguing that social pressure, not abstract group interest, is what keeps Black voters in the Democratic fold. Black voters are keenly aware of the community's support for the Democratic Party and hold each other accountable for upholding that support. Terms like "Uncle Tom" or "sellout" are often directed at defectors. Joe Biden expressed a version of this thinking on Charlamagne tha God's podcast in 2020, saying, "If you have a problem figuring out whether you're for me or Trump, then you ain't Black." Such social sanctions are also reported in surveys: just 20 percent of Black Obama voters reported that their family or friends wouldn't have cared if they supported Romney over Obama in 2012, compared to 46 percent of white Obama voters who said the same.

Even more revealing is the fact that Black voters often switch political sides based on whether they are talking to another Black person or not. In face-to-face survey interviews, Black respondents were 13 points more likely to identify as a Democrat in the presence of a Black interviewer than they were to a non-Black interviewer. In online surveys, where there is no interviewer, Democratic support levels were nearly equal to the non-Black interviewer scenario. In an experiment the authors conducted in 2012 simulating the effect of peer pressure on political support, Black students were much more likely to donate to Obama in the presence of a Black Obama-supporting confederate—that is, one secretly hired for the experiment—than if they were alone or with a white Obama-supporting confederate. The difference in likelihood of donating to Obama was greatest among cross-pressured conservatives.

Black churches have also been instrumental in maintaining Democratic unity. Their members defy political stereotypes as an older and relatively conservative group with more traditional views on issues like abortion or gay rights, who are nonetheless more likely to actively support a party espousing liberal social attitudes than are non-churchgoers in the Black community. Ryan Burge, a political scientist and pastor who tracks religious voting trends, finds that 48 percent of Black Christians consider themselves strong Democrats, compared to 31 percent of secular Blacks. The Black church has historically been a space for politics and organizing, starting in the civil rights era, and today Black church congregants are more likely to hear political sermons than are other churchgoers. This gap in church attendance also represents a generational divide, where younger, more secular Blacks are most likely to depart from the Democratic voting norm.

Social ties within the Black church not only predict Democratic support in the general election but support for the consensus candidate in Democratic primaries. Burge found notably higher support for Biden over Sanders in the Democratic primary among Black Christians than secular Black voters. High social cohesion means that the word about a preferred candidate spreads fast. As a result, the Black vote in primaries can turn quickly, as it did for Obama in 2008, or when Jim Clyburn, the highest-ranking Black member of the House, boosted Joe Biden's campaign with his endorsement ahead of the South Carolina primary.

Bloc voting has given Black voters an effective veto in every Democratic presidential nominating contest over the last thirty years. When Black voters rally behind a Democratic candidate, it is usually the candidate strongest with the party's moderate or establishment wing, like Hillary Clinton in 2016 or Joe Biden in 2020, with Obama in 2008 standing out as the obvious exception. This pragmatic streak shows that the politics of Black America, while solidly Democratic, are also nonprogressive.

When Black voters have a choice between a moderate and a progressive in the Democratic primary and race is not a factor, the moderate usually wins. This was exemplified in a high-profile primary rivalry where Democratic regular Shontel Brown defeated Bernie Sanders supporter Nina Turner for a Cleveland, Ohio, House seat.

Conservatives are only too eager to point to their moderation as a reason Black voters could support Republicans should Democrats veer too far left. Despite their recent gains in Black support, this ignores two important realities. First is the social pressure that keeps Democratic support high. Second is the fact that this bloc voting works so well in primaries that Democrats usually avoid nominating candidates not favored by Black voters. A contingent of ideologically mixed voters representing nearly a quarter of the Democratic primary electorate and voting cohesively has a moderating effect on the candidates Democrats nominate—a counterweight absent in the Republican Party. The fact that Black voters usually get their way in primaries limits the potential for mass defection in the general election, even if those consensus candidates have turned in uninspiring general election performances with Black voters as of late. Had Bernie Sanders won the Democratic nomination in 2016 or 2020 against the will of the Black primary electorate, this would have proven a major test for how high the Republican share of the Black vote could go.

Absent Democrats nominating a further-left progressive, hopes for Republican gains rest on the Black vote becoming more ideological, like the white vote has fully become and the Hispanic and Asian American vote seems on its way to becoming. While Republicans might take heart in the fact that Black conservatives realigned in 2020, fewer Black voters called themselves conservatives than had in 2016. Self-identified conservatives are, on their own, too small a group on which to build a Black voting base. Black moderates are where the votes are.

Returning to a piece of data first examined in chapter 5, fully 83 percent of Black voters are neither consistently conservative nor consistently liberal on policy, a higher share than any other group in the electorate. That's defined by not giving consistently liberal or conservative survey answers more than three-quarters of the time, a threshold above which one can predict voting for Democrats or Republicans with near-total accuracy. Whites, who are the most ideological group, occupy this middle ground 51 percent of the time. Whites with a college degree are the only group with an ideologically motivated majority, with just 38 percent in this broadly-defined middle ground. If we analyze these non-ideological voters in more detail, breaking down the ideological spectrum into ten segments from left to right, we see vast differences in the voting behavior of Black voters and those of every other group.

Figure 10.2: Even Conservative-Leaning Black Voters Supported Biden

Net Trump-Biden margin by race and conservative ideology score

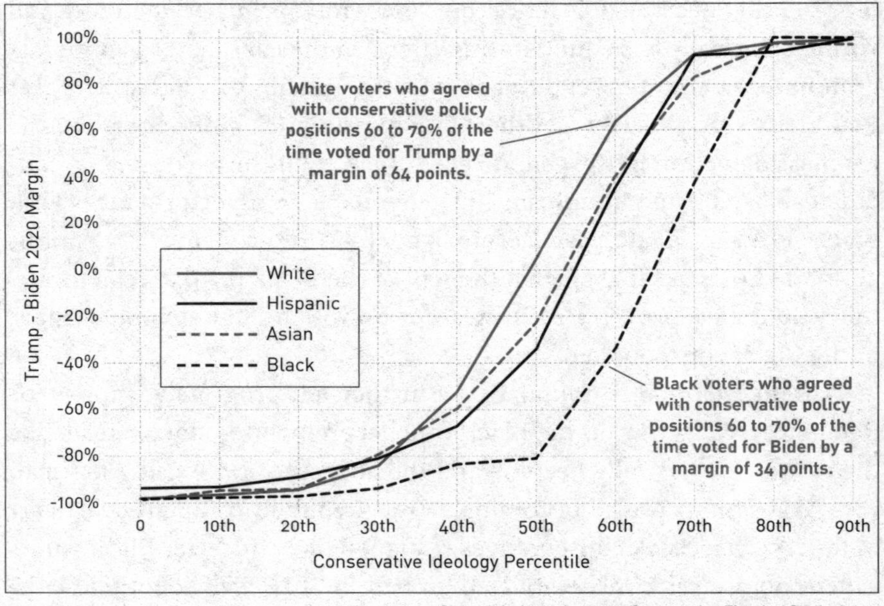

Source: Index using 2020 Cooperative Election Study data

The voting preferences of most voters in the middle progress in logical fashion according to whether they take more liberal or conservative positions, but the curve for Black voters is shifted downward in a much more pro-Democratic direction. More than nine in ten African Americans who are not consistent ideologues voted for Joe Biden, a group that includes around 25 percent of the Black electorate that leans slightly in a conservative direction on policy issues. By contrast, Hispanic and Asian American voters who leaned a bit to the right supported Trump by more than two-to-one margins. In the 50th to 60th percentile of conservative ideology, where a voter tilts ever so slightly right on policy questions, white voters supported Trump by four percentage points, while Black voters supported Biden by 82 points, a racial margin gap of 86 points. By comparison, Hispanic voters in this slice of the electorate voted for Biden by 36 points and Asian Americans did so by 24 points. When things are shifted a little further right, toward conservative scores in the 60 to 70 percent range, white voters chose Trump by a margin of 64 points, while Black voters opted for Biden by 34 points, for an even larger margin gap of 98 points. That two groups of voters with identical views of public policy issues can vote so differently is one of the most striking phenomena observable in public opinion research.

To be clear: If Black voters simply voted as their policy views suggested, this would not make them a Republican group. Assuming polarization took hold in the same way as it has among whites at all points along the ideological spectrum, they would still vote Democratic by around 70 to 30 percent. That may sound like cold comfort for Republicans, but not if you think about it in terms of margins and swings, not absolute support levels. Such an outcome would represent a margin shift of 40 points from the 90 to 10 percent baseline—good for a shift of nearly 5 points in the national popular vote margin. Of course, there are clear and obvious problems with expecting Black voters, with their unique experience in America, to mirror the political preferences of white voters. But even if we use other nonwhite groups as a point of comparison, shifting Black voter preferences along the ideological spectrum to reflect those of Hispanics or Asian Americans, the Democratic to Republican margin would move to 75 to 25 percent, for a margin shift of 30 points, the equivalent of 3 to 4 points of the popular vote margin. The effect of the social trends unique to African Americans is clear and significant: an often-decisive boost for Democratic candidates in national elections.

PERSUASION

I offer no prediction about whether Black social pressure to vote Democratic will fade anytime soon. As a social phenomenon, it's proven to be quite durable, without equal in American politics, with the possible exception of the rural South Texas politics discussed earlier. But the fact that this, at its root, is a social phenomenon does create an opening that Republicans would not have if their problem were an ideological one.

Keeping up this social pressure means sanctioning defectors, which comes at a social cost. Right now, that's relatively easy to do when fewer than one in ten defect. It becomes harder to do when one in eight, one in six, or one in five dissent. Even a tiny shift in the Black vote, on the order of two or five points, would result in dramatically higher odds of encountering a Black Republican. And potentially, this could mean that a tipping point is reached where the norm is no longer enforceable. Such an outcome is known in the social sciences as a preference cascade, where, faced with new facts, large populations previously immovable in their views change their minds all at once. If this were to occur, the most likely result would be a shift in the partisan balance from nine to one Democratic to about three to one. This would have a transformative effect on national politics. And all it might take to set it off is a concerted effort to increase the Black Republican vote share by those first few crucial percentage points.

Given what's at stake, the Republican and conservative approach has fallen woefully short. This starts with how Black Republicans are often presented in conservative media: as iconoclasts and independent thinkers who got off the Democratic "plantation." Besides the problematic analogy to slavery, this has the unintended consequence of presenting the party's Black supporters as somehow rare or heroic. That's not the right persuasion strategy. Few people want to be this kind of hero, boldly defying a majority of their peers. Talking about how switching is easy—and increasingly common, as in the case of younger Black men—would be by far a more appealing message. Of course, this approach suffers from a chicken-or-the-egg problem. Republican support has to grow for it to work. But this nonetheless underscores the importance of Republicans talking up their every success with Black voters, however small, just as they've done with Hispanic voters.

The stridently pro-Trump Black conservative commentator Candace Owens is in many ways not the model for how Republicans can persuade moderate Black voters, trafficking in the "plantation" stereotype, for instance. But Chryl Laird pinpoints something that's unique about Owens's approach: she's trying to get people to switch *as a group*. "Seeing a lot of her commentary, she is actually operating with a Black model," Laird tells me. "What she's doing with her organization is creating a Black collective. She's creating a set of people who've all agreed we're defecting, and we're going to defect together." Creating alternative social ties is important, Laird argues, because Black Republicans are often penalized in Black social networks. Black conservatives, she says, often manage to replace these ties with support from white conservatives. But this model doesn't work for regular people who are not public figures. What you need to inspire a large-scale switch is safety in numbers. The key element, Laird says, is "people getting people connected with one another, so that if I am somebody who's decided to defect, there are other Black people with me who have also decided to defect, and we have collectively now created our own social tie together that allows them not to be worried, even as they will still probably deal with a lot of pushback from the larger group."

There is also a lack of attention to this problem at the highest levels in the party. Because Black voters will likely never be a Republican group, simply improving performance on the margin doesn't seem to be worth trying. Better to focus on closely divided constituencies like white suburbanites, or Hispanics, who are actually swing voters or becoming ones.

Basic arithmetic exposes the flaw in this thinking: even small shifts have the same effect on the underlying electoral calculus, regardless of whether the voter shifting is white, Black, Hispanic, or Asian American. Going from 48 to 52 percent is more satisfying than going from 10 to 15 percent, because the former turns a loss into a win, but this logic doesn't apply to subgroups within the electorate. There, every new voter you can win on the margin matters just as much.

The parties' targeting algorithms further exacerbate this problem. Campaigns survey the electorate and draw up models ranking voters from a 0 to 100 probability of support. Voters in the 30 to 70 percent range are then drawn into "persuasion" universes, the focus of multimillion-dollar advertising campaigns waged through television, mail, and digital ads. By default, this excludes nearly all Black voters from Republican persuasive communications, as their probability of support is generally lower than 30 percent, and excludes them from all but get-out-the-vote appeals from Democrats. Targeting decisions by both parties make campaign persuasion universes overwhelmingly white, overlooking nonwhite voters in general and Black voters especially.

A voter who ranks somewhere in the middle of the probability distribution—55 percent likely to support the Democrat, 45 percent likely to support the Republican—does not turn out to be more persuadable than someone with an 85 percent chance of supporting the Democrat. Persuadability is not defined by where someone starts out, but by their likelihood of shifting when presented with new information. If new information moves someone with a high partisanship score, they are persuadable. This simple change in emphasis by candidates would instantly result in the Black vote being more heavily courted by both parties. Given the significant gains Republicans would be poised to make simply by convincing Black conservatives, actively campaigning for Black votes with advertising, campaign stops, and door-to-door canvassing might be the highest-possible leverage step Republicans could take to expand their multiracial populist coalition. This starts with no longer limiting ourselves to talking to stereotypical "swing voters," but also those likely to switch if contacted. It also means identifying ideological conservatives in the Black community and targeting them with ads and grassroots voter contact.

The largest question in any campaign is what to say. Here, the answer is simpler than it would be if the voter in question were a white suburbanite or a down-the-line political independent. Black voters agree with the Republican Party on policy issues much more than they vote for them, so among Black voters, Republicans stand to benefit the most from a substantive, issue-heavy style of campaign. The flip side for Democrats when speaking to Black voters, David Shor tells me, is that "if you talk about policy content to some degree, you're probably going to lose votes." Consider an issue like defunding the police, which many progressive institutions adopted in solidarity with the racial justice protests in 2020. Not only was this an unpopular position among voters in the general electorate, but the progressive position badly underperformed underlying Democratic partisanship among Black voters. "If you look at polling, defunding the police has like 40 to 45 percent support among African Americans," notes Shor. "When you campaign on an issue that 45 percent of a group supports, you're going to lose votes, that's just a reality."

Of course, Republicans should not be indiscriminate in their approach. They should pick issues where there is the least distance between Black voters and Republicans. One useful place to start is by looking at issues where Black public opinion is close to that of the population as a whole, or even a bit to the right of it. On most issues tested in the Cooperative Election Study, Black voters don't look like down-the-line partisan Democrats. They take positions to the right of white Democrats. Abortion rights and the environment are two issues where Black voters lean even further right—and to the right of the country as a whole. On immigration, Black voters lean just slightly left of the nation, and to the right of Hispanics. On criminal justice issues, Black voters tend to lean a bit more to the left, with Hispanics considerably to the right of them. The issue set that Black voters are furthest left on is old-school economic populism. One such issue is raising the minimum wage, where Black support for the left-leaning position is 23 points higher than the country as a whole. Another example is a Medicare for All plan. Contrary to the conventional wisdom, economics—not any issue commonly linked to a progressive agenda on race—turns out to be the best bet for Democrats to rally Black voters. This is why Trump's approach to these issues—like making sure Republicans didn't get caught on the wrong side of cutting Social Security and Medicare—is one worth duplicating for the Republicans vying to take the party in a different direction in 2024.

Environmental issues are a relatively under-discussed vulnerability for Democrats. In Echelon Insights polling before the 2020 primaries, white college graduates in the Democratic Party were nearly twice as likely to say they were extremely concerned by climate change—at 71 percent—than Black Democrats—at 38 percent. Perhaps sensing a disconnect, progressives have started to stress the concept of "environmental justice" to engage nonwhite communities on the issue. But this has proven to be a challenge. A series of focus groups by the public policy think tank Third Way in 2020 showed tangible quality-of-life concerns like crime and the cost of living overshadowing a long-range threat like climate change. "I'm worried about, you know, going to the store and back in one piece," said one woman in Philadelphia. "Truthfully, I can go worry about global warming and all that, but that's not going to feed my kids," reported a non-college-educated male, also in Philadelphia. This is part of a larger class divide among Democrats: Biden voters making more than $200,000 a year were more than 20 points more likely to rate climate change as more important than the cost of living than their lower-income counterparts. A push for net-zero carbon emissions resulting in a sudden rise in the cost of living for working families could pave the way for new populist revolts like those we've seen on immigration worldwide. And in America, the multiracial working class stands far apart from the upper middle class on climate change. Compared to the electorate as a whole, both Black and Hispanic voters stand to the right, or slightly left of center, on environmental regulation. Figure 10.3 shows the gap between these groups and overall public opinion on a range of topics, also including crime, immigration, Medicare for All, and the minimum wage.

Of course, even if Republicans were able to make a concerted effort to appeal to Black voters, they would still have history to overcome. The belief that Republicans benefited from a "Southern Strategy" of appealing to anti-Black southern whites is firmly ingrained and remains a barrier to winning more voters today. A more formal mea culpa for the party's actions during that era seems to be in order, as well as more regular acknowledgment of racial disparities in the present. Liberals in the twentieth century and early twenty-first argued that an immediate emphasis on curing current racial disparities would ultimately lead to a day of full

Figure 10.3: Black Voters Lean Right on Abortion and the Environment
Average Black and Hispanic conservatism on issues vs. the overall electorate

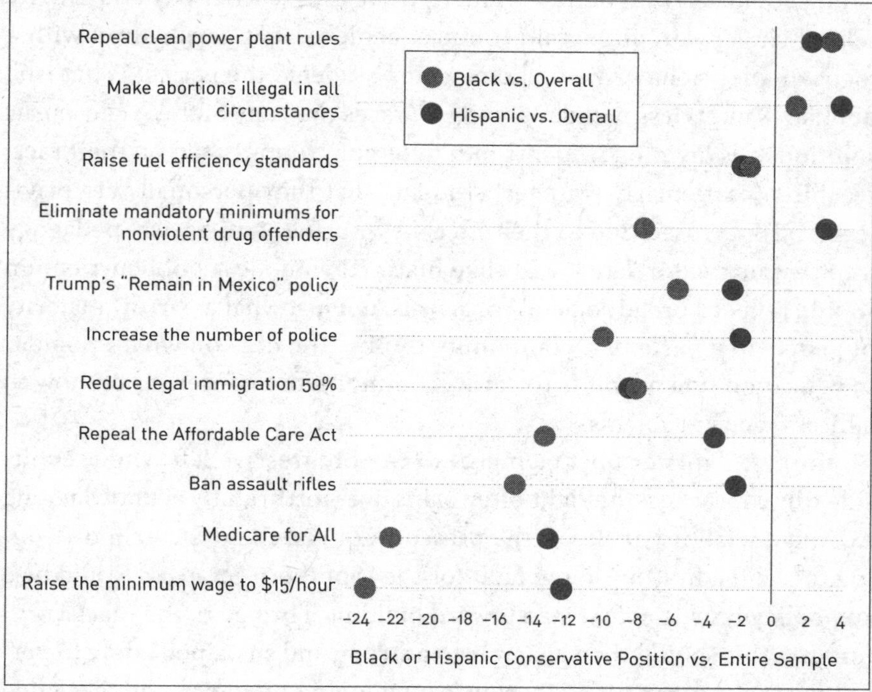

Source: Cooperative Election Study, 2020

equality where all could ultimately be known as Americans, not by racial or ethnic labels. New ideologies on the left seem to reject this ideal end state, seeking a permanently heightened and bureaucratically enforced race consciousness throughout society and institutions. That is a change for the worse and one conservatives are right to speak out against.

K–12 education is a flash point in this new culture war, but one where there is—contrary to media narratives—an underlying consensus on how to address questions of inequality. Specifically, there is broad agreement in polling for teaching about slavery or racism in American history, despite attempts to play off objections to critical race theory as a rejection of such teachings. Acknowledgment of racial achievement gaps is also not controversial: it was a focus of George W. Bush's and present in conservative discourse about pandemic learning loss and school choice. Do both sides agree on a set of solutions? Broadly speaking, yes. Voters support a range of ideas from both left and right: higher teacher pay and greater school choice, attention paid to racial achievement gaps paired with a focus on high achievement and teaching students the basics. What isn't popular—and is less popular among *all* races than any of these consensus solutions—is dividing students into different groups based on their race, teaching (particularly younger) students that they personally are privileged or oppressed due to their race, or infusing "anti-racist" pedagogy into seemingly unrelated fields like math. The public school curriculum should reflect a broad societal consensus, not just what a narrow majority of people in a particular community thinks. The data on what's popular in education policy points toward a commonsense consensus on how to address racial problems.

In their fights against elements of the progressive left who are outside this consensus, the right often skips over forthrightly acknowledging existing racial disparities in the present, not just the past. Acknowledging this and admitting some fault for the "Southern Strategy" could be a symbolically crucial first step toward building a bridge to the Black community. This should then give way to a strong and sustained effort to persuade Black voters, with vigorous campaigning on conservative agenda items where Black voters are closest to Republicans. It's true that the Republicans' 2013 apology for their immigration rhetoric didn't amount to much. But that issue seems nowhere near as defining for Hispanics as the history of civil rights is for African Americans.

It's no secret that when Black voters first moved into the Democratic fold, Republicans had an interest in realigning conservative white Democrats. Some of these voters—but not all—had racist views. It's also true the Democratic Party of the period placed an outsized emphasis on keeping these voters in the fold, with some success when they ran southern Democrats like Jimmy Carter and Bill Clinton. But for the most part, it was Republicans who benefited. The conservative southerner, voting Republican for president, but Democratic for Congress, was the ultimate cross-pressured voter of the late twentieth century.

The most important cross-pressured voter in America today is no longer the conservative white Democrat. It is the conservative Black Democrat. There are barriers the Republican Party needs to overcome before it can make significant gains in the Black community. And some of this may already be happening naturally, in the emergence of a younger and less partisan generation, less tied to traditional Black institutions. As White and Laird write in the conclusion to *Steadfast Democrats*, "We believe that increased contact with non-blacks and a decline in attendance at black institutions, in favor of more integrated spaces, would threaten the stability of black Democratic partisan loyalty." That partisan loyalty does not stem from ideology, but from a social environment that spurs political cohesion under the Democratic banner. Understanding these social forces and promoting a homegrown civil society on the right are essential next steps in the work of building a stronger party that truly represents the interests of working people across the racial divide. This is not just a question of winning elections. For the Party of Lincoln, it is also the right thing to do.

11.

THE MULTIRACIAL POPULIST FUTURE

I now turn to my final question: Where do the Republicans go from here? To answer this, we must reflect briefly on where they've been over the last few years. The Trump presidency should have served as the ideal testing ground for how the populist party I'm describing would govern. Instead, Trump's populist reshaping of the Republican Party proceeded in fits and starts, to no satisfying conclusion. Trump placed the issue of immigration center stage, waged trade wars, and refused to be tagged as a stingy, Scrooge-like budget cutter, ballooning the deficit in response to the COVID-19 pandemic. But he also passed a tax cut heavily weighted toward corporations and the wealthy, and in numerous ways governed like a traditional economic conservative. He went along with the ill-fated Obamacare repeal effort staged by the GOP's anti-government wing, a political disaster that caused his approval ratings to drop more quickly than any event of his presidency until January 6, 2021.

And yet: Trump's failure to deliver on his populist commitments did not appear to cost him support. His coalition, though weaker in 2020, was more heavily weighted toward economically downscale voters. His lost votes were upscale whites exhausted by four years of nonstop chaos, not the working-class voters for whom the free-wheeling Trump remained the preferred choice. Meanwhile, Thomas Frank's paradox, of the party of corporate tax cuts winning the support of the blue-collar worker, remained stubbornly unresolved.

A polling experiment run during the 2020 election helps answer why. In 2019, a weekly sample of more than six thousand voters who were part of the Democracy Fund + UCLA Nationscape survey was asked, in addition to the normal polling questions, to pick between one of two randomly generated issue platforms. One such hypothetical platform might include building a border wall, passing a Medicare for All plan, and raising taxes on the wealthy. Looking at how often statements containing any one position won their respective matchups would uncover the "revealed importance" of each position. What the researchers found was that meta-partisan issues like impeaching Trump or cultural issues like building the border wall mattered more to what voters would pick than economic or social welfare questions like tax cuts or health care. So while polls might show Republicans supporting a tax hike for people making over $600,000 a year, few actually changed their votes on that basis. As long as Trump stayed true on the commitments his base *actually* cared about—controlling immigration or fighting the Beltway "swamp"—his support would remain solid.

We should also consider another oft-dismissed possibility: that being in the working class is not necessarily incompatible with being an economic conservative. They are not necessarily so in the sense of a hardened belief in the specifics of the Laffer curve, but in a basic faith in the ability of people to get ahead through hard work without government handouts. That a group of people valuing social stability would also adopt an economic philosophy centered around personal responsibility to provide for themselves and their families, should not surprise us. It is only surprising to those who overthink these things, who view everything through the lens of people's relationships to the state, rather than their relationships to each other in society. If the entirety of how workers view the economy boils down to the availability of government benefits, then economic conservatism is not in their interests. But if their view of the economy is more than that: the ability to find a good job at a decent wage, the cost of gas and the grocery bill, or the opportunity to own a home, then there is no contradiction. A narrow government-centered view is all-consuming for wonks who care about the size of the federal budget. The latter is what matters to ordinary Americans.

And this is what ideologues on both sides completely miss: voters don't particularly care about the government's size, but they do care about government decisions that go against their *moral* sensibilities, like paying people not to work or giving bailouts to big banks. What is profoundly a *moral* fight is obscured by a wonky twentieth-century debate between Team Government and Team Capitalism. This fight matters a lot to true believers like Thomas Frank on the left or Paul Ryan on the right. It mattered a lot to me—starting in high school when I would voraciously follow the debates in the pages of *National Review* and the *New Republic*, closely tracking the latest developments of Newt Gingrich's Contract with America. As late as the 1990s, honest philosophical differences over the role of government were at the center of the partisan debate. Republicans sincerely pushed for a balanced budget, even at the cost of their own popularity, and Democrats pushed back with a vision of a robust social safety net. The debate, central to the politics of the Reagan era and its aftermath, was deftly satirized by the late, great P. J. O'Rourke, who wrote, "Democrats are . . . the party that says government can make you richer, smarter, taller, and get the chickweed out of your lawn. Republicans are the party that says government doesn't work, and then they get elected and prove it."

I come to tell the younger me that the libertarian dream of smaller government is dead. And so, for that matter, is the progressive dream of turning America into a Scandinavian workers' paradise. The voters don't particularly care about whether the disciples of Milton Friedman or John Maynard Keynes are right—and today, neither party pretends that this is what the fight is about. Republicans, for their part, are happy to spend like drunken sailors when in power, having learned the hard way that changes to Social Security and Medicare are not political winners. Donald Trump himself signed the death warrant for a unilateral Republican push for entitlement reform in 2016. As far as the Democrats go, the push for bigger government has of late been more successful, but only because of "never let a good crisis go to waste" spending during the pandemic. The inflation it's given us seems poised to return us to something resembling the austerity politics of the post–Great Recession period.

To the extent Americans have broader ideals about how the economy should work, they are encompassed in brand labels like "capitalist" and "socialist" that themselves allow for a broad range of interpretation.

Underpinning this are contrasting sets of values and impulses—values shaped by people's intuitions and experiences rather than economics texts. The social psychologist Jonathan Haidt's moral foundations framework is a useful place to start examining these values and how our political beliefs ultimately flow through from them. Haidt lays out five distinct moral taste buds: care versus harm, fairness versus cheating, loyalty versus betrayal, authority versus subversion, and sanctity versus degradation. And while conservatives value all of the positive ones listed equally, liberals disproportionately value those of care and fairness, giving less priority to loyalty, authority, and sanctity.

For the working class, the ideal of hard work associated with the values of authority and loyalty remains central. This is the idea of paying your dues and following the rules. A second idea about how society can achieve economic security revolves around the ideas of fairness and compassion, manifested in support for raising taxes on the rich to provide a fairer distribution of wealth, or providing health care access for those who cannot fend for themselves. Both of these basic tendencies exist within all of us. Few are moral absolutists. Even the most unshakable party loyalists embrace parts of both.

Given this choice, the working class will often choose the party of the right. In a postmaterialist world, social values matter more than economic ones. But social values also influence economic values. In the Rio Grande Valley and elsewhere, you see it in the deep moral aversion toward government handouts. Indeed, it is the very success of the New Deal programs and America's partial safety net that has given working-class voters license to vote for the party of the right. It's an axiom in politics that voters seldom if ever vote to say, "Thank you." They will zero in on whatever problems remain. And if their neighborhood is being ravaged by crime or by opioid addiction, the last thing one can expect are good feelings for the technocrats who were in charge as these problems got worse. It is why more voters cluster in the populist quadrant, not the libertarian one. Hands-off ideologies, be they the social libertinism of the left or the free-market libertarianism of the right, don't have much purchase with the working class. None of this is new. It basically describes the consensus in a place like Bay Ridge in the 1960s. Economically, this consensus is anti-welfare and pro–Social Security. Shorn of its hard-core libertarianism, the Republican Party is becoming a natural home for working-class voters.

REVISITING THE "GRAND NEW PARTY"

The belief that the Republicans might someday evolve into a working-class party of the people saw a revival in the waning days of the George W. Bush presidency, in the work of two young conservative thinkers, Ross Douthat and Reihan Salam. Like Thomas Frank, they took note of a Republican coalition that was becoming less the party of the country club and more the party of Sam's Club, borrowing a phrase coined by Minnesota governor Tim Pawlenty. Their 2008 book, *Grand New Party*, was an effort to sketch out a working-class vision for the Republican future. While other conservatives were focused on recapturing the Reagan-era magic, Douthat and Salam argued that this approach did not address the real problems of the working and middle classes. Thanks to Reagan, these problems were no longer ones of crippling high taxation. The GOP's continued focus on low-tax growth had little to say about problems like family breakdown. Lacking were conservative programs to alleviate the financial hardships faced by young couples in raising children, for instance. Such programs would support conservative goals of allowing more children to grow up in stable, two-parent households, letting one parent stay home. But it would also require an investment of tax dollars, so it was easily dismissed as "big government."

This initial effort to rethink Republican policy for the twenty-first century would take a backseat to all-out opposition to Obama and the far-reaching government response to the financial crisis. The Tea Party movement, with its anti-government message and "Don't Tread on Me" flag, was as much about working out its angst at the big spending of the Bush years as it was proximately about Obama. For these conservatives, a fresh start meant going back to the basics, which meant total opposition to government action on all fronts. When Tim Pawlenty, the original "Sam's Club Republican," ran for president in 2012, I worked for his campaign. His emphasis on bread-and-butter working-class concerns did not break through the small-government ardor of 2010 and 2012, and he left the race before Iowa.

During Obama's second term, the *Grand New Party* vision morphed into "reform conservatism." The Reformicons distinguished themselves in their willingness to rethink rigid conservative orthodoxy, but there was a bit of a nibbling-around-the-edges quality to it, offering targeted spending programs and tax credits as worker-friendly alternatives to wholesale economic redistribution. In their belief that government was not always the enemy, the Reformicons departed from the conservative policy apparatus in Washington. But their vision was not different enough to grab the attention of the Republican primary electorate. A version that was descended a golden escalator at Trump Tower on June 16, 2015.

In a party dominated by stale establishment thinking or reform proposals too easily dismissed as Democrat-lite, Trump offered frustrated Republicans something more thrilling: the prospect of unrestricted partisan combat against the media and political elite. That is the way it usually is with working-class populist movements, who win support with bold rhetorical thrusts, not detailed policies that hew toward the political center. And Trump's army of common folk was not being riled up on economic grounds, for class war of rich and poor, but to smash the political establishment—to drain the proverbial swamp.

After Trump's election, the effort to build a lasting apparatus around his upending of the conservative establishment gained steam. Oren Cass founded American Compass, a think tank focused on the American worker, from which he would launch salvos against the remaining vestiges of free-market worship on the right. Well into Trump's term, the conservative policy universe still had not adapted to this new reality. "It's one thing if that were the case in 2012 or 2013," Cass told me. "But here we were most of the way through the Trump administration and the attitude [in conservative think tanks] is pretty much: This too shall pass. If we keep our heads down and get through this term, we can go back to doing exactly what we were doing in 2014."

In the Senate, Trump's 2016 primary rival Marco Rubio advanced pro-worker policies such as placing workers on corporate boards and briefly held up Trump's tax cut bill until it did more for those at the bottom of the income distribution. Collectively, these efforts sought to build what was termed "Trumpism after Trump," keeping the good about Trump—his realignment of working-class voters into the GOP—without the chaos or election denial or bad tweets.

A harder-edged vision for the future of the right after Trump is provided by the New Right, alternatively flying under the banner of national conservatism ("NatCon") or national populism ("NatPop"). This was the latest iteration of an actually quite-old faction of the right, advancing isolationism, no-holds-barred cultural warfare, and opposition to immigration and free trade. One can argue to what extent Trump is a New Right true believer, but those on the former "paleoconservative" right—associated with the presidential bids of Pat Buchanan and with the writings of not-so-borderline white nationalists like Samuel Francis—clearly viewed him as one of them. Where Trump was first and foremost a political improviser, one who challenged Buchanan from the left for the 2000 Reform Party nomination, the New Right operates at the level of high ideology, aiming for a root-and-branch redefinition of what the right is. On Twitter, its devotees rail against "Zombie Reaganism," the so-called three-legged stool that countenanced free trade, open immigration policies, and "forever wars." Where the high-minded traditional right is committed to the ideal of America as a global bastion of liberty, the New Right sees the country as something like an Old European ethnostate, the kind where only an ethnic Gaul could be a true Frenchman. Discarding the tenets of classical liberalism, these nationalists find common ground with authoritarian strongmen who vigorously defend their lands from Western cosmopolitan influence—Vladimir Putin among them. The New Right cares little for free-market economics, gladly endorsing aggressive antitrust enforcement to punish woke corporations. As a movement with more support online than in the real electorate, much of what it does feels performative. "Medicare for All, abortions for none" is the a-little-too-on-the-nose description of the alt-right presidential hopeful on HBO's *Succession*, one that's become an inside joke among the rabble-rousers of the New Right.

In the real world, voters care very little about raging online debates between the various ideological subvariants on the right. Just as the pre-

Trump fights over the future of conservativism proved irrelevant to the direction of politics under Trump, so it is with the intra-right skirmishes today. Yes, there is a populist center of gravity in American politics, one that represents most swing voters. But they are hardly New Right ideologues, espousing a combination of hard-left economic views and hard-right cultural views. The key point about these voters is that they are only slightly off-center in their views on either dimension, hardly good recruits for a new ideological vanguard.

Grand ideological gestures and policy briefs play a secondary role in the work of building durable political majorities. More important are the leaders who actually put themselves forward to do the job. It is these leaders who catalyze movements around a set of policies, attracting new constituencies to the cause. We will examine these three key ingredients of realignment in turn: the candidate, the policies, and the voters.

THE CANDIDATE

In the last generation, we've seen two presidents win by forging an intimate connection with blue-collar workers. The first hailed from Hope, Arkansas. In his 1992 and 1996 campaigns, Bill Clinton came close to winning the white working class, and won large parts of the rural South and border states. In his speeches, Clinton revealed himself as a master at holding a mirror up to the struggles of everyday Americans. Late in the 1992 campaign, he campaigned in Albany, Georgia, deep in the state's rural southwest. Here is some of what he had to tell the crowd assembled at the city's train station that September day:

> In the morning I go running on the streets in Little Rock and all sorts of people come up to me. I knew how important the family leave bill was a couple of years ago when I stopped my morning jog at the local McDonald's about two blocks from a homeless shelter and a young couple came up to me living in a homeless shelter because they both had to give up their jobs when their kid got cancer and they had to bring their child to the Arkansas

> Children's Hospital and there was no medical and family leave provision in our law to protect people like that. I want you to know that I may not have all the answers and I won't always tell you what you want to hear, but I will wake up every day thinking about you, and your interests, and your hopes, and your children, and your future.

Clinton concluded his remarks: "Now you are being called upon, every one of you, to secure a better future for your children and your grandchildren, and to make America great again, economically, educationally, and socially." It was a familiar refrain the country would hear again in 2016.

While most political speeches are drab litanies of policy laundry lists and rote commentaries on the state of political affairs, Clinton's were something different. He was serving as the voice of the people, channeling their emotions and frustrations. And in doing so, he fused together both liberally coded and conservative-coded values. He "felt your pain," tying back to Jonathan Haidt's liberal moral foundation of care and compassion, but was also standing up for people who "worked hard" and "played by the rules" who could no longer make it in America, drawing on conservative values of hard work and rule-following.

There is a direct through line from Bill Clinton's "feel your pain" campaigns to the one a Fifth Avenue real estate mogul waged in 2016. "To every voter in Milwaukee, to every voter living in every inner city, or every forgotten stretch of our society," Trump would say on the campaign trail, "I am running to offer you a better future." In a memorable and evocative passage from his November victory speech, Trump vowed that "[t]he forgotten men and women of this country will be forgotten no longer." The phrase "forgotten men and women" had begun making its way into Trump's economic speeches during the general election campaign, and it fundamentally shows how one wins an economic debate: not simply by proposing popular, poll-tested policies, but simply by standing beside the average American, showing that you think like they do. Hillary Clinton, too, promised to help regular people, but often these promises in her speeches came across as litanies of proposals, trying to touch every base, rather than extended stories like the one her husband told about the people he met outside the McDonald's in Little Rock. Worse still, she appeared to impugn Trump supporters—not unlike the way Mitt Romney slighted Obama's working-class supporters—calling them a "basket of deplorables." Trump had an easy layup when he was able to frame her comments as an attack on ordinary working Americans, as he did in a speech in the fall of 2016, declaring, "The hardworking people she calls deplorable are the most admirable people I know: they are cops and soldiers, teachers and firefighters, young and old, moms and dads, blacks, whites and Latinos—but above everything else, they are all American."

This side of Trump's campaign is often forgotten in the torrent of insults that marked much of the rest of his campaign. I realized it when I turned on the radio late in the 2016 campaign to hear one of his speeches before an Ohio crowd using the "forgotten men and women" refrain. That was at that moment that I revised my assessment of Trump's odds of victory dramatically upward. His working-class rhetoric was not just a refreshing pivot for his campaign, but for the Republican Party.

And if you knew where to look, this rhetoric was there all along. It was there in an early Trump visit to Flint, Michigan, an auto town that exemplified all the ways that the working class has seen their future diminished. It was the hometown that left-wing filmmaker Michael Moore chronicled in 1989's *Roger & Me*, about the plant shutdowns that reduced the General Motors workforce in the town from a high of 80,000 to 50,000. By 2015, the GM workforce in and around Flint had fallen even more steeply, to 7,200. Recall the Flint water crisis, when the mostly Black population within the city lines was forced to consume lead-poisoned drinking water, a moral touchstone of Hillary Clinton's primary campaign. For decades, Democrats were the ones who told the story of Flint and the corporate raiders responsible for its plight. Republicans before Trump were mostly on the defensive about places like Flint.

Trump visited the Flint Assembly Plant in August 2015, a place well off the beaten path from the early state primary hustings in Iowa and New Hampshire. His visit, documented at the time by the *Washington Post*'s David Weigel, showed how adaptable Trump's base-pleasing rhetoric on immigration and China could be to a general election battleground dominated by blue-collar voters who had trended toward Obama in 2008 and 2012. Trump in Flint talked not only about immigration but about bringing auto industry jobs back to the United States, promising that as president he wouldn't allow Ford to relocate a plant to Mexico. "So then I only have one question," Trump jabbed. "Do they move the plant to the United States the same day or a day later?" This was music to Flint's ears. "A lot of what he says hits a chord with me," said a former Buick City plant worker. "Immigration and jobs going to China—this area's really suffered from that. I just like somebody that stands up for what he speaks about." "I've been waiting for a stronger president, somebody that I could look up to and respect again. He could stand up to those other countries," said another rally attendee. "It's wrong when they can build furniture in China and ship it here cheaper than it costs us to build it here." While Romney came to Michigan four years earlier promising managerial wizardry to save the auto industry, Trump's business acumen was more about his rule-breaking mojo. "He's a businessman," Brenda Parsons told Weigel. "Being a businessman, he knows the ways around. I don't think he'd go to Congress and ask. I think he'd just do it." In the fall of 2016, Trump posted a double-digit improvement over Mitt Romney's 2012 performance in Flint.

The populist coalition Trump was able to capture in 2016 was defined by its anger at elites, but the elite in question was the political establishment more than the economic one. Trump recast the villain in the Flint story from Wall Street profiteers to an easily fooled Washington establishment trading away American jobs to other countries. In the end, Trump's was the more compelling story. Americans hate Wall Street but they love entrepreneurial success stories. By contrast, they have only disdain for the political class.

This is not a new phenomenon. Lance Tarrance, the veteran Republican pollster, identified this populist undercurrent in the party almost forty years ago, in numerous campaigns that saw more populist ex-Democrats go toe-to-toe with the GOP's old-line country-club establishment. This description of the voter Tarrance relied on, from a 1986 profile by Ronald Brownstein, could double up as a profile of the Obama-to-Trump voter from 2016:

> Unlike traditional Republicans, the conservative populists are not reflexively antigovernment, they see "a role for the government protecting the individual against economic hardship and promoting economic change." Culturally, they are conservative, holding "values that are somewhat nostalgic" though they don't necessarily support the religious right agenda on specific issues such as abortion or back aggressive foreign intervention, Tarrance maintains. And in pure populist tradition, they are skeptical of big institutions, "including big business as well as big labor and big government."

In the 1980s, it was unknown which side in the Republican civil war would prevail. In 1986, a populist client of Tarrance's failed to derail the comeback bid of William P. Clements Jr., the first Republican governor of Texas since Reconstruction. "The Republican Party is still a suburban, upper-income, upper-educated party," noted Stuart Rothenberg, who would become one of the nation's leading political handicappers. "Let's face it, [Clements] the old-time Republican won." The suburban, upper-income, upper-educated Republicans aren't winning many of those same intraparty battles today.

Despite the strength of the Republican establishment in those days, Tarrance in 1980 identified a group numbering around a third of the Republican primary electorate who would rally behind a populist outsider, a "white knight" riding in on horseback, casting aside the career politicians. Of the five candidate archetypes identified in open-ended responses to Tarrance's survey of Republicans, the populist outsider had the most theoretical support. Yet in the decades that followed, none of the avatars of conservative primary resistance to the establishment perfectly fit the bill of the populist outsider. It took until 2016 for one such candidate to quickly rally the support of a third of Republicans against a fractured field.

The very early days of the Trump candidacy are remembered for his rhetoric on immigration and his pledge to build a wall. But that is not the lens through which Trump's earliest supporters saw him. We asked people supporting Trump in August 2015 to write a few words about why they were doing so. Immigration was mentioned far more than any other issue—but it fell far down the list, much lower than voters' visceral reactions to Trump the man. The most dominant theme we heard, by far, was that he was not a career politician. Other words used more commonly than "immigration" were "businessman," "truth," "balls," and yes, "hair."

When voters talk about politicians, policy is rarely what they talk about. Alignment on a certain set of principles are table stakes, not enough on their own to win. A winning set of personal attributes is what distinguishes the victors from the also-rans. And for a populist candidate, that means a convincing ability to channel the experiences of the large majority of Americans who are not high in education or income.

THE POLICIES

Donald Trump waged one successful campaign on populist themes, yet failed to translate this energy into a consistently populist governing agenda. Trump or another Republican could win with a populist coalition in 2024. Without further efforts to develop such a governing agenda, they, too, will face the same problem.

Specific policies seldom determine electoral success, but Republicans should nonetheless reorient their policy priorities to reflect the makeup of their voting coalition. This task is not about electoral advantage, but about actually delivering for the people who vote for them. Beyond a few broad thoughts on how to level the economic playing field for the multiracial working class, and some dos and don'ts, I don't come bearing a policy laundry list for the next Republican administration. Contrary to public belief, dictating to politicians what policies they should pursue is not what pollsters do. That task must ultimately be left to elected leaders themselves. My job is to help them communicate those priorities, while pointing out any pitfalls along the way. Ultimately, the ability to deliver good policy depends on winning elections. And election victories are driven less by policy specifics than the overarching story a candidate is able to tell, their gut-level connection with the average American, and underlying events and conditions in the country. On the policy front, the task of the candidate while campaigning for higher office is to avoid mistakes, like supporting policies that will actively alienate key voting blocs.

Once victory is achieved, they have broader latitude to fill in policy specifics. When Donald Trump took office, his governing agenda was mostly a blank sheet of paper. For Republicans today, it needs to be something more.

When people hear about Republicans as a working-class party, they might assume this means an embrace of left-wing ideas about government spending, taxation, and regulation. But the new Republican voters are not demanding this, and the current working-class realignment is happening under the umbrella of a pro-capitalist, moderate-to-conservative politics of aspiration. Are there areas of economic policy where the party needs to be less dogmatically right wing? Sure. But what is needed in these instances is a move to the middle—not a surrender to the left. And much of this shift toward the economic center has already happened.

The first step is to correctly identify where the divides in our economy and society are coming from, and then to adopt policies to help those disadvantaged by those divides. The major divide that underlies all the others is education. It's the variable that means the most about how people live their daily lives, as evidenced by how voters are sorting themselves politically and geographically. If the Republican base now consists of a majority of people who did not graduate college, the party's job is to stand up for them. And this means not only giving voice to their cultural concerns, but pursuing policies that would better their economic lot.

If this sounds like old-fashioned income redistribution, read on. What this would actually mean is a direct assault on the social status and winner-take-all privilege of the educated elite, addressing the social inequality between graduates and non-graduates that makes racial and income disparities worse. Recall Charles Murray's Newton, Iowa, where the CEO lived on the same block as the factory worker. Economically, the two were unequal. But socially, this was a broadly egalitarian society where both lived by the same communal norms. This was an America where both the economic elite and the working class were not only surrounded by people just like themselves. It should be our goal to move toward a multiracial version of that America.

This starts with combating discrimination against the non-graduate with every ounce of the zeal we combat discrimination on the basis of race or gender, and with the same level of intention that the government targets assistance to low-income Americans. We currently bemoan the lack of diversity in the upper ranks of corporate America. A big reason behind this lack of diversity are requirements that every white-collar job—even for the most entry-level position—be filled with someone with a college diploma. These requirements exclude roughly three-quarters of Black and Hispanic applicants from even being considered, as compared to just over half of white applicants. Unnecessary degree requirements are the textbook definition of a policy that produces disparate racial impacts, impacts that liberals argue need to be urgently addressed.

Other societies, Germany for instance, do this better, with widespread apprenticeships in lieu of four years in a college classroom. Just 31 percent of twenty-five to sixty-four-year-olds in Germany have any kind of postsecondary credential, compared to 50 percent here, and their economy is on par with our own. To the extent U.S. policymakers have a solution to these disparities, it is to adopt racial quotas for admission to elite universities. The problem is that this benefits a microscopically small share of the population, who are likely to do well in life anyway. In the grand scheme of things, the question of who can go to Harvard doesn't matter much. The larger problem lies in those who don't go to college, or drop out, because they judge—not wrongly—that the exorbitant cost of a college diploma isn't worth it.

The ultimate goal is to ensure that more people can rise high up the economic ladder without a college diploma, just as they used to. Of course, some fields like law or medicine will continue to require advanced degrees. Some people will want exposure to academic life. But college should not be an all-purpose economic sorting machine.

This starts with rethinking—and, wherever possible, eliminating—degree requirements for employment in both the public and private sectors. Hiring people from working-class backgrounds, without a degree, should be a goal for businesses, akin to hiring racial minorities or veterans. Struggling with labor shortages during the pandemic, many companies were already eliminating degree requirements for "middle skill" positions, providing on-the-job training instead. Requiring that an applicant have a BA simply as a throwaway line in a job description, not because they followed a relevant course of study in college, should be ended as a practice. We have stopped doing so at my company, since the skills needed can be learned anywhere, not just in a classroom.

Government can lead the way, too, by reducing degree requirements for its own workers. States from Maryland to Pennsylvania to Utah have already ended these requirements for state government jobs. This model should also be extended to the teaching profession, starting in elementary school education. It is a good thing for teachers to come from all corners of society, not just from the minority of families who could afford to send their children to college. Before college education was widespread, we had teachers colleges and other ways of training teachers that didn't require a one-size-fits-all, four-year degree. Replacing our overreliance on college for career preparation should be a multiplicity of one- to two-year professional certification programs that won't bankrupt the middle-class family trying to give their children a leg up after high school. Policy should also work to dismantle unreasonable barriers to employment for the working class, like excessive licensing requirements for jobs such as hairdressing or cosmetology. Under the umbrella of the Alliance for Opportunity, a group of state-level conservative think tanks have come together around a bipartisan set of solutions to encourage more employment opportunities for the working class, including criminal justice reform policies that help former inmates reintegrate into the workforce. The idea here is not merely to talk up vocational and technical education in high school, already a popular talking point for politicians. It is to dismantle the gating mechanism for most desirable, professional careers, one that has reinforced an informal caste system in America.

Where the economic gaps between classes and racial groups are largest is in wealth, a reflection not only of the economic divides of the present but also those of the past. In 2016, the average white family had a net worth of $171,000, ten times that of the average Black family, at $17,150. The picture is different when one includes the future value of Social Security benefits, which, if calculated as a source of wealth, would dramatically increase the net worth of Black, Hispanic, and lower-income families. According to one study, the average net worth of late boomers, age fifty-one to fifty-six, increases by between $150,000 to $200,000 across racial groups when one factors in Social Security. The racial wealth gap is a less daunting $377,800 for whites to $172,700 for Blacks under this measure, with more than 80 percent of the wealth of Blacks and Hispanics in the middle of the income distribution tied up in future Social Security benefits. Why not allow more ways for workers to unlock that wealth, either in their lifetimes or for their children? Proposals have been made for workers to be able to tap into these future benefits for childcare or paid family leave. A more ambitious proposal would allow for adult children to inherit a portion of their parents' unused Social Security benefits, letting them build a nest egg or fund the down payment on a home, beyond the current Social Security death benefit. Such a policy would especially help Black families, but also those in lower-income brackets, whose lower life expectancy means they are not able to tap into all of their promised benefits. In the arena of family policy, Mitt Romney, whose infamous "47 percent" comment in the 2012 campaign branded him as out of touch with working families, has led the charge to replace the current child tax credit with larger monthly installment payments to young families.

Many ideas like this circulated in the George W. Bush administration under the moniker of the "ownership society." Making it easier for the working class to acquire assets has long been a tenet of conservative thinking, with Margaret Thatcher's policy to allow council estate tenants the right to buy their homes at a discount being one of the defining policies of her tenure. But the Bush-era "ownership society" fell short mostly by focusing on lowering the threshold for making mortgage payments, leaving workers exposed when the subprime market collapsed. The goal instead should have been to allow people to accrue tangible assets, not making it easier to finance debt.

One could go on and on about various proposals to reorient conservative policy toward the working class. My focus here is mostly on politics, so I will gladly leave the detailed mechanics of overhauling entitlements and social welfare programs to the policy experts. I will, however, conclude this policy discussion with a short list of don'ts. To the extent policy makes an impression on voters, it is usually when politicians make careless mistakes.

The key principle to remember when pushing for policy change is that of loss aversion: voters value losses more than equally sized gains. Policy shifts that change existing benefits but don't ultimately result in people receiving *more*—either benefits or tax cuts—are political losers. Here, voters calculate that no change at all is better than an uncertain future state. This includes the idea of replacing most government welfare programs with a universal basic income, which in addition to triggering negative emotional responses around incentivizing idleness, violates this rule by zeroing out existing benefits people have grown accustomed to. Voters have a deep status quo bias, and proposals to change existing benefit structures start out at a disadvantage.

Another don't is more basic, yet even small-government Republican politicians still run afoul of it: don't raise taxes on the middle class. Republicans have historically been the party of tax cuts, arguing that broadly based tax cuts that include the wealthy and entrepreneurs can spur job creation for the working class. With tax rates near historic lows and deficits high, tax cuts have played less of a role in the Republican policy playbook. From a political-economy standpoint, the realignment of wealthy voters to the Democrats makes cutting taxes for them even less appealing as a strategy. But there is no reason Republicans can't apply their tax-cutting zeal to earners at the bottom of the income distribution. Oddly, some Republicans have proposed doing the opposite, grumbling that barely half of Americans pay federal income taxes and proposing that all pay a nominal amount so that they have "skin in the game." This was the subject of a proposal made in 2022, one that would be quickly denounced by Republican leadership—but not before it became a subject of incessant Democratic attacks in the midterm elections. It was also the impetus behind Romney's famous "47 percent" comments. Proponents of the so-called Fair Tax want to eliminate income taxes entirely, moving to broad-based consumption taxes instead, a political disaster that would make those at the bottom pay more.

Just because many working Americans don't pay federal income taxes doesn't mean they don't pay other kinds of taxes, many of them regressive, taking more of a percentage of income from the poor than the rich. These include payroll taxes, sales taxes, property taxes, and gasoline taxes. Virginia's Glenn Youngkin had the right idea when he campaigned on eliminating the sales tax for groceries, responding to high inflation hitting low-income workers hardest. For a populist Republican, a progressive tax system is a political and policy opportunity, just as it is for the left. Instead of tax hikes for the rich, they can fight for tax cuts for the poor. But that is only possible if the right ends its singular obsession with income taxes, changing the way government programs are funded to allow for regressive taxes—like payroll and gasoline taxes—to also be cut.

Of course, opportunities for fiscal expansion will be few and far between in the era of limits we are now entering. While they are out of power, Republicans may be tempted to go back to the well of cutting spending. They would do well to recall how badly this approach backfired in attempts to cut Medicare in the 1990s or overhaul Social Security in the 2000s. The country may well need to reform entitlements to ensure their fiscal solvency, but there are substantial political costs for Republicans who try to go it alone. Until and unless a bipartisan solution avails itself, Republicans would be wise to tread lightly.

Republicans should be bolder in advocating for new public spending in one area they all agree is a legitimate function of government: ensuring public safety. Campaigns to defund the police may have failed politically and in actually cutting police budgets, but the campaigners succeeded in all the ways that mattered: demoralizing police officers, causing them to leave their jobs in record numbers, and curtailing routine neighborhood policing. There is abundant evidence now that reductions in policing since 2020 have made urban communities less safe, with disproportionate negative impacts in the Black community. The 1990s crime bill may have erred in its focus on tough sentencing guidelines and incarceration, but an effective selling point of the legislation was its funding for one hundred thousand new police officers, the goal of which is to prevent crime and the resulting costs of imprisonment. We need an effort on a similar scale today, with a surge of traditional neighborhood policing, paired with police reforms like those proposed by South Carolina senator Tim Scott.

The content of the issue page on a candidate's website might matter little to the ultimate outcome of an election, but it matters a lot to how the country is governed. The political shifts we've seen in recent years—and in particular, the one that gave us Donald Trump—scream out for a policy response. First and foremost are policies to tackle social inequality, boosting prospects of the country's non-college-graduate majority.

THE VOTERS

Even the most charismatic candidate with the best policies must still assemble a winning coalition. For Republicans, increasing support from the multiracial populist coalition is the key to winning elections in the future.

The two components of the multiracial populist coalition, the white working class and nonwhites, are often thought of as opposites. Though I believe that the evidence is strong that both groups will move closer together in their voting behavior over the long term, currently they remain quite far apart. Rates of demographic growth and decline within the various groups will matter a lot to both parties' electoral prospects. Thus far, Republicans have been able to stave off demographic demise by increasing their support levels from nonwhite voters. This, I have argued, is part of a natural convergence toward the social, cultural, and economic mainstream, one that we can expect to continue into the future. But if Republicans falter for any reason, a demographic winter may still be at hand and the prophets of the Emerging Democratic Majority may yet be proven right. The time horizon on which to judge this is not the next election: demographic change over a short, four-year election cycle is likely to be washed out by shifts in public sentiment. But over a long-enough period, the effects are clear. And so, to determine what a future-proof Republican majority coalition might look like, we need to look beyond the election of 2024, to the election of 2036.

By one measure, the Emerging Democratic Majority, driven by the country's changing demographics, has already arrived: Republicans have lost the popular vote in seven of the last eight presidential elections. The one candidate who was the exception, George W. Bush, won it on the basis of a unique ability to win over Hispanic voters. Nonetheless, if you squint, Republicans are still competitive at the presidential level, winning three of these eight elections, with some extra assistance from the Electoral College. This is indeed the system the Founders intended, not a direct democracy, but a system designed to balance the interests of different states and regions. Nonetheless, a future where Republicans win only by the good graces of the Electoral College is untenable. The result of this continuing trend will be a kind of learned helplessness that optimizes for winning 48 not 51 percent of the vote, resulting in the selection of more extreme candidates that will place the party on the back foot when real popular majorities do matter—as in all the individual House, Senate, gubernatorial, and down-ballot elections. To some extent, perverse non-majoritarian incentives have already taken over, in how candidates win primaries in ways that render them toxic to general election swing voters, in the failure to win the 2020 election despite a winning economic record, and in the party's 2022 failures attributable to the 2020 election loser. It may be easier said than done, but Republicans need to get serious and learn how to win popular majorities again, now and in the more diverse America to come. That will require the party to move beyond its present dysfunction, one personified by the post-2016 Donald Trump, but not limited to him alone.

Winning a popular majority in the 2036 election will require the Republican candidate doing even better among Hispanic, Asian American, and especially Black voters, continuing to naturally expand its margins among the white working class, and maintaining some semblance of support among whites with a college degree. To understand just how much, we first need to quantify the share of the 2036 electorate that different groups will make up. Work done by the States of Change project, a joint effort by the left-leaning Center for American Progress, the right-leaning American Enterprise Institute, and the Bipartisan Policy Center has created such projections going out to 2036. It's doubtful that this specific projection, assuming 2016 turnout levels by different groups, will prove to be exactly on the mark, but directionally, most of its conclusions will be: in the lower share of working-class whites as a share of the electorate or in the higher share of Hispanics. Table 11.1 shows Echelon Insights' estimates of the demographic makeup of the 2020 electorate side by side with the future 2036 electorate.

Table 11.1: The Makeup of the American Electorate, 2020 and 2036

Group	2020	2036
White Non-College	42.9%	35.3%
White College	28.5%	29.0%
Nonwhite Non-College	18.8%	24.4%
Nonwhite College	7.7%	11.2%
Multiracial Populist **(White Non-College + Nonwhite)**	**71.4%**	**71.0%**
Non-College	***62.4%***	***59.7%***

Sources: Echelon Insights demographic estimates for 2020 and States of Change projections for 2036

From 2020 to 2036, whites without a college degree are predicted to drop as a share of the electorate by nearly eight points, from 43 to 35 percent, while nonwhite voters will rise from 27 to 36 percent. These gains nearly cancel each other out, so the size of the multiracial populist coalition changes barely at all in this period, staying steady at 71 percent. This also means the rest of the electorate—whites with a college degree—hardly qualifies as "ascendant" or "rising," staying constant at 29 percent. The share of the electorate without a college degree will tick down a little, from 63 to 60 percent, with large drops in the white non-college-educated electorate, offset by a considerable increase in the nonwhite, non-college-educated electorate. At the end of this process, the Hispanic electorate is projected to rise from about 10 percent today to 14 percent, the Black share of the electorate will tick up slightly from 12 to 13 percent, and Asian Americans and other groups, including those of two or more races, will go from 6 to 8 percent of the electorate.

With the Republicans' strongest group shrinking and their weakest set of groups growing, Republicans will need to increase their support levels across all parts of the multiracial populist coalition just to keep pace with where they are today. And since Republicans were not in a winning position in 2020, they will need a further improvement to get back to a winning baseline. Table 11.2 shows scenarios for the percentage of the vote Republicans would need to receive within all demographic groups to win the 2036 popular vote.

Table 11.2: Winning Republican Scenarios for 2036

Republican vote share by group in 2020 and under 2036 demographics

Group	2020	2036 Republican Victory Scenarios			
White Non-College	*62%*	*70%*	*68%*	*71%*	*71%*
White College	*45%*	*40%*	*45%*	*45%*	*48%*
White	55%	56%	58%	59%	61%
Black	8%	24%	20%	18%	15%
Hispanic	36%	50%	48%	46%	42%
Asian/Other	39%	45%	45%	42%	40%

Sources: AP/NORC VoteCast for 2020 and author calculations based on 2036 States of Change demographic share estimates

Because the white vote is likely to prove less reliable for Republicans over time, thanks to higher rates of college education and cultural liberalism, future conservative majorities will depend on culturally right-leaning nonwhites riding to the rescue. In all of these scenarios, Republicans are able to win while achieving less of the two-party share of the white vote they achieved in 2016—61 percent. But this will require strong increases in nonwhite support. Republicans may still win more of the white vote, as the Trump elections might have constituted a nadir among suburban whites, but they shouldn't count on this, and should instead focus on the larger opportunity of continuing to realign culturally conservative nonwhite voters—especially Black conservatives.

Within the white vote, Republicans should naturally be able to further consolidate their position among white non-college-educated voters, rising to around 70 percent support by 2036. Much of this will be a function of generational turnover: nearly all of the white working class in the electorate by then will have come of age in an era of high political polarization between graduates and non-graduates. Among the youngest set of fully post-college-age white voters, thirty- to forty-four-year-olds, political divides between white graduates and non-graduates are the widest of any age group. In the first, wildest scenario, the education gap balloons to 60 points on the margin and 30 points in support levels for each party—70 percent Republican among non-college-educated whites and 40 percent among those with a college degree. That's an increase of about 20 points from the 40-point margin gap today. If education polarization continues in this vein, with Republicans gaining among non-college-educated voters, but losing among college graduates, they will be limited to no more than 56 percent of the white vote, barely above 2020's losing level.

To make up for it, they will need to post some spectacular gains with racial and ethnic minorities: drawing even among Hispanic voters, winning 24 percent of the Black vote, doubling or tripling their 2020 Black support, depending on which exit poll you believe is correct, and improving further among Asian American, Pacific Islander, Native American, and mixed-race voters. Before we dismiss this possibility out of hand, we should pause to consider that shifts of this magnitude over the course of a decade or two are not uncommon. In the sixteen years between 2000 and 2016, we went from an electorate where there was only a modest gap between whites by education to one where the gap was nearly 40 points on the margin and 20 points in terms of the shares of the vote earned by each party. In 2000, there was no age gap between the youngest and the oldest voters, and now there is a big one. Electoral forecasts generally tend to play it too safe, so it is a useful thought experiment to first game out scenarios with bigger rather than smaller shifts. In all likelihood, one or more of the numbers in this scenario will change even more than these projections.

While Republicans could make improvements of that magnitude among nonwhite voters in this period, these are admittedly aggressive estimates. They would also make nonwhites as a group nearly as Republican (39 percent) as whites with a college degree (40 percent), an outcome I think I will see within my lifetime, though maybe not in the next decade or two. Republicans' share of the nonwhite vote is naturally on the rise, since the fastest-growing groups within it—Hispanics, Asian Americans, and voters of two or more races—vote more Republican than slower-growing African Americans. But a shift to Republicans winning four in ten nonwhite voters would certainly be remarkable. Whether they arrive by 2036 or not, these are the numbers we could one day expect if Hispanics do come to fully resemble white Catholics in their voting patterns and if Black voters start voting mostly according to their ideological leanings and stances on issues.

Of course, it would be better for Republicans if they did not lose support in any demographic, but all coalitional shifts generally involve tradeoffs. If they are going to lose voters or show only modest gains, whites with college degrees seem like the most logical sacrifice. I will nevertheless issue a warning similar to that issued by John Judis and Ruy Teixeira about Democratic support in the white working class: Republicans cannot afford to write off the white suburban college-educated voter entirely. A key property of all majority coalitions is that they don't entirely make sense—as when FDR was able to unite African Americans and white Southerners or when Barack Obama was able to unite parts of the midwestern white working class with his "rising American electorate." A winning Republican coalition will require some mix of both upper- and working-class voters, of cosmopolitans and traditionalists.

Should Republicans manage to recover some lost white suburban support, they would still have to increase their nonwhite support, but the need would not be as great. In the least aggressive scenario, where white education polarization is just a touch more than it is today, and the party performs at 2016 levels with white voters, they would require 15 percent of the Black vote, 42 percent of the Hispanic vote, and 40 percent of Asian Americans and others. These are roughly the levels achieved by the party in the 2022 midterms, which, while not comparable to a presidential-year electorate, show that these goals are within reach.

What I've laid out so far are optimistic scenarios. The pessimistic ones for the party are that they cannot keep up with shifting demographics and begin to lose—or that they continue to win in the most chaotic and shambolic ways possible, never truly achieving a secure governing majority. Perhaps with lower immigration levels and falling rates of college attendance, demographic change won't happen as quickly, allowing the party to muddle through for longer. And the possibility remains that Republicans can continue to win without winning the popular vote. Going by demographics alone, a Republican Electoral College advantage is likely to persist in some form, though this prediction is more uncertain, depending on the exact partisan rank ordering of large states. Too many Republicans moving to Florida or Democrats improving their fortunes in Texas could radically alter these calculations.

Nevertheless, states competitive in either 2016 or 2020 will continue to have a more Republican-leaning demographic mix in 2036, containing more white non-college-educated voters, 37.9 percent, than the country as a whole, at 35.3 percent. The future demographic mix of the battleground states—conceding that the exact list of states in this group is likely to change some in the next decade—much more closely resembles that of red states than blue states.

In the 2020-era electoral battlegrounds, the Black vote in 2036 will matter more than the Hispanic vote, outvoting it 15 to 12 percent. Thanks to the influence of California, Hispanics will be concentrated more strongly outside of battleground states than inside them. This fact

Figure 11.1: Battlegrounds Look More Like Red States in 2036

Projected demographic makeup of the electorate in 2036, by 2016–2020 state competitiveness

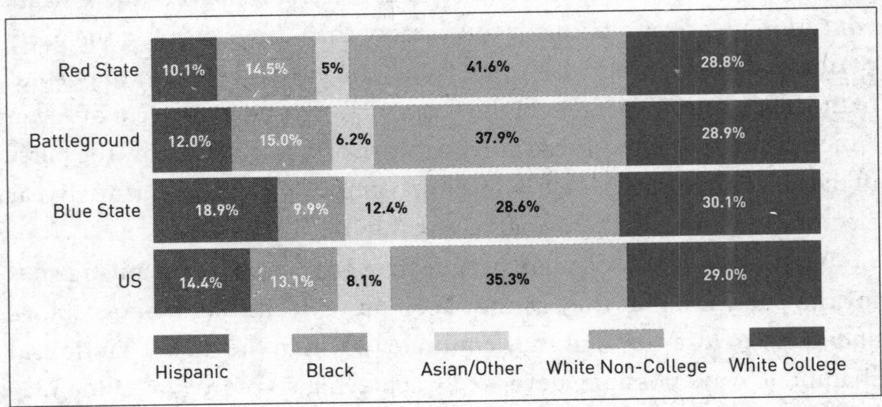

Source: States of Change Project

makes improvements in the African American vote—and among Black conservatives especially—paramount for Republican success in 2036 and beyond. At the state level, the battlegrounds will continue to be divided between a northern tier, including Maine, Michigan, Minnesota, and New Hampshire, where working-class whites will continue to form majorities or near-majorities in 2036, and a group of Sunbelt states where large Black and Hispanic populations combine with the working-class majority among whites to produce multiracial populist concentrations above the national average of 71 percent.

The electoral battlegrounds with the largest multiracial populist coalitions in 2036 will be Nevada (81.5 percent), New Mexico (80.6 percent), Florida (78.2 percent), and Georgia (76.9 percent). This list itself shows that this coalition of voters is very much up for grabs. Florida is the model for the Republican multiracial future, a rising Republican bastion where nonwhite voters will be close to a majority in 2036 and where Hispanics vote close to how the state as a whole does. Georgia represents the limitations and frustrated ambitions of this coalition, where Republican gains won't be possible without a breakthrough among Black voters. The Southwest rests on a knife's edge: Republican gains among Hispanics there lag behind those in Florida or Texas. The low number of whites with degrees in working-class Nevada now means that the state votes to the right of the country as a whole, though often Democratic, while the relative strength of this demographic in the Phoenix metro has shifted Arizona toward the Democrats. And New Mexico rests on the outer edge of this frontier, leaning more Democratic, thanks to a plurality Hispanic population, one largely without immigrant origins, but within striking distance under the right circumstances. Bush's 2004 sweep of all three swing states in the region, and not Trump's performance either in 2016 or 2020, remains the model.

There are proponents of the Democratic majority hypothesis still biding their time, believing that the electorate will become educated enough or nonwhite enough to at last assure a generational progressive majority. They are likely to be frustrated yet again. The changing size and character of groups will in turn change who those groups support, likely leading us back to a competitive equilibrium. And the most competitive states will

Figure 11.2: The 2036 State Landscape

Projected demographic makeup of the 2036 electorate, by state

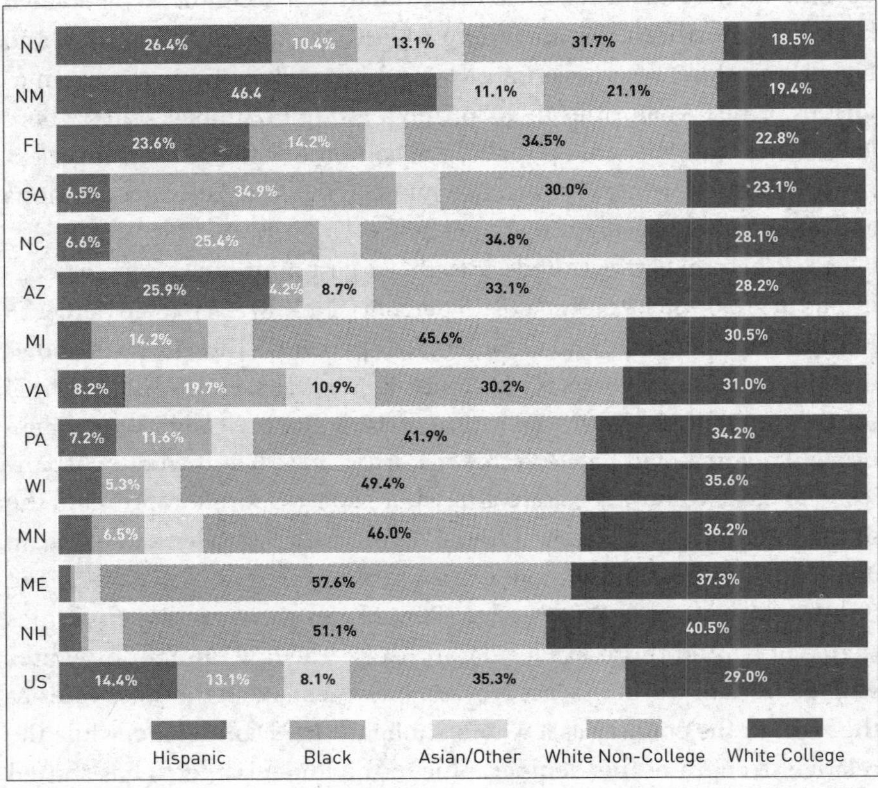

Source: States of Change Project

likely be those with a stronger working-class electorate—defined by the white working class in the North and a more diverse working class in the South and West. The road to a majority in 2036 will run straight through the working class, not through the college-educated avante-garde cordoned off in the blue states.

A NATION UP FOR GRABS

Our current politics is often described as increasingly polarized. Each year, the two sides grow further apart and partisans are increasingly willing to embrace logical fallacies and conspiracy theories to "own the libs"—or "cons." On the surface, there is plenty of supporting evidence for this view: in the disappearance of landslide national elections, in the consistency in which voters support the same party for all offices, by the absurd lengths to which voters will go to line up their views on everything, even assessments of their own personal well-being, with who happens to be in power at the moment.

But this is not the entire story. Telling a story about how partisan alignment has gotten more predictable over the years ignores what's happening under the surface. The bias toward telling a straightforward polarization story is largely a reflection of a peculiar information environment inhabited by Twitter-addled national reporters and analysts. This group rarely if ever encounter people without college degrees in their daily work, people who are more unpredictable in their political views. Among people with college degrees, particularly those interested in politics, one's choice of candidate is almost always a settled question. Changing one's mind or going against one's team is never an option. To the extent swing voters exist, they are a theoretical abstraction in the latest poll; the rare moments one encounters them viscerally in the flesh can be a revelation.

Politics is polarized, but, from election to election, the people subject to being polarized in either direction can change in sometimes subtle, sometimes dramatic ways. These shifts usually have clear demographic or regional explanations. It is not just about red areas getting redder, and blue areas getting bluer. Judged by aggregate voting statistics, places like the Rio Grande Valley *depolarized* in 2020, becoming something akin to a swing region after being one of the most Democratic in the nation.

The election of 2012 between Barack Obama and Mitt Romney was, up until that point, the modern high-watermark of lockstep polarization: 92 percent of Democrats voted for Obama and 93 percent of Republicans voted for Romney. Four years later, a radically different kind of candidate on the ballot triggered a sudden change in what the parties represented to their voters. Wealthy white voters in the suburbs rethought their allegiance to the Republican Party. Former autoworkers from the Midwest abandoned the former "party of the people." Large swaths of the country saw double-digit shifts in candidate support going in both directions.

Partisan alignment went down from 2012 levels, reflecting a temporary moment of misalignment—before zooming back to new highs of 94 percent of Democrats and Republicans respectively voting for their party's presidential nominee in 2020. Partisans became more aligned, but who was in the parties changed.

The fact that these changes continue to occur shows that there are still large numbers of voters in flux or even misaligned in the "wrong" party. The classic historical examples of misalignment were the northern liberal Republicans and the Southern conservative Democrats. These voters realigned over time in a long process of partisan re-sorting. Today, there is a smaller, but potentially decisive, misalignment among moderate-to-conservative nonwhite Democrats. This misalignment seemed like a permanent state, until it started to crack in 2020.

These Americans defy the social media–fueled stereotype of voters today as hardened ideologues completely closed off to appeals from the other side. They are moderate in the positions they take on issues and open to persuasion. When they choose a side, they will serve as a moderating force within that party, a needed antidote to the polarized hellscape of national politics and on social media today.

We would all be better off if politics in the coming years prioritized this commonsense majority, consisting mainly of people who did not graduate college. It's the right thing to do to bridge the partisan divide, elevating the perspectives of voters who do not live and breathe politics twenty-four seven and are not down-the-line partisans. And it's right in terms of helping the people in society who need help the most. A focus on the needs and priorities of the multiracial working class will address a currently under-addressed form of inequality, one where non-graduates have artificially limited job opportunities and struggle with high rates of addiction and illegitimacy. Jump-starting social mobility means policies targeted specifically at non-graduates, reversing the economic calcification and social division that came about as a result of the college sorting machine in postwar America.

This book has focused primarily on the Republican Party, as they seem to be the beneficiaries of many trends now playing out among the working-class electorate, but the Democrats also have a chance to become a stronger and better party if they dedicate themselves anew to the middle- and working-class voters who were their focus in the 1990s. That will mean casting aside some newer elements empowered by the rise of social media and the internet. Easier said than done, though. Republicans have similar problems with extremist elements that might prevent them from completely winning over the multiracial populist electorate.

This is also a story about the country, not just about partisan politics. A multiracial, mainstream, middle-class majority is emerging, one defined by closer social and family bonds between people of different racial and ethnic backgrounds. This is a welcome development, regardless of your party. Recognizing that there is still much work to be done should not blind us to the progress our country has made on numerous fronts in the struggle for equality, from housing to employment to educational opportunity.

In a multiracial democracy, having an electorate that is no longer as divided along racial lines should be a cause for celebration. If one could hold the partisan strength of the parties constant so that neither would be more likely to lose out as a result, this is a principle that both Democrats and Republicans should be able to easily agree on. In the end, what has set our country apart is its ability to overcome the blood-and-soil ethnic rivalries that marked Old Europe and early America. No, the work here is not done, something conservatives should more vocally recognize. More broadly, Republicans should not be averse to talking about race. Contrary to the conventional wisdom about such a prospect a decade or so ago, the diversification within their ranks is not coming about because the party has gone squishy or soft, but because a clearer populist message activated underlying conservative tendencies in nonwhite former Democrats.

This underlying conservatism is the same that brought into the party the descendants of the nineteenth-century immigrants who transformed the country for the better. It is not one of ideological litmus tests or economic orthodoxies, but of simple love of country, respect for those who put their lives on the line to protect it, a belief that hard work alone should determine success, and a refusal to be divided or defined purely based on one's race or ethnic background.

ACKNOWLEDGMENTS

As a first-time author, I quickly learned that the work that goes into a book extends far beyond the typing of words. The tasks are varied, from nurturing the initial seed of an idea, to writing the proposal, to delivering the pitch, and then to the whirlwind of researching, interviewing, writing, rewriting, and the nagging details of endnotes, tables, and charts. That doesn't even cover the work of getting the book out into the world, which at the moment is still somewhere off in the future for me, but approaching quickly.

At the outset, there was one team I knew who could turn a long-shot book proposal into a reality. Dylan Colligan, Keith Urbahn, and their team at Javelin performed masterfully throughout. Dylan was a calming and steadying presence, rolling the ball patiently uphill until we got a yes. Keith is a virtuoso at under-promising and over-delivering. Together, they found the perfect editor for this work in Robert Messenger, someone every bit as passionate about the ideas expressed here as I am. Robert is a pure delight to talk to, his every suggestion moving the book in a better direction. It was a privilege working with him and his entire team at Simon & Schuster.

Many of the ideas for *Party of the People* first originated in a paper for the States of Change project in 2019, exploring the potential impact of demographic change on the Republican Party. For inviting me to write this paper and for her unfailing kindness over the years, I owe a debt to Karlyn Bowman, as well as to another former American Enterprise Institute colleague, John Fortier, for pulling it all together, and to the Cato

Institute's Emily Ekins, for filling in for me on such short notice. From 2017 through its retirement in 2021, I was honored to serve on the Voter Study Group's advisory board, giving me exposure to an unparalleled and unique source of polling, exposing me to the country's best minds on voting trends, and helping me develop many of the ideas contained in this book. Joe Goldman, Robert Griffin, and Alicia Prevost deserve praise for their leadership of this work over the years.

A big thank-you to everyone who took time to talk to me and offer their advice, among them Michael Barone, Ross Barrera, Jorge Bonilla, Oren Cass, Chryl Laird, Steve Le, Sam Oh, Oscar Rosa, Leslie Sanchez, David Shor, Giancarlo Sopo, Lance Tarrance, Ruy Teixeira, and Javier Villalobos. Conversations with my friend Reihan Salam were the perfect bookends to the process. I'm grateful to very-much-not-Donald-Trump's-fixer Michael Cohen for being generous with his advice on the mechanics of writing while holding down a day job in political consulting, and for reminding me to just be myself in these pages. A special thank-you goes out to Orlando Sanchez and Shannon Vrba for their leadership of Texas Latino Conservatives and allowing me to be part of a team conducting original voter research of Texas Hispanics and the Rio Grande Valley. To all who put up with my emails, texts, and DMs for extra comments and clarifications, an added thanks.

None of this would have been possible without the entire team at Echelon Insights, where I spend my time professionally. You all have lightened the load in ways you might not have fully understood. My cofounder, Kristen Soltis Anderson, who knows what being a first-time author is like, was amazing in her advice and encouragement throughout. Echelon partner Kai Chen Yeo gave me confidence that I could step away for long spells of writing and that we wouldn't miss a beat. Special thanks go out to our dedicated staff, current and former, who put up with me throughout, including Eleanor O'Neil, Nolan Combs, Stephen Kent, Jonathan De Troye, Ryan Doogan, Victor Lue, Meaghan Bowman, Shaun Saluja, Avery James, Mike Wiley, Sander Eizen, Samuel Owens, and Benjamin Khoshbin.

I would not be writing this, at the end of a long road, without the love and support of one very special person, my wife, Maggie. Time is the one truly limited resource we all have, and this book took a lot of it, much of it in the form of time away from family. Maggie, your patience and understanding is something I will be forever grateful for. When I was so deep into the process that I could not remember the beginning nor see the end, you reminded me to celebrate the small milestones and, with Maddy's help, dropped everything to make sure I had whatever I needed. I don't think I can fully express what your support has meant, and I love you.

NOTES

ABOUT THE NUMBERS

Where another analyst had already done the work of surfacing the right fact or figure, my job was relatively easy: citing their work and moving along. It was not always quite that simple. Many of the analyses you see in these pages involved tapping into raw data sources themselves, running SQL queries, R plots, or exploring the data in Tableau, my data visualization tool of choice.

Where data used in these pages is not directly cited, it comes from countless hours spent in software, wrangling data. Here I'll provide a summary of the methods I've used. The good news is that you don't have to be a pollster to check my work. Most of the data sources I'll list below are freely available online.

Dave Leip's Atlas of U.S. Presidential Elections (https://uselectionatlas.org) remains an unparalleled source for county-level election results going back decades. Throughout this work, I had an open browser tab for the *New York Times*'s precinct-level election maps for the 2016 (https://www.nytimes.com/interactive/2018/upshot/election-2016-voting-precinct-maps.html) and 2020 (https://www.nytimes.com/interactive/2021/upshot/2020-election-map.html) elections. I routinely cross-referenced this with Justice Map's maps of race and income by census tracts or blocks (http://www.justicemap.org/). Election Twitter (#ElectionTwitter) provided gems throughout my research, especially from user Cinyc (https://

cinycmaps.com), whose tract-level ancestry map helped me identify neighborhoods and spot hyper-localized trends.

No one survey is able to answer all the questions an analyst might have. Some surveys are topically on-point, delving deep on the issues of any given point in time, but have smaller sample sizes that limit subgroup analysis—which is important when you're focused on the voting behavior of subgroups of Asian American voters, for instance. Meanwhile, very large-sample surveys are typically conducted throughout the election season and are more limited in the range of questions they consistently ask.

Out of all of these surveys, the Cooperative Election Study (https://cces.gov.harvard.edu/), going back several election cycles, hits high notes both on sample size (sixty thousand respondents) and topical depth. I also find its demographic subgroup estimates to be more consistent with other high-quality sources. With the exception of the ideological scoring of racial groups, most CES data cited in these pages is filtered to validated 2020 voters, lining up with the Biden +4.4 result in the popular vote. The Democracy Fund + UCLA Nationscape survey (https://www.voterstudygroup.org/data/nationscape) was another impressive project, interviewing more than five hundred thousand subjects throughout the 2020 election cycle. Due to its smaller sample size, I have not personally delved deeply into the American National Election Studies (ANES) data, though it is an invaluable one for its longevity, dating back to 1948, and is relied upon by others I have quoted (https://electionstudies.org/). Elsewhere, I relied on data from Echelon Insights' monthly surveys (https://echeloninsights.com/products/voter-omnibus/).

I have long been an exit poll skeptic, but they are useful for time-series analysis going back decades. In more recent elections, I consider the AP/NORC VoteCast exit poll to be more reliable (https://www.foxnews.com/elections/2022/midterm-results/voter-analysis). Using both voter file and survey data, the duo of Yair Ghitza and Jonathan Robinson from the Democratic firm Catalist has created an impressive alternative to the exit polls, projecting both the size of groups within the electorate and their choices at the ballot box (https://catalist.us/wh-national/). Using a combination of both census and voter file data, Jonathan De Troye at

Echelon Insights has created preelection projections for the size of different groups in both 2020 and 2022, data used to quantify the size of the multiracial populist coalition all the way down to the precinct level (https://medium.com/echelon-indicators/3432deb9fe05). The States of Change project has provided similar estimates of the demography of the electorate projected all the way out to 2036 (https://www.americanprogress.org/series/states-of-change/).

The work of the U.S. Census Bureau remains indispensable for the kinds of analysis I've done, with countless data sets downloaded and custom tables built at https://data.census.gov.

Last but not least, one of the more unique data sources I've been able to tap into, one not publicly available in every state, is an enhanced national voter file provided by L2 Inc. (https://l2-data.com/). Voter files can't tell you with perfect accuracy who one has voted for, but they are the only data source we have about all voters as individuals, enabling us to examine tiny differences from block to block—all in a privacy-safe manner. L2 is to be applauded for their work supporting election analysis across the political spectrum.

Foreword

xv *I explored this possibility in a 2019 paper*: Patrick Ruffini, "Two Perspectives on Demographic Changes in the States Ahead of the 2020 Presidential Election," States of Change, June 2019, https://bipartisanpolicy.org/download/?file=/wp-content/uploads/2019/06/Two-Perspectives-on-Demographic-Changes-in-the-States-Ahead-of-the-2020-Presidential-Election.pdf.

1. Party of the People

1 *"For us, it is the Democrats"*: Thomas Frank, *What's the Matter with Kansas? How Conservatives Won the Heart of America* (New York: Picador, 2005), 1.

2 *The idea that the Democrats*: Matt Grossmann, Twitter, November 22, 2016, https://twitter.com/MattGrossmann/status/801068032399245313.

2 *In the 1996 election*: "Exit Polls 2016," CNN Politics, November 8, 2016, https://www.cnn.com/election/2016/results/exit-polls.

2 *In the 2020 election*: "Live Exit Polls 2020: Election Day Exit Polls for Trump

vs. Biden," NBC News, November 3, 2020, https://www.nbcnews.com/politics/2020-elections/exit-polls.

5 *Ohio State political scientist Tom Wood*: Tom Wood, Twitter, March 25, 2021, https://twitter.com/thomasjwood/status/1375231548237213699.

6 "Vote *to stop abortion*": Frank, *What's the Matter with Kansas?*, 7.

8 *"Democrats cannot aspire to dominate this period"*: Stanley B. Greenberg, *Middle Class Dreams: The Politics and Power of the New American Majority* (New Haven, CT: Yale University Press, 1996), 305.

13 *"Barack Obama won because he recognized a new America"*: Page Gardner, Stanley B. Greenberg, Erica Seifert, and David Walker, "The Role of the Rising American Electorate in the 2012 Election," Democracy Corps, November 14, 2012, https://democracycorps.com/national-surveys/the-role-of-the-rising-american-electorate-in-the-2012-election/.

14 *"When it comes to social issues"*: "Growth and Opportunity Project," Republican National Committee, March 18, 2013, https://online.wsj.com/public/resources/documents/RNCreport03182013.pdf.

14 *"He had a crazy policy of self deportation"*: Jonathan Capehart, "Trump Knows 'Mean-Spirited,'" *Washington Post*, November 27, 2012, https://www.washingtonpost.com/blogs/post-partisan/post/donald-trump-knows-mean-spirited/2012/11/27/008cf4b4-3821-11e2-a263-f0ebffed2f15_blog.html.

16 *An analysis by the American Enterprise Institute's Philip Wallach*: Philip Wallach, "Look at the Data to See How Trump Weighed Down Republican Candidates," *Washington Post*, November 15, 2022, https://www.washingtonpost.com/opinions/2022/11/15/data-trump-weighed-down-republican-candidates/.

17 *The biggest surprise was the victory of Lester Chang*: Wilfred Chan, "The Other New York: How Republicans Made 'Shocking' Gains in the Empire State," *The Guardian*, November 28, 2022, https://www.theguardian.com/us-news/2022/nov/28/new-york-republicans-midterm-elections-brooklyn-crime.

21 *"College-educated whites, especially those with higher incomes"*: Thomas Edsall, "How Much Longer Can 'Vote Blue No Matter Who!' Last?," *New York Times*, February 1, 2023, https://www.nytimes.com/2023/02/01/opinion/democratic-party-coalition.html.

21 *"The big-picture problem"*: Lisa Lerer, "Joe from Scranton Didn't Win Back the Working Class," *New York Times*, December 5, 2020, https://www.nytimes.com/2020/12/05/us/politics/biden-blue-collar-voters.html.

22 *"Those of you"*: Perry Bacon Jr., "4 Major Flaws in Calling Republicans the 'Working Class' Party," *Washington Post*, March 7, 2023, https://www.washingtonpost.com/opinions/2023/03/07/college-degree-status-working-class-blue-collar-politics/.

2. The Cosmopolitan Trap

29 *And in a place like*: "U.S. Census Bureau QuickFacts: Falls Church city, Virginia," U.S. Census Bureau, https://www.census.gov/quickfacts/fact/table/fallschurchcityvirginia.

32 *By Wasserman's tabulations*: Dave Wasserman, Twitter, December 8, 2020, https://twitter.com/Redistrict/status/1336349272950890497.

33 *In 2000*: Hannah Gilberstadt and Andrew Daniller, "Liberals Make Up the Largest Share of Democratic Voters, but Their Growth Has Slowed in Recent Years," Pew Research Center, January 17, 2020, https://www.pewresearch.org/fact-tank/2020/01/17/liberals-make-up-largest-share-of-democratic-voters/.

34 *where they trailed conservative-identifiers*: Lydia Saad, "Democrats' Identification as Liberal Now 54%, a New High," Gallup, January 12, 2023, https://news.gallup.com/poll/467888/democrats-identification-liberal-new-high.aspx.

35 *The company's president*: Charles A. Murray, *Coming Apart: The State of White America, 1960–2010* (New York: Crown Forum, 2012), 74.

35 *"If somebody with an MBA degree applies for a job"*: Letters of Note, Twitter, November 4, 2018, https://twitter.com/lettersofnote/status/1062751597053337602.

36 *So long as one belonged to the right social circles*: David Brooks, "'The Chosen': Getting In," *New York Times*, November 6, 2005, https://www.nytimes.com/2005/11/06/books/review/the-chosen-getting-in.html.

36 *In just eight years, from 1952 to 1960*: Murray, *Coming Apart*, 55.

37 *Up until 1980*: Bill Bishop and Robert G. Cushing, *The Big Sort: Why the Clustering of Like-Minded America Is Tearing Us Apart* (Boston: Houghton Mifflin Harcourt, 2009), 131.

37 *In* The Rise of the Creative Class: Richard Florida, *The Rise of the Creative Class, Revisited* (New York: Basic Books, 2014), 237–49.

38 *Those purely in the ranks of the middle class*: Stephen Rose, "Squeezing the Middle Class," Brookings Institution, August 10, 2020, https://www.brookings.edu/research/squeezing-the-middle-class/.

38 *In 2000*: Murray, *Coming Apart*, 78.

39 *Using class directories*: Ibid., 86.

40 *Satellite imagery from 2005 to 2015*: Patrick Ruffini, Twitter, April 16, 2021, https://twitter.com/PatrickRuffini/status/1383245523314888707.

40 *The county has the highest median household income*: "U.S. Census Bureau QuickFacts: Loudoun County, Virginia," U.S. Census Bureau, https://www.census.gov/quickfacts/loudouncountyvirginia.

41 *"postindustrial metropolitan area"*: John B. Judis and Ruy Teixeira, *The Emerging Democratic Majority* (New York: Scribner, 2004), 8.

41 *"Anti-racism" training for teachers*: "In Wealthy Loudoun County, Virginia, Parents Face Threats in Battle over Equity in Schools," NBC News, June 1, 2021, https://www.nbcnews.com/news/us-news/wealthy-loudoun-county-virginia-parents-face-threats-battle-over-equity-n1269162.

41 *School board members themselves*: Emily Jacobs, "Virginia Parents Bullied by Other Parents for Stance against Critical Race Theory," *New York Post*, June 3, 2021, https://nypost.com/2021/06/03/virginia-parents-bullied-by-other-parents-for-stance-against-critical-race-theory/.

43 *Whatever hiatus Shor may have had planned*: Eric Levitz, "David Shor's Unified Theory of the 2020 Election," *New York*, July 17, 2020, https://nymag.com/intelligencer/2020/07/david-shor-cancel-culture-2020-election-theory-polls.html.

43 *"Over the past 60 years"*: Levitz, "David Shor's Unified Theory of the 2020 Election."

44 *voters who agreed with Democrats*: David Shor, Twitter, September 17, 2021, https://twitter.com/davidshor/status/1438920804952068099.

45 *A 2021 study by the progressive polling firm Data for Progress*: Alexander C. Furna and Timothy M. LaPira, "Political Elites Are More Supportive of Progressive Policies Than the Average Voter," Data for Progress, December 9, 2021, https://www.dataforprogress.org/blog/2021/12/9/political-elites-are-more-supportive-of-progressive-policies-than-the-average-voter.

45 *A term coined by political scientist Ronald Inglehart*: Ronald Inglehart, "Values, Objective Needs, and Subjective Satisfaction among Western Publics," *Comparative Political Studies* 9, no. 4 (January 1977): 429–58.

47 *A cross-national study by Amory Gethin, Clara Martínez-Toledano, and Thomas Piketty*: Amory Gethin, Clara Martínez-Toledano, and Thomas Piketty, "Brahmin Left Versus Merchant Right: Changing Political Cleavages in 21 Western Democracies, 1948–2020," *Quarterly Journal of Economics* 137, no. 1 (February 2022): 1–48.

47 *This is the politics of*: Benjamin Enke, Mattias Polborn, and Alex A. Wu, "Values as Luxury Goods and Political Polarization," Washington State University, October 25, 2021, http://ses.wsu.edu/wp-content/uploads/2021/10/Morals_polarization.pdf.

3. The Majority That Failed

52 *"While corporate and financial executives"*: John B. Judis and Ruy Teixeira, *The Emerging Democratic Majority* (New York: Scribner, 2004), 67.

53 *"[I]t is fair to assume"*: Ibid., 42.

54 *The Democratic group Women's Voices, Women Vote*: "Women's Voices

Women Vote Action Fund (WVWVAF)," InfluenceWatch, https://www.influencewatch.org/non-profit/womens-voices-women-vote-action-fund/.

54 *"millennials, minorities, and socially liberal whites"*: Ronald Brownstein, "The Clinton Conundrum," *The Atlantic*, April 16, 2015, https://www.theatlantic.com/politics/archive/2015/04/the-clinton-conundrum/431949/.

55 *his team confidently predicted a victory*: Ginger Gibson, "Beeson Predicts 300 Electoral-Vote Win for Romney," Politico, November 4, 2012, https://www.politico.com/blogs/politico-now/2012/11/beeson-predicts-300-electoral-vote-win-for-romney-148323.

56 *A thorough analysis*: Nate Cohn, "There Are More White Voters Than People Think. That's Good News for Trump," *New York Times*, June 9, 2016, https://www.nytimes.com/2016/06/10/upshot/there-are-more-white-voters-than-people-think-thats-good-news-for-trump.html.

57 *"America's a country of strong families"*: "2008—Country I Love," Presidential Campaign Commercials 1952–2020, Living Room Candidate, Museum of the Moving Image, http://www.livingroomcandidate.org/commercials/2008/country-i-love#.

58 *"skinny kid with a funny name"*: Barack Obama, "Keynote Address at the 2004 Democratic National Convention," July 27, 2004, https://www.presidency.ucsb.edu/documents/keynote-address-the-2004-democratic-national-convention.

58 *Obama ran 155,452 ads on health care*: Andrei Scheinkman, Xaquîn G.V., Alan McLean, and Stephen Weitberg, "The Ad Wars—Election Guide 2008," *New York Times*, https://www.nytimes.com/elections/2008/president/advertising/index.html.

58 *Obama's most-aired ad*: Sean Sullivan, "This Is the Single Most-Aired Political Ad in the Last 10 Years," *Washington Post*, April 8, 2014, https://www.washingtonpost.com/news/the-fix/wp/2014/04/08/watch-obama-hit-mccain-in-the-single-most-aired-campaign-ad-of-the-past-decade/.

59 *Two weeks after the 2008 election*: Mitt Romney, "Let Detroit Go Bankrupt," *New York Times*, November 18, 2008, https://www.nytimes.com/2008/11/19/opinion/19romney.html.

59 *"Turns out that when we built that stage"*: Maggie Haberman, "New Anti-Bain Ad: 'My Own Coffin' (Updated)," Politico, June 23, 2012, https://www.politico.com/blogs/burns-haberman/2012/06/new-anti-bain-ad-my-own-coffin-updated-127072.

59 *"I do not think that Mitt Romney cares"*: "Priorities USA Ad Featuring Joe Soptic," Politico, August 8, 2012, https://www.politico.com/video/2012/08/priorities-usa-ad-featuring-joe-soptic-011475.

60 *"In Mitt Romney's world"*: Tommy Christopher, "Jennifer Granholm: In Romney's World, 'Cars Get The Elevator And Workers Get the Shaft,'"

Mediate, September 6, 2012, https://www.mediaite.com/tv/jennifer-granholm-in-romneys-world-cars-get-the-elevator-and-workers-get-the-shaft/.

60 *"There are 47 percent of the people"*: Lucy Madison, "Fact-Checking Romney's '47 Percent' Comment," CBS News, September 25, 2012, https://www.cbsnews.com/news/fact-checking-romneys-47-percent-comment/.

60 *In the exit poll*: "Exit Polls 2012: How the Vote Has Shifted," *Washington Post*, November 6, 2012, https://www.washingtonpost.com/wp-srv/special/politics/2012-exit-polls/table.html.

60 *"Who will do more for the auto industry?"*: Angie Drobnic Holan, "Lie of the Year: The Romney Campaign's Ad on Jeeps Made in China," PolitiFact, December 12, 2012, https://www.politifact.com/article/2012/dec/12/lie-year-2012-Romney-Jeeps-China/.

61 *"There's a tradition of equal rights"*: Michael Barone, author interview, September 22, 2021.

64 *"After Obama's historic victory"*: Ruy Teixeira, "Demography Is Not Destiny," *Persuasion*, July 16, 2020, https://www.persuasion.community/p/demography-is-not-destiny.

64 *"The voters you romanticize"*: Peter Birkenhead, "Democrats: The White Working Class Isn't Voting for You, So Stop Pandering to Them," Daily Beast, June 30, 2016, https://www.thedailybeast.com/democrats-the-white-working-class-isnt-voting-for-you-so-stop-pandering-to-them?ref=scroll.

65 *"The country is under conservative assault"*: Steve Phillips, "The Democratic Party's Billion-Dollar Mistake," *New York Times*, July 20, 2017, https://www.nytimes.com/2017/07/20/opinion/democrats-midterm-elections-black-voters.html.

65 *"Ppl. worry the concern with working-class whites"*: James Surowiecki, Twitter, November 13, 2016, https://twitter.com/JamesSurowiecki/status/797926644514177026.

66 *"The white working class and the upper middle class"*: Sean Trende, *The Lost Majority: Why the Future of Government Is Up for Grabs—and Who Will Take It* (New York: St. Martin's Press, 2012), Kindle edition, 168.

66 *"cultural hegemony of the professional class"*: Ruy Teixeira, author interview, December 1, 2021.

4. The Working-Class Majority

71 *She lives in the county*: "Middle America Project," Echelon Insights, https://echeloninsights.com/map.

72 *"a middle-aged married woman"*: Richard M. Scammon and Ben J. Wattenberg, *The Real Majority* (New York: Coward-McCann, 1970), 70.

73 *Charles Murray's "Bubble Quiz"*: Charles A. Murray, *Coming Apart: The State of White America, 1960–2010* (New York: Crown Forum, 2012), 107–9.

74 *Using zip-code-level quiz data*: Charles Murray, "Why Should I Have All the Fun? More from the Bubble Quiz," American Enterprise Institute, April 25, 2016, https://www.aei.org/economics/why-should-i-have-all-the-fun-more-from-the-bubble-quiz/.

75 *The 10023 zip code*: Charles Murray, "Lessons from the Bubble Quiz #2: The Bubbliest Zip Codes for Growing Up," American Enterprise Institute, April 7, 2016, https://www.aei.org/economics/lessons-from-the-bubble-quiz-2/.

76 *In the 1963–64 season*: "Top-Rated United States Television Programs of 1963–64," Wikipedia, https://en.wikipedia.org/wiki/Top-rated_United_States_television_programs_of_1963%E2%80%9364.

76 *Ratings for the top-rated show have declined*: "Top-Rated United States Television Programs of 2018–19," Wikipedia, https://en.wikipedia.org/wiki/Top-rated_United_States_television_programs_of_2018%E2%80%9319.

76 *"The success of 'Yellowstone'"*: Roger Friedman, "TV: 'Yellowstone' Gets Network-Like Numbers, 'Succession' Has No Traction, 'Curb' Collapsing," Showbiz411, November 9, 2021, https://www.showbiz411.com/2021/11/09/tv-yellowstone-gets-network-like-numbers-succession-has-no-traction-curb-collapsing.

76 *Google search interest lets us see*: Search data in this section is from a twelve-month trailing Google Trends search accessed on March 28, 2022. "Yellowstone vs. Succession," Google Trends, https://trends.google.com/trends/explore?geo=US&q=%2Fg%2F11c37_t1x9,%2Fg%2F11g88f7vxw.

77 *In the 2021 ratings*: "Streaming Grew Its Audience in 2021; Drama, Reality and Kids' Programming Led the Content Wars," Nielsen, January 2022, https://www.nielsen.com/insights/2022/streaming-grew-its-audience-in-2021-drama-reality-and-kids-programming-lead-the-content-wars/.

77 *As of 2016*: Andrew Perrin, "Appendix A: Additional Demographic Tables and Charts," Pew Research Center, September 1, 2016, https://www.pewresearch.org/internet/2016/09/01/book-reading-2016-appendix-a/.

77 *Traveling abroad at one point*: Laura Silver, "Most Americans Have Traveled Abroad, but This Varies by Income, Education, Race," Pew Research Center, August 12, 2021, https://www.pewresearch.org/fact-tank/2021/08/12/most-americans-have-traveled-abroad-although-differences-among-demographic-groups-are-large/.

78 *In Pennsylvania*: Nick Anderson and Danielle Douglas-Gabriel, "College Enrollment Drop Sparks Recruitment Scramble," *Washington Post*, March 31, 2022, https://www.washingtonpost.com/education/2022/03/31/college-enrollment-down-recruitment-freshmen/.

79 *the University of California, Berkeley*: Christian Britschgi, "California NIMBYs Are Ruining U.C. Berkeley. Stop Them Before They Kill Again," *Reason*, March 14, 2022, https://reason.com/2022/03/14/california-nimbys-are-ruining-u-c-berkeley-stop-them-before-they-kill-again/.

80 *At Harvard*: Hannah J. Martinez and Meimei Xu, "Freshmen Split on Defunding Police, Other Hot-Button Political Issues," *Harvard Crimson*, September 9, 2021, https://www.thecrimson.com/article/2021/9/9/freshman-survey-defund-politics/.

80 *At the top twenty schools*: Matthew Yglesias, "Education Polarization Is Only Growing," *Slow Boring*, September 27, 2021, https://www.slowboring.com/p/education-polarization.

81 *The typical college experience in America*: College graduation statistics are from the U.S. Department of Education's College Scorecard.

82 *In 2022, the* Wall Street Journal: Douglas Belkin, "To Get into the Ivy League, 'Extraordinary' Isn't Always Enough These Days," *Wall Street Journal*, April 21, 2022, https://www.wsj.com/articles/to-get-into-the-ivy-league-extraordinary-isnt-always-enough-these-days-11650546000.

83 *According to a 2021 survey*: Erika Giovanetti, "Money Is the Top Reason Why Students Are Dropping Out of College, Study Finds," Fox Business, January 14, 2022, https://www.foxbusiness.com/personal-finance/students-drop-out-of-college-financial-reasons.

83 *Debunking some common misconceptions*: Melanie Hanson, "College Dropout Rates," Education Data Initiative, June 17, 2022, https://educationdata.org/college-dropout-rates.

83 *About half of title examiners*: Data in this discussion of the makeup of the American workforce is from the Bureau of Labor Statistics' Employment Projections program, accessed in April 2022. "Employment by Detailed Occupation: U.S.," Bureau of Labor Statistics, https://www.bls.gov/emp/tables/emp-by-detailed-occupation.htm.

87 *From May 2020 to April 2021*: Elise Gould and Jori Kandra, "Only One in Five Workers Are Working from Home Due to COVID: Black and Hispanic Workers Are Less Likely to Be Able to Telework," Economic Policy Institute, June 2, 2021, https://www.epi.org/blog/only-one-in-five-workers-are-working-from-home-due-to-covid-black-and-hispanic-workers-are-less-likely-to-be-able-to-telework/.

5. The Political Center of Gravity

91 *announcing that Starbucks*: Phil Wahba, "Donald Trump Muslim Ban: Starbucks Will Hire Refugees in Response," *Fortune*, January 29, 2017, https://fortune.com/2017/01/29/donald-trump-muslim-ban-starbucks/.

91 *criticizing Donald Trump's border wall*: Howard Schultz, "Our Path," *Medium*, February 14, 2019, https://medium.com/@Howardschultz/ourpath-9164e18bdb98.

92 *At Echelon Insights*: Echelon Insights, Twitter, November 8, 2022, https://twitter.com/EchelonInsights/status/1590005397321981952.

94 *Using public opinion data from the Voter Study Group*: Lee Drutman, "Political Divisions in 2016 and Beyond," Democracy Fund Voter Study Group, June 2017, https://www.voterstudygroup.org/publication/political-divisions-in-2016-and-beyond.

96 *In 2021*: Xenocrypt, "Revisiting the Famous 2016 'Economic Views vs. Social Views' Scatterplot," *Medium*, April 8, 2021, https://medium.com/@xenocryptsite/revisiting-the-famous-2016-economic-views-vs-social-views-scatterplot-55016c1b8888.

97 *My colleagues at Echelon Insights*: "June Verified Voter Omnibus—The 4 Quadrants of American Voters," Echelon Insights, June 29, 2022, https://echeloninsights.com/in-the-news/june-22-omnibus-quad-2/.

99 *In* Alienated America: Timothy P. Carney, *Alienated America: Why Some Places Thrive While Others Collapse* (New York: HarperCollins, 2019).

100 *and that a ban on travel from specific countries*: Steven Shepard, "Poll: Majority of Voters Back Trump Travel Ban," Politico, July 5, 2017, https://www.politico.com/story/2017/07/05/trump-travel-ban-poll-voters-240215.

101 *"There is a religious war"*: "Pat Buchanan on the Culture War (1992)," American Yawp Reader, https://www.americanyawp.com/reader/29-the-triumph-of-the-right/pat-buchanan-on-the-culture-war-1992/.

106 *An analysis by Ruy Teixeira*: Ruy Teixeira, "Working Class and Hispanic Voters Are Losing Interest in the Party of Abortion, Gun Control and the January 6th Hearings," *Liberal Patriot*, July 14, 2022, https://theliberalpatriot.substack.com/p/working-class-and-hispanic-voters.

108 *liberal analyst Steve Phillips writes*: Steve Phillips, *Brown Is the New White: How the Demographic Revolution Has Created a New American Majority* (New York: New Press, 2016).

109 *A 2020 Pew Research Center study found that*: "About One-in-Four U.S. Hispanics Have Heard of Latinx, but Just 3% Use It," Pew Research Center, August 11, 2020, https://www.pewresearch.org/hispanic/2020/08/11/about-one-in-four-u-s-hispanics-have-heard-of-latinx-but-just-3-use-it/.

109 *When we asked in a 2022 survey*: "January Verified Voter Omnibus—What to Call People of Spanish Speaking Heritage?" Echelon Insights, https://echeloninsights.com/in-the-news/hispanic-latino-latinx/.

109 *Democratic representative Ruben Gallego of Arizona*: Ruben Gallego,

Twitter, December 6, 2021, https://twitter.com/RubenGallego/status/1467920180135276554.

109 *but another Pew Research Center study published in 2020*: "Black and White Democrats Differ in Their Media Diets, Assessments of Primaries," Pew Research Center, March 11, 2020, https://www.pewresearch.org/journalism/2020/03/11/black-and-white-democrats-differ-in-their-media-diets-assessments-of-primaries/.

109 *This comes at a time when coverage*: Zach Goldberg, "How the Media Led the Great Racial Awakening," *Tablet*, August 4, 2020, https://www.tabletmag.com/sections/news/articles/media-great-racial-awakening.

111 *But white Democrats go further*: Patrick Ruffini, Twitter, July 20, 2021, https://twitter.com/PatrickRuffini/status/1417512351218163719.

111 *In the American National Election Studies' 2018 survey*: Asma Khalid, "How White Liberals Became Woke, Radically Changing Their Outlook on Race," NPR, October 1, 2019, https://www.npr.org/2019/10/01/763383478/how-white-liberals-became-woke-radically-changing-their-outlook-on-race.

112 *Zach Goldberg uses the term*: Zach Goldberg, "Is Defunding the Police a 'Luxury Belief'?" Manhattan Institute, September 8, 2022, https://www.manhattan-institute.org/is-defunding-the-police-a-luxury-belief.

113 *And yet, driven by Democratic coalition politics*: Roque Planas, "2020 Democrats Overwhelmingly Back Decriminalizing Border Crossings in Thursday Debate," *HuffPost*, June 28, 2019, https://www.huffpost.com/entry/decriminalizing-border-crossing-democrats-2020_n_5d15884ee4b03d6116392906.

113 *"It is hard to avoid the conclusion"*: Ruy Teixeira, "The Democrats' Hispanic Voter Problem," *Liberal Patriot*, December 9, 2021, https://www.liberalpatriot.com/p/the-democrats-hispanic-voter-problem-dfc.

114 *A* New York Times *report in July 2022*: Zolan Kanno-Youngs, "Democrats Navigate Nuanced Views on Abortion Among Black Voters," *New York Times*, July 18, 2022, https://www.nytimes.com/2022/07/18/us/politics/abortion-black-voters-democrats-biden.html.

115 *That's similar to the margin of support for a fifteen-week ban*: Echelon Insights, Twitter, July 20, 2022, https://twitter.com/EchelonInsights/status/1549862759013253121.

116 *A prime example of this came when Planned Parenthood*: "Planned Parenthood Stands with the Movement for Black Lives' Call to Defund the Police," Planned Parenthood Action Fund, https://www.plannedparenthoodaction.org/planned-parenthood-pennsylvania-advocates/planned-parenthood-stands-movement-black-lives-call-defund-polic.

116 *The survey also found that a federal jobs guarantee for all Americans*: Patrick Ruffini, Twitter, March 3, 2021, https://twitter.com/PatrickRuffini/status/1367254977849282561.

117 *Using American National Election Studies data*: Matt Grossmann, Twitter, November 22, 2016, https://twitter.com/MattGrossmann/status/801068032399245313.

117 *According to IRS data*: Gregory Korte, "Democrats' Tax-Hike Bet Relies on Their New $500,000-Plus Voters," Bloomberg Tax, April 19, 2021, https://news.bloombergtax.com/daily-tax-report/democrats-tax-hike-bet-relies-on-their-new-500-000-plus-voters.

6. The New American Mainstream

121 *The Irish quickly became the majority in Boston*: Michael Barone, *The New Americans: How the Melting Pot Can Work Again* (Washington, DC: Regnery, 2001), 30.

121 *A row of classified ads*: Mark Bulik, "1854: No Irish Need Apply," *New York Times*, September 8, 2015, https://www.nytimes.com/2015/09/08/insider/1854-no-irish-need-apply.html.

122 *Where they excelled was in fields*: Barone, *The New Americans*, 37.

123 *Their darker complexion*: Robert Orsi, "The Religious Boundaries of an Inbetween People: Street *Feste* and the Problem of the Dark-Skinned Other in Italian Harlem, 1920–1990," *American Quarterly* 44, no. 3 (September 1992): 313–47, https://www.jstor.org/stable/2712980.

123 *"There has never been since New York was founded"*: Brent Staples, "How Italians Became 'White,'" *New York Times*, October 12, 2019, https://www.nytimes.com/interactive/2019/10/12/opinion/columbus-day-italian-american-racism.html.

123 *"They are of a very low order of intelligence"*: "Report of the Select Committee of the House of Representatives to Inquire into the Alleged Violation of the Laws Prohibiting the Importation of Contract Laborers, Paupers, Convicts and Other Classes, Together with the Testimony, Documents and Consular Reports Submitted to the Committee," United States, U.S. Government Printing Office, 1889.

123 *This became enough of a political issue*: Brando Simeo Starkey, "White Immigrants Weren't Always Considered White—and Acceptable," Andscape, https://andscape.com/features/white-immigrants-werent-always-considered-white-and-acceptable/.

124 *While mistreatment of African Americans*: Staples, "How Italians Became 'White.'"

124 *The animosity was such*: Paul Moses, "Immigrants: Irish-Italian Love-Hate Relations (Opinion)," CNN, December 1, 2015, https://www.cnn.com/2015/12/01/opinions/moses-irish-italian-immigrant-experience/index.html.

124 *"transformed by influences of American society"*: Daniel Patrick Moynihan and Nathan Glazer, *Beyond the Melting Pot: The Negroes, Puerto Ricans, Jews, Italians, and Irish of New York City* (Cambridge, MA: MIT Press, 1963), 13.

124 *After the war*: Barone, *The New Americans*, 146.

125 *by the 1960s*: Ibid.

125 *"Italian Americans have risen"*: Ibid.

125 *"Just remember"*: Michael Barone, *Our Country: The Shaping of America from Roosevelt to Reagan* (New York: Free Press, 1990), 310.

126 *"On the day [Kennedy] died"*: Moynihan and Glazer, *Beyond the Melting Pot*, 287.

126 *Within the Irish community*: Ibid., 266–67.

127 *"From these multiplying examples"*: Daniel Bell, *The Radical Right*, 3rd ed. (New York: Routledge, 2017), 140.

128 *From Kennedy's time to today*: Eric Kaufmann, "Hispanic Americans Are No Longer 'Minority Voters,'" *UnHerd*, December 9 2021, https://unherd.com/thepost/hispanic-americans-are-no-longer-minority-voters/.

130 *In the five years from 2014 to 2019*: Noah Smith, "Median Household Income Grew More in the '10s than the '90s," Bloomberg, September 23, 2020, https://www.bloomberg.com/opinion/articles/2020-09-23/median-household-income-grew-more-in-the-10s-than-the-90s?sref=R8NfLgwS#xj4y7vzkg.

130 *Extensive analysis of individual and household data*: Raj Chetty, Nathaniel Hendren, Maggie R. Jones, and Sonya R. Porter, "Race and Economic Opportunity in the United States: An Intergenerational Perspective," *Quarterly Journal of Economics* 135, no. 2 (May 2020): 711–83.

131 *One in eight Hispanics worked*: "The Economic Contributions of Hispanic Americans," New American Economy Research Fund, September 15, 2021, https://research.newamericaneconomy.org/report/hispanic-spending-power-2021/.

131 *According to one report*: Victoria Arena, "Key Insights from the 2020 State of Latino Entrepreneurship Report," Latinas in Business, April 8, 2021, https://latinasinbusiness.us/2021/04/08/key-insights-from-the-2020-state-of-latino-entrepreneurship-report/.

132 *While surveys of Hispanic adults*: Jens Manuel Krogstad and Mark Hugo Lopez, "Most Latinos Say U.S. Immigration System Needs Big Changes," Pew Research Center, April 20, 2021, https://www.pewresearch.org/fact-tank/2021/04/20/most-latinos-say-u-s-immigration-system-needs-big-changes/.

132 *From 1998 to 2008*: Rakesh Kochhar, "Latinos' Incomes Higher than before Great Recession, but U.S.-Born Latinos Yet to Recover," Pew Research Center, March 7, 2019, https://www.pewresearch.org/hispanic/2019/03/07/latinos-incomes-higher-than-before-great-recession-but-u-s-born-latinos-yet-to-recover/.

134 *As law professor David Bernstein writes*: David Bernstein, *Classified: The Untold Story of Racial Classification in America* (New York: Bombardier Books, 2022).

134 *Richard Alba cites*: Richard Alba, *The Great Demographic Illusion: Majority, Minority, and the Expanding American Mainstream* (Princeton, NJ: Princeton University Press, 2020), Kindle edition, 125.

136 *Standing at 14 percent in 2015*: Gretchen Livingston, "The Rise of Multiracial and Multiethnic Babies in the U.S.," Pew Research Center, June 6, 2017, https://www.pewresearch.org/fact-tank/2017/06/06/the-rise-of-multiracial-and-multiethnic-babies-in-the-u-s/.

137 *Mixed-white and minority voters*: Kim Parker, Juliana Menasce Horowitz, Rich Morin, and Mark Hugo Lopez, "Multiracial in America: Proud, Diverse, and Growing in Numbers," Pew Research Center, June 11, 2015, https://www.pewresearch.org/social-trends/2015/06/11/multiracial-in-america/.

138 *The typical white student*: "Miseducation: Henry County School District," ProPublica, https://projects.propublica.org/miseducation/district/1302820.

139 *Contrast this with the Atlanta city schools*: "Miseducation: Atlanta City School District," ProPublica, https://projects.propublica.org/miseducation/district/1300120.

140 *Oxford scholar Benjamin Elbers calculates*: Benjamin Elbers, "Trends in U.S. Residential Racial Segregation, 1990 to 2020," *Socius* 7 (January–December 2021), https://journals.sagepub.com/doi/epub/10.1177/23780231211053982.

140 *Brookings Institution demographer William H. Frey*: William H. Frey, "Black-White Segregation Edges Downward Since 2000, Census Shows," Brookings Institution, December 17, 2018, https://www.brookings.edu/blog/the-avenue/2018/12/17/black-white-segregation-edges-downward-since-2000-census-shows/.

141 *Raj Chetty's research team found*: Chetty et al., "Race and Economic Opportunity in the United States," 711–83.

142 *Further studies by Chetty*: Claire Cain Miller, Josh Katz, Francesca Paris, and Aatish Bhatia, "Vast New Study Shows a Key to Reducing Poverty: More Friendships between Rich and Poor," *New York Times*, August 1, 2022, https://www.nytimes.com/interactive/2022/08/01/upshot/rich-poor-friendships.html.

7. Hardhat Conservatives

149 *Not just in the United States*: Bill Bishop and Robert G. Cushing, *The Big Sort: Why the Clustering of Like-Minded America Is Tearing Us Apart* (Boston: Houghton Mifflin Harcourt, 2009), 87.

149 *Richard Scammon and Ben Wattenberg tracked this shift*: Richard M. Scammon and Ben J. Wattenberg, *The Real Majority* (New York: Coward-McCann, 1970), 37–39.

150 *"The man who works hard"*: Ibid., 43.

151 *In Orange County, Vermont*: Kevin Phillips, *The Emerging Republican Majority* (Princeton, NJ: Princeton University Press, 2015), 75.

151 *"Back in 1960"*: Ibid., 32–33.

153 *His policy papers were unusually detailed*: William F. Buckley, Jr., *The Unmaking of a Mayor* (New York: Encounter Books, 2015), 305.

153 *In places like the Staten Island–based 64th Assembly District*: "NY Historic Elections Multimap," Cinyc Maps, June 19, 2022, https://cinycmaps.com/index.php/8-new-york/113-ny-historic-elections-multimap.

154 *In December 1964*: Kenneth J. Heineman, "Protests at the University of California, Berkeley," Bill of Rights Institute, https://billofrightsinstitute.org/essays/protests-at-the-university-of-california-berkeley.

154 *"Look, I don't care if I'm in the mountains"*: Gerard J. De Groot, "Ronald Reagan and Student Unrest in California, 1966–1970," *Pacific Historical Review* 65, no. 1 (February 1996): 107–29.

154 *More people voted*: Michael W. Flamm, "'Law and Order' At Large: The New York Civilian Review Board Referendum of 1966 and the Crisis of Liberalism," *The Historian* 64, no. 3–4 (Spring & Summer 2002): 643–65.

154 *conservative, but not* "a *conservative"*: William F. Gavin, *Street Corner Conservative* (New Rochelle, NY: Arlington House, 1975), 69.

155 *In the city*: Thorongil, Twitter, April 15, 2022, https://twitter.com/Thorongil16/status/1515058691875213322.

157 *These numbers were considered significant:* Everett Carll Ladd Jr., "Liberalism Upside Down: The Inversion of the New Deal Order," *Political Science Quarterly* 91, no. 44 (Winter 1976): 577–600.

157 *"The size of the upper classes is new"*: Ibid., 593.

157 *The gap was just as wide by education in 1975*: Ibid., 595.

158 *Median-income families*: Ibid., 591.

159 *"Labor, to some extent"*: "Excerpts from Interview with Meany on Status of Labor Movement," *New York Times*, August 31, 1969, 44.

159 *"Much of the working class"*: Ladd, "Liberalism Upside Down," 590.

160 *"Everything I got I worked for"*: David Paul Kuhn, *The Hardhat Riot: Nixon,*

New York City, and the Dawn of the White Working-Class Revolution (New York: Oxford University Press, 2020), 18.

160 *A cover spread*: Ibid., 63.

160 *"The working class earns its living"*: Pete Hamill, "The Revolt of the White Lower Middle Class," *New York*, April 14, 1969, https://nymag.com/news/features/46801/.

162 *When hardhats clashed with student protesters*: Kuhn, *The Hardhat Riot*, 367.

162 *A poll by Daniel Yankelovich*: Gavin, *Street Corner Conservative*, 120.

163 *"Blacks, too"*: Scammon and Wattenberg, *The Real Majority*, 240.

164 *Figures compiled by David Paul Kuhn*: Kuhn, *The Hardhat Riot*, 70.

164 *Fifteen million young men*: Ibid., 78.

164 *Of the 210,000 evaders*: Ibid., 74.

164 *"afraid to ask"*: Christopher Caldwell, *The Age of Entitlement: America Since the Sixties* (New York: Simon & Schuster, 2020), 78.

164 *At St. Paul's*: Ibid., 69.

164 *A young man of draft age*: Ibid., 69–70.

165 *"Part of the brutality"*: Ibid., 76.

165 *"From the point of view"*: Kuhn, *The Hardhat Riot*, 117.

166 *Twelve days later*: Ibid., 243.

166 *"[I]t should be our focus"*: Ibid., 250.

166 *"This display of emotional activity"*: Ibid., 251.

167 *In a national address*: Richard M. Nixon, "The Great Silent Majority," American Rhetoric, November 3, 1969, https://www.americanrhetoric.com/speeches/richardnixongreatsilentmajority.html.

167 *Within a week*: Kuhn, *The Hardhat Riot*, 252.

167 *"They were clearly coming unmoored"*: Ibid., 251.

167 *Nixon refused to endorse*: "White House Has No Comment on Senatorial Race," *Times Record*, September 25, 1970, 13.

167 *"an electorate in motion"*: Phillips, *The Emerging Republican Majority*, 33.

168 *"contains a credible and workable blueprint"*: Kuhn, *The Hardhat Riot*, 267.

8. The 2020 Surge

173 *"When Mexico sends its people"*: "Full Text: Donald Trump Announces a Presidential Bid," *Washington Post*, June 16, 2015, https://www.washingtonpost.com/news/post-politics/wp/2015/06/16/full-text-donald-trump-announces-a-presidential-bid/.

174 *by the time the 2020 election came around*: Ruy Teixeira, "Did the Democrats Misread Hispanic Voters?" *Liberal Patriot*, February 4, 2021, https://www.liberalpatriot.com/p/did-the-democrats-misread-hispanic.

174 *In Echelon Insights polling*: Echelon Insights, Twitter, November 23, 2020, https://twitter.com/EchelonInsights/status/1330974953571823619.

176 *So eager was the community*: Edward Cody, "In Miami, It's 'Reagan, Si,'" *Washington Post*, May 21, 1983, https://www.washingtonpost.com/archive/politics/1983/05/21/in-miami-its-reagan-si/dea90bd9-3c35-4a35-a64d-ab18670b18b2/.

176 *"Superstar Wows Little Havana"*: "President Reagan Visits Little Havana," Flashback Miami, May 20, 2016, https://flashbackmiami.com/2016/05/20/president-reagan-visits-little-havana-may-20-1983/.

177 *Florida International University's survey*: Cuban Research Institute, Florida International University, "2016 FIU Cuba Poll: How Cuban Americans in Miami View U.S. Policies Toward Cuba," September 14, 2016, *Cuban Research Institute Events*, 293, https://digitalcommons.fiu.edu/cri_events/293/.

177 *"America will never be a socialist country"*: "Remarks by President Trump to the Venezuelan American Community," February 18, 2019, U.S. Mission to the Organization of American States, https://usoas.usmission.gov/remarks-by-president-trump-to-the-venezuelan-american-community/.

177 *"One of the things that pushed me over the edge"*: Giancarlo Sopo, author interview, March 23, 2021.

178 *The Trump campaign first waded*: "Goya," YouTube, July 22, 2020, https://www.youtube.com/watch?v=eHib1OWSW_s.

179 *In early October*: "Castrochavismo," YouTube, October 12, 2020, https://www.youtube.com/watch?v=rBnbIttz2fc.

179 *Sopo's final ad*: "Por Trump," YouTube, October 20, 2020, youtube.com/watch?v=X-ZwOfaTMBc.

179 *The pre-election FIU poll*: Guillermo Grenier and Qing Lai, *2020 FIU Cuba Poll: How Cuban Americans in Miami View U.S. Policies Toward Cuba*, 2020, Florida International University.

182 *But in the next forty years*: Jens Manuel Krogstad, "Florida's Puerto Rican Population Rivaling New York's," Pew Research Center, October 30, 2015, https://www.pewresearch.org/fact-tank/2015/10/30/in-a-shift-away-from-new-york-more-puerto-ricans-head-to-florida/; César J. Ayala, "Puerto Rico and Its Diaspora," https://www.sscnet.ucla.edu/soc/faculty/ayala/prdiaspora/index-english.html.

182 *"The dirty little secret is"*: Jorge Bonilla, author interview, September 7, 2022.

184 *There, the Republican share*: Florida Politics Enjoyer, Twitter, November 21, 2022, https://twitter.com/FLPolEnjoyer/status/1594846865136431104.

184 *The VoteCast exit poll*: "Fox News Voter Analysis," Fox News, https://www.foxnews.com/elections/2022/midterm-results/voter-analysis?year=2022&state=FL.

184 *Even as he gained ground*: Ibid.

187 *"There are people like myself"*: Sam Oh, author interview, March 26, 2021.

188 *Kim's race attracted*: Richard Cohen and Charlie Cook, ed., *The Almanac of American Politics, 2022* (Arlington, VA: Columbia Books, 2021), 295.

189 *Among new 2020 voters*: Ruth Igielnik, Scott Keeter, and Hannah Hartig, "Behind Biden's 2020 Victory," Pew Research Center, June 30, 2021, https://www.pewresearch.org/politics/2021/06/30/behind-bidens-2020-victory/.

189 *"Working-class nonwhite voters really do not agree with us"*: David Shor, author interview, August 31, 2021.

190 *A postmortem by the Democratic firm Equis Labs*: "2020 Post-Mortem (Part One): Portrait of a Persuadable Latino," Equis Research, April 2, 2021, https://equisresearch.medium.com/2020-post-mortem-part-one-16221adbd2f3.

191 *During these school closures*: Gary Kamiya, "San Francisco's Ridiculous Renaming Spree," *The Atlantic*, February 2, 2021, https://www.theatlantic.com/ideas/archive/2021/02/san-francisco-renaming-spree/617894/.

191 *In the year following the end of merit-based admissions*: Carl Samson, "Top SF High School Sees Record Spike in Failing Grades after Dropping Merit-Based Admission System," Yahoo News, May 26, 2022, https://news.yahoo.com/top-sf-high-school-sees-192303605.html.

192 *California especially*: Patrick Ruffini, Twitter, October 18, 2022, https://twitter.com/PatrickRuffini/status/1582492066256285697.

192 *Though not closely contested*: Adrian IAB, Twitter, March 7, 2021, https://twitter.com/adriaeln/status/1368771897387810820.

9. Realignment on the Rio Grande

197 *"Mexicans here cling to the customs"*: Michael Barone and Grant Ujifusa, *The Almanac of American Politics, 1990: The Senators, the Representatives and the Governors: Their Records and Election Results, Their States and Districts* (Washington, DC: National Journal Group, 1989), 1193.

197 *The illegal population lives the entirety of their lives*: Manny Fernandez, "This Is America. Do You Belong Here? Navigating the Checkpoints of the Southwest Border," *New York Times*, March 28 2019, https://www.nytimes.com/2019/03/28/us/border-checkpoints-mexico.html.

198 *Among those casting a straight-ticket ballot*: "General Election Summary Report," Starr County, Texas, November 8, 2016, https://www.co.starr.tx.us/upload/page/6487/docs/a0016.pdf.

198 *The "Duke of Duval" consolidated his power*: Hernán Contreras, "Origins of Boss Rule in Starr County," RealStarr, https://realstarr.net/linked/origins_of_boss_rule_in_starr_county_texas.pdf.

199 *"We had the law to ourselves there"*: "Ex-Official Says He Stole 1948 Election for Johnson," *New York Times*, July 31, 1977.

199 *"our own form of racism"*: Ross Barrera, author interview, October 26, 2022.

200 *In the 2022 primary*: Carla Astudillo, "Election Results: How Texas Voted in the 2022 Primary," *Texas Tribune*, March 1, 2022, https://apps.texastribune.org/features/2022/texas-election-results-2022-primary/.

202 *"There's not many jobs out here"*: Oscar Rosa, author interview, November 17, 2022.

202 *This is an updated version*: John Burnett and Marisa Peñaloza, "In Rio Grande Valley, Some Campaign Workers Are Paid to Harvest Votes," NPR, July 7, 2015, https://www.npr.org/2015/07/07/413463879/in-rio-grande-valley-some-campaign-workers-are-paid-to-harvest-votes.

203 *In the two years from 2019 to 2021*: "Personal Income by County, Metro, and Other Areas," Bureau of Economic Analysis, November 16, 2022, https://www.bea.gov/data/income-saving/personal-income-county-metro-and-other-areas.

204 *the third safest in fact*: "McAllen Once Again Named in Top 10 Safest Cities in America," *Texas Border Business*, July 21, 2022, https://texasborderbusiness.com/mcallen-once-again-named-in-top-10-safest-cities-in-america/.

204 *"We realized we were not dependent on Mexico"*: Javier Villalobos, author interview, October 31, 2022.

208 *"If I went and earned a college degree"*: Leslie Sanchez, author interview, December 12, 2022.

208 *One also sees it*: Sebastián Osorio Idárraga, "Remittances Remain Vital Source of Revenue for Latin America's Economies," *Bloomberg Línea*, October 27, 2022, https://www.bloomberglinea.com/english/remittances-remain-vita-source-of-revenue-for-latin-americas-economies/.

210 *In total*: "Southwest Land Border Encounters," Customs and Border Protection, https://www.cbp.gov/newsroom/stats/southwest-land-border-encounters.

211 *Today, an estimated one in eight people*: "County Data (48215): Unauthorized Population," Migration Policy Institute, https://www.migrationpolicy.org/data/unauthorized-immigrant-population/county/48215.

10. Black Politics

215 *when Gallup asked*: Christopher Caldwell, *The Age of Entitlement: America Since the Sixties* (New York: Simon & Schuster, 2020), 20.

216 *"[I]n the years since"*: Ismail K. White and Chryl N. Laird, *Steadfast*

Democrats: How Social Forces Shape Black Political Behavior (Princeton, NJ: Princeton University Press, 2021), 5.

219 *In Philadelphia*: Patrick Ruffini, Twitter, December 15, 2016, https://twitter.com/PatrickRuffini/status/809605590309883904.

219 *The steepest turnout declines*: Patrick Ruffini, "Black Voters Aren't Turning Out for the Post-Obama Democratic Party," FiveThirtyEight, May 30, 2017, https://fivethirtyeight.com/features/black-voters-arent-turning-out-for-the-post-obama-democratic-party/.

219 *In Nevada*: Patrick Ruffini, Twitter, January 30, 2017, https://twitter.com/PatrickRuffini/status/826268326720598020.

219 *In North Carolina*: Patrick Ruffini, Twitter, January 29, 2017, https://twitter.com/PatrickRuffini/status/825891101081030656.

220 *According to the 2016 Cooperative Election Study*: Alexander Agadjanian, "How the 2016 Vote Broke Down by Race, Gender, and Age," *Agadjanian Politics*, March 8, 2017, https://agadjanianpolitics.wordpress.com/2017/03/08/how-the-2016-vote-broke-down-by-race-gender-and-age-decision-desk/.

221 *As the Democratic nominee*: Victoria M. Massie, "Hillary Clinton Said 'Systemic Racism' in Tonight's Speech. That's Major," *Vox*, July 29, 2016, https://www.vox.com/2016/7/29/12320118/hillary-clinton-speech-systemic-racism.

221 *In doing so*: Farah Stockman, "The Subtle Phrases Hillary Clinton Uses to Sway Black Voters," *New York Times*, September 29, 2016, https://www.nytimes.com/2016/09/30/us/politics/hillary-clinton-black-voters.html.

221 *The second was activist pressure*: Allison Graves, "Did Hillary Clinton Call African-American Youth 'Superpredators'?" PolitiFact, August 28, 2016, https://www.politifact.com/factchecks/2016/aug/28/reince-priebus/did-hillary-clinton-call-african-american-youth-su/.

222 *Such an example came*: Barack Obama, "Remarks by the President on Trayvon Martin," The White House, July 19, 2013, https://obamawhitehouse.archives.gov/the-press-office/2013/07/19/remarks-president-trayvon-martin.

222 *"Is it more important for me"*: Ezra Klein, "Barack Obama Interview: Joe Biden Is 'Finishing the Job,'" *New York Times*, June 1, 2021, https://www.nytimes.com/2021/06/01/opinion/ezra-klein-podcast-barack-obama.html.

224 *"Barack Obama plans to win South Carolina"*: Helen Kennedy, "Obama's Beauty Parlor Strategy for S.C.," *New York Daily News*, January 21, 2008, https://www.nydailynews.com/news/politics/obama-beauty-parlor-strategy-s-article-1.344177.

224 *"The rise of Jim Crow laws"*: Joyce Balls-Berry, Lea C. Dacy, and James Balls,

"'Heard it through the Grapevine': The Black Barbershop as a Source of Health Information," National Library of Medicine, https://www.ncbi.nlm.nih.gov/pmc/articles/PMC4749262/.

225 *she also led by 24 points*: Paul Steinhauser, "Poll: Obama Makes Big Gains among Black Voters," CNN, January 18, 2008, https://www.cnn.com/2008/POLITICS/01/18/poll.2008/index.html.

225 *"And so what then becomes"*: Chryl Laird, author interview, February 16, 2023.

226 *In the early 1970s*: White and Laird, *Steadfast Democrats*, 8–9.

226 *With legislation pomoting the creation*: "African American Members of the U.S. Congress: 1870–2020," Congressional Research Service, December 15, 2020, https://sgp.fas.org/crs/misc/RL30378.pdf.

226 *By 2021, there were fifty-seven*: "Black Americans 117th Congress," House Press Gallery, https://pressgallery.house.gov/black-americans-117th-congress.

226 *"Linked fate" is one explanation*: Michael C. Dawson, *Behind the Mule: Race and Class in African-American Politics* (Princeton, NJ: Princeton University Press, 1994).

227 *Deeper social ties*: White and Laird, *Steadfast Democrats*, 32.

227 *To take one example*: Ibid., 108.

227 *Terms like "Uncle Tom"*: Ibid., 39.

227 *Joe Biden expressed*: Eric Bradner, Sarah Mucha, and Arlette Saenz, "Biden: 'If You Have a Problem Figuring Out Whether You're for Me or Trump, Then You Ain't Black,'" CNN Politics, May 22, 2020, https://www.cnn.com/2020/05/22/politics/biden-charlamagne-tha-god-you-aint-black/index.html.

227 *Such social sanctions*: White and Laird, *Steadfast Democrats*, 81.

227 *In face-to-face survey interviews*: Ibid., 121.

227 *In an experiment the authors conducted*: Ibid., 159.

228 *Ryan Burge, a political scientist and pastor*: Ryan Burge, "Black Christians and Black 'Nones' Show Little Ideological Divide," Religion Unplugged, January 22, 2021, https://religionunplugged.com/news/2021/1/21/how-the-black-christian-vote-compares-to-secular-black-americans.

228 *today Black church congregants are more likely to hear*: Besheer Mohamed, Kiana Cox, Jeff Diamant, and Claire Gecewicz, "Black Religion and Politics," Pew Research Center, February 16, 2021, https://www.pewresearch.org/religion/2021/02/16/religion-and-politics/.

235 *"if you talk about policy"*: David Shor, author interview, August 31, 2021.

236 *In Echelon Insights polling*: Patrick Ruffini, Twitter, September 24, 2019, https://twitter.com/PatrickRuffini/status/1176571728362909699.

236 *A series of focus groups*: "Black Americans Care about Climate Change (But

It's Complicated)," Third Way, July 9, 2020, https://www.thirdway.org/memo/black-americans-care-about-climate-change-but-its-complicated.

236 *Biden voters making more than $200,000*: David Shor, Twitter, July 3, 2022, 236://twitter.com/davidshor/status/1543714344164364289.

239 *"We believe"*: White and Laird, *Steadfast Democrats*, 205.

11. The Multiracial Populist Future

243 *"Democrats are . . . the party"*: P. J. O'Rourke, *Parliament of Whores: A Lone Humorist Attempts to Explain the Entire U.S. Government* (New York: Viking, 1991), 19.

244 *The social psychologist Jonathan Haidt's*: Moral Foundations Theory, https://moralfoundations.org/.

245 *Their 2008 book*: Ross Douthat and Reihan Salam, *Grand New Party: How Republicans Can Win the Working Class and Save the American Dream* (New York: Knopf Doubleday, 2008).

246 *"It's one thing"*: Oren Cass, author interview, October 13, 2022.

247 *"Medicare for All, abortions for none"*: James Pogue, "What Peter Thiel, J. D. Vance, and Others Are Learning from Curtis Yarvin and the New Right," *Vanity Fair*, April 20, 2022, https://www.vanityfair.com/news/2022/04/inside-the-new-right-where-peter-thiel-is-placing-his-biggest-bets.

248 *"In the morning I go running"*: "Clinton Campaign Speech," C-SPAN, September 23, 1992, https://www.c-span.org/video/?32698-1/clinton-campaign-speech.

249 *"To every voter in Milwaukee"*: "Full Text: Donald Trump Campaign Speech in Wisconsin," Politico, August 17, 2016, https://www.politico.com/story/2016/08/full-text-donald-trumps-speech-on-227095.

249 *In a memorable and evocative passage*: "Donald Trump Remarks in New York City Accepting Election as the 45th President of the United States," American Presidency Project, November 9, 2016, https://www.presidency.ucsb.edu/documents/remarks-new-york-city-accepting-election-the-45th-president-the-united-states.

250 *"The hardworking people she calls deplorable"*: "Donald Trump Remarks to the Economic Club of New York at the Waldorf Astoria in New York City," American Presidency Project, September 15, 2016, https://www.presidency.ucsb.edu/documents/remarks-the-economic-club-new-york-the-waldorf-astoria-new-york-city.

250 *By 2015*: "GM to Invest $877M in Flint Truck Plant," *Detroit News*, August 4, 2015, https://www.detroitnews.com/story/business/autos/general-motors/2015/08/04/gm-invest-flint-truck-plant/31095645/.

250 *Trump visited the Flint Assembly Plant*: David Weigel, "Why Donald Trump Makes Sense to Many Voters—Even Some Democrats," *Washington Post*, August 15, 2015, https://www.washingtonpost.com/politics/why-donald-trump-makes-sense-to-a-lot-of-voters--even-some-democrats/2015/08/15/cee648f0-42bf-11e5-8ab4-c73967a143d3_story.html.

252 *"Unlike traditional Republicans"*: Ronald Brownstein, "The GOP's Modern Populist Pollster," *National Journal*, June 14, 1986, 1492–93.

252 *Despite the strength of the Republican establishment*: Lance Tarrance, author interview, May 11, 2022.

255 *Just 31 percent*: "International Educational Attainment," National Center for Education Statistics, May 2022, https://nces.ed.gov/programs/coe/indicator/cac/intl-ed-attainment#:~:text=Across%20OECD%20countries%2C%20the%20average,42%20percent%20to%2050%20percent.

256 *In 2016*: Kriston McIntosh, Emily Moss, Ryan Nunn, and Jay Shambaugh, "Examining the Black-White Wealth Gap," Brookings Institution, February 27, 2020, https://www.brookings.edu/blog/up-front/2020/02/27/examining-the-black-white-wealth-gap/.

256 *According to one study*: Wenliang Hou and Geoffrey T. Sanzenbacher, "The Importance of Social Security as an Equalizer," ASA Generations, https://generations.asaging.org/importance-social-security-equalizer.

257 *In the arena of family policy*: "The Family Security Act 2.0: A New National Commitment to Working American Families," Office of U.S. Senator Mitt Romney, https://www.romney.senate.gov/wp-content/uploads/2022/06/family-security-act-2.0_one-pager_appendix.pdf.

261 *To understand just how much*: Rob Griffin, William H. Frey, and Ruy Teixeira, "States of Change," Center for American Progress, June 27, 2019, https://www.americanprogress.org/article/states-of-change-3/.

269 *The election of 2012*: "President Exit Polls—Election 2012," *New York Times*, November 6, 2012, https://www.nytimes.com/elections/2012/results/president/exit-polls.html.

270 *before zooming back*: "National Results 2020 President Exit Polls," CNN Politics, November 3, 2020, https://www.cnn.com/election/2020/exit-polls/president/national-results.

INDEX

Page numbers followed by *f* or *t* refer to figures and tables, respectively.